Praise for the
Bad Girls of the Bible series

"Liz Curtis Higgs's unique use of fiction combined with Scripture and modern application helped me see myself, my past, and my future in a whole new light. A stunning, awesome book."
>—ROBIN LEE HATCHER
>author of *Whispers from Yesterday*

"In her creative, fun-loving way, Liz retells the stories of the Bible. She delivers a knock-out punch of conviction as she clearly illustrates the lessons of Scripture."
>—LORNA DUECK
>former co-host of *100 Huntley Street*

"The opening was a page-turner. I know that women are going to read this and look at these women of the Bible with fresh eyes."
>—DEE BRESTIN
>author of *The Friendships of Women*

"This book is a 'good read' directed straight at the 'bad girl' in all of us."
>—ELISA MORGAN
>president emerita, MOPS International

"With a skillful pen and engaging candor Liz paints pictures of modern situations, then uniquely parallels them with the Bible's 'bad girls.' She doesn't condemn, but rather encourages and equips her readers to become godly women, regardless of the past."
>—MARY HUNT
>author of *Mary Hunt's Debt-Proof Living*

"*Bad Girls* is more than an entertaining romp through fascinating characters. It is a bona fide Bible study in which women (and men!) will see themselves revealed and restored through the matchless and amazing grace of God."

> —ANGELA ELWELL HUNT
> author of *The Immortal*

"Liz had me from the first paragraph. I was continually amazed how skillfully she dressed the biblical characters in contemporary garments. She made the old stories live again. An exciting work."

> —KALI SCHNIEDERS
> author of *Truffles from Heaven*

"Liz has brought a blended format of fiction, biblical commentary, and thought-provoking questions to each of these characters. I love the way Liz slips 'modern-day flesh' on biblical truth."

> —DARLENE HEPLER
> Church of the Open Door, Elyria, Ohio

"With great insight into the challenges faced by ten women who have gone before us, Liz analyzes the driving forces in women's lives that can cause them to make bad decisions. Invite a group of friends to join you in discussing the issues presented in this book—your lives may be changed forever!"

> —VICKY WAUTERLEK
> The Village Church of Barrington, Illinois

"I loved the down-to-earth realism. Instead of having an airbrushed, plastic feel, Bad Girls of the Bible jumps off the pages with fresh, relevant, and engaging applications."

> —BECKY MOLTUMYR
> director of women's ministries, Brookside Church,
> Omaha, Nebraska

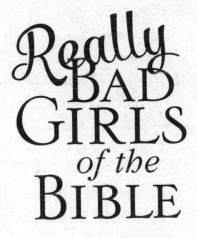

Really
BAD
GIRLS
of the
BIBLE

OTHER BOOKS BY LIZ CURTIS HIGGS

NONFICTION
Bad Girls of the Bible
Unveiling Mary Magdalene
Slightly Bad Girls of the Bible
Rise and Shine
Embrace Grace
My Heart's in the Lowlands
The Girl's Still Got It
The Women of Christmas
It's Good to Be Queen

HISTORICAL FICTION
Thorn in My Heart
Fair Is the Rose
Whence Came a Prince
Grace in Thine Eyes
Here Burns My Candle
Mine Is the Night
A Wreath of Snow

CONTEMPORARY FICTION
Mixed Signals
Bookends
Mercy Like Sunlight

CHILDREN'S BOOKS
The Pumpkin Patch Parable
The Parable of the Lily
The Sunflower Parable
The Pine Tree Parable

LIZ CURTIS HIGGS

Really BAD GIRLS of the BIBLE

More Lessons *from* Less-Than-Perfect Women

WATERBROOK

REALLY BAD GIRLS OF THE BIBLE

The contemporary story in each chapter is fiction. The characters and events are fictional and are not intended to parallel exactly the biblical story.

Trade Paperback ISBN 978-1-60142-861-5
eBook ISBN 978-0-307-44617-6

Copyright © 2000, 2016 by Liz Curtis Higgs

Cover design by Kelly L. Howard

Published in the United States by WaterBrook, an imprint of the Crown Publishing Group, a division of Penguin Random House LLC, New York.

WATERBROOK® and its deer colophon are registered trademarks of Penguin Random House LLC.

The Library of Congress has catalogued the original edition as follows:
Higgs, Liz Curtis.
    Really bad girls of the Bible: more lessons from less-than-perfect women / Liz Curtis Higgs. — 1st ed.
        p.   cm.
    Includes bibliographical references.
    ISBN 978-1-57856-126-1 (pbk.)
    1. Women in the Bible—Biography. 2. Christian women—Religious life. I. Title.
    BS575.H56   2000
    220.9'2'082—dc21   00043247

Printed in the United States of America
2019—Revised Edition

10 9 8 7 6

SPECIAL SALES

Most WaterBrook books are available at special quantity discounts when purchased in bulk by corporations, organizations, and special-interest groups. Custom imprinting or excerpting can also be done to fit special needs. For information, please e-mail specialmarketscms@penguinrandomhouse.com or call 1-800-603-7051.

For every woman whose note to me began,
"Dear Liz:
You don't know who I am, but you wrote
Bad Girls of the Bible for me…"

I do know who you are, dear sister,
and I did write that book for you.
This one, even more so.

My heart beats with yours as we turn toward the
only One who can save us from ourselves.

Contents

Introduction: Nightfall 1

One: Dead Man Talking
Medium of En Dor: *Bad Moon Rising* 11

Two: Lethal Weapon
Jael: *Bad for a Good Reason* 37

Three: Peculiar Grace
The Adulteress: *Bad, but Not Condemned* 63

Four: Blood Will Tell
Athaliah: *Bad and Proud of It* 89

Five: Bathing Beauty
Bathsheba: *Bad Moon Rising* 116

Six: Just Desserts
Herodias: *Bad and Proud of It* 153

Seven: Veiled Threat
Tamar the Widow: *Bad for a Good Reason* 180

Eight: Tears of a Clown
The Bleeding Woman: *Bad, but Not Condemned* . . . 214

Conclusion: Rebel's Heart 240

Spoken Word: Lord, We're Talking Some Really Bad Girls Here . . . 242

Discussion Questions. 243

Study Guide 245

Notes 273

Acknowledgments 287

Nightfall

Everyone is a moon,
and has a dark side
which he never shows to anybody.
MARK TWAIN

Beth awoke with the twittering birds in the predawn darkness. It took her a few seconds to figure out where she was. Sitting in her car—that much was certain. Parked sideways in the gravel lot behind her apartment building. She'd driven there apparently. But when? And how? From where?

The driver's door was hanging wide open. One blue-jeaned leg was draped out the car door, toes pointed north. Her blouse was half-undone and covered with a horrid-smelling, sticky substance. Remnants of red lipstick were smeared all over her face.

Or was that shame?

Nah. She didn't have any shame left.

She ran a hand through her hair out of habit, then swore at her disheveled image in the rearview mirror. *Disgusting, Beth.*

What day was it anyway? Her throbbing head fell back against the headrest. *Saturday.* The day after Friday, the day after she'd acted like a complete idiot in front of the sales team at work. Lost it, big time. Absolutely *blasted* their ears off. If word got back to her boss, she could kiss this gig good-bye.

Beth groaned and squinted at her watch. *Five something.* The early morning chill seeped through her jeans, making her shiver. Her bladder was screaming for attention, but she ignored it, trying to get her bearings, sort things out, fill in the blank spaces.

Twelve hours ago she'd come stomping into her living room after work, spitting mad, embarrassed over her anger and angry over her embarrassment. Without even shrugging off her jacket, she'd rolled a thimbleful of grass into a tight little joint and dragged hard on it as if it were a cigarette, nearly choking.

Suddenly the blare of a car horn cut through the silent morning darkness and interrupted her thoughts, making her jump with a hungover shudder. Beth sank back in her seat, feeling her heartbeat slowly return to normal. *Easy does it, kid.*

After she'd gotten high last night, then what?

In disjointed pieces more memories shifted into place. She'd fallen asleep on the couch, only to wake up bleary-eyed and stupid around eight. After a hot shower and a cold beer, she'd headed for the club and run into Tee.

Tee. Even now, still semiwasted in her car, she mustered a smile at the memory of Tee looking *fine* in his painted-on jeans. Not the man she'd been looking for, but she'd decided on the spot that he'd do nicely. They'd downed a couple of pitchers of Miller, danced a little, gotten high in the parking lot.

And then…nothing. Did they go to his place? To another bar? Why couldn't she remember? Where did those hours go?

Beth banged the palm of her hand on the steering wheel in frustration, avoiding a second glance in the rearview mirror. Whatever had happened last night, she'd made a spectacle of herself—that was pretty obvious.

C'mon, Beth. Time to go inside. Grabbing her purse, she swung her other leg out of the car and stumbled toward her apartment, fumbling for the keys. Her hands were shaking so badly it was all she could do to get inside before her heaving stomach sent her in search of a trash can, pronto.

Sprawled on the kitchen floor minutes later, every inch of her body in pain, Beth fought against the sobs that pressed against her chest. She'd had bad nights before, but not this bad. Not whole hours lost in the blackness, not driving a car blind drunk, risking her life and the lives of others. How could Tee have let her drive home? Had they argued?

What had happened? *What had happened?*

Beth forced herself to stand up, clutching the edge of the faded Formica counter to keep from falling to her knees. *Enough.* Twenty-seven years was enough, wasn't it? If a chick couldn't get her act together after all that time, she oughta hang it up, right?

Right.

She made her way down the hall, toward a shower and a bed, hoping to wash away her pain and sleep away the shadowy, shameful memories, yet knowing it wouldn't help.

What did she have to live for anyway? No real friends, probably no job come Monday morning, no decent man in her life, no future whatsoever.

Nothing but to get out of bed, get to work, get home, get drunk, get lucky.

Bag it, girl.

Depositing her clothes in an untidy heap on the linoleum floor, Beth fell into the shower. Scalding hot water slapped her across the face. Numb with pain, she simply stood there and took it.

Pills would be the easiest way. No pain, no hassle, just sleep.

Endless sleep.

She turned her back on the water as a flood of unwelcome tears streamed down her cheeks. The pulsating water lashed against her shoulders like a leather strap, a much-deserved punishment.

Death couldn't come soon enough for Beth…

What's So Bad About Being a Bad Girl?

Beth has a problem, but it's not the one you might think of first.

Her problem isn't drinking, drugs, or promiscuity. That's the outside stuff, the part most folks agree makes her a Bad Girl.

But here's the deal: You can straighten up your external act and still be dying inside. People applaud 'cause you're "clean," but inside you feel dirtier than ever.

Beth's problem also isn't low self-esteem, unresolved anger, or feelings of abandonment. Those things may fuel her Badder-Than-She-Wants-to-Be lifestyle, but they aren't at the heart of it. When you get such psychological issues worked out, people mistakenly think you're "cured," an emotionally healthy woman ready to face the world.

Our girl Beth knows better. She knows that identifying—even discussing at length—those prickly core issues doesn't make them go away, no matter how many books you read or sermons you hear.

Her problem is simply this: Beth is in a pit, and she can't climb out.

Those who've never been in that particular pit have little patience with Beth. They lean over her abyss and shake their finger at her. "Don't you know that's a pit? What kind of fool gets herself in that much trouble? You've shamed your whole family. Don't you know that?"

Listen to me: This will not help Beth. She is already covered with shame and self-loathing; she doesn't need more added on top. Judgment isn't a lifeline; it's a death sentence.

Good people—parents, spouses, friends, well-meaning folks, Christians—may venture near the edge of Beth's pit, not to judge, but to encourage. They call down to her, "Just climb out, Beth. You can do it! We're all waiting up here for you, sweetie. Come on, take that first step."

Oh dear. This won't help Beth either. It's too dark down there even to see a toehold or feel a rope bouncing off your shoulder or hear a ladder being lowered rung by rung. It's especially tough when you've been crying for a good while.

Besides, Beth already *knows* she can't do it. She's tried again and again to climb out of her pit of despair, each time slipping deeper into the muck. It may be pitch-black in that hole, but she's been down there so long the darkness feels like home.

Some kind believers may gather in a circle around the top of her pit. They pray that Beth will wake up and climb out—"Dear Lord, let Beth see her sins clearly. Tell her we love her"—before heading to Denny's for brunch, convinced they've done all they could for poor, misguided Beth.

Is this woman beyond reach, beyond hope?

Here's the rest of her story…

Beth fell into bed, sinking into the mattress, a damp towel still wrapped around her body, her arms limp and outstretched, her cheeks ruddy with shame. She would buy those pills when she woke up, but for the moment she was in no shape to drive.

Instead she would sleep.

A little sleep now. A forever sleep soon.

The sleep of the dead.

Little did Beth know that while she planned her own unhappy ending, far above her someone was circling her pit, waiting for the opportune moment. Waiting until she hit bottom. Waiting until she looked up. That time finally came when Beth realized where she was—buried deep in a pit—and how much she hated being there.

On that sacred day, when nothing could be heard but Beth's weeping in that grim and desolate place, a man lowered himself over the side. He eased down the walls of the pit—not in a hurry but not stalling either—giving Beth time to see him coming, to watch his descent and reflect on who he was.

Finally he stood before her and breathed one syllable into the darkness. "Beth."

He knows my name. Stunned, she merely nodded, squinting to see him better.

His eyes were kind. "I came for you."

She stared at the familiar stranger but said nothing.

He brushed a smudge of dirt off her sleeve. "You think I came only for those people up there, don't you?"

"Yes," she managed to croak, hating the sound of her voice.

"I did come for them. But I also came for you."

"No." She shook her head, certain on this one. "I'm not good enough."

"That's true, you're not. Neither are they. But I am." He held his arms out, as if to cradle something. "Are you ready?"

She shrank back. "Ready for what?"

"For me." He regarded her without judgment or disgust. "I'm here to carry you out of your pit."

Her eyes narrowed. "Who says I want out?"

He gazed at the cramped, bleak space that surrounded them. "Nobody really wants to live in a place like this. People convince themselves they do, but they don't."

"I dunno…" She peered upward, aware for the first time that light was seeping in from above. "What if I don't like it…up there?"

"You will," he assured her with a gentle smile. "I promise."

A spark of defiance crept into her voice. "What's so good about it?"

"That's where I live." He touched her hand. "Come with me, Beth. I love you."

He *loved* her? Boy, that was a new one. Not guilt or shame or shoulda-woulda-coulda stuff. *Love.* Hard to say no to that one.

Beth exhaled, preparing for a long haul. "Tell me what I have to do."

He gathered her into his arms like a babe. "What you have to do is simply this: Believe in me. Trust that I can carry you without letting go."

She swallowed hard. "Are you strong enough?"

"I am." He started moving upward without so much as a grunt.

"Are you brave enough?"

"I am." They were halfway to the top.

Her quivering voice was barely above a whisper. "Do you love me enough?"

"I do." He looked straight at her when he said it, and despite the knot in her stomach, she believed him.

The truth was undeniable. *He loves me. He loves me!*

All at once they were out of the pit and on solid ground. She blinked at the brightness of the sun. Or was it his face, shining like that?

The man slid her gracefully to her feet. "Welcome home, Beth."

"Th-thank you," she stammered.

And then she cried with her whole heart...

Praise the LORD,...
who forgives all your sins
    and heals all your diseases,
who redeems your life from the pit
    and crowns you with love and compassion. *Psalm 103:2–4*

Sometimes I still cry. I'm crying now. Weeping, in fact, with joy and gratitude. You've guessed by this point, I imagine, that Beth's story is my own. Though I'm Eliza*beth*, everybody calls me Liz.

I know what you're thinking.

How did you end up in that pit, Liz? Were you tossed in against your will? Did you crawl in on purpose? Or did you wake up there one morning, dazed and confused?

Yes, yes, and yes. Don't waste any energy on questions like these.

It doesn't matter how we get down in a pit. *It only matters that we get out of it.*

Not all pits are dark either. Some are neon bright, filled with the spoils of materialism or the trophies of worldly success.

The ten years I spent in the pit are my hardest-earned credentials for writing *Really Bad Girls of the Bible,* the stories of eight biblical women who lived in pits of one design or another. They had some all-too-obvious sins going on in their lives as well. Public sins. Nasty sins. Murder. Sorcery. Adultery. Deceit.

One writer observed, "Life hasn't changed a great deal in over two thousand years. The images of the good girl and the bad girl are still very much with us."[1] They sure are. We'll save the Good Girls for another time. I always learn more from women who are less than perfect, simply because we have much more in common.

Try as I might (and I did!), I couldn't change their lives to have happy endings. The Lord himself did so in several cases. In others, although the women made poor choices, God worked through their situations anyway. They were Bad Girls—but he is a good and sovereign God.

When I wrote *Bad Girls of the Bible,* I never dreamed there were so many other Former Bad Girls like me out there who needed to know they are not alone. These precious sisters sent letters and e-mails, which I read in private, then prayed over and tucked in a safe place. I treasure their confessions, knowing the courage it took to write them.

Carefully keeping their identities close to my heart, I'll share only a few words so you'll know that *you* are not alone as well. Three women wrote:

- It's nice to know I'm not as hopeless as I once thought and God does have a special plan for each of us.
- Though most people have not forgiven me, God certainly has.
- When you are on the bottom, God can still reach down and bring you up.

Yes, he can! What words of comfort for us pit dwellers. Now it's time to meet our historical counterparts.

Athaliah and Herodias were *Bad and Proud of It.* "Make no apologies" and "take no prisoners" were the mottoes of these two vengeful females.

The Medium of En Dor and Bathsheba both experienced a *Bad Moon*

Rising. A royal pain came knocking on their doors one moonlit night—different nights, different kings, but double trouble just the same.

Our two *Bad for a Good Reason* Girls, Jael and Tamar the widow, were used by God despite their highly unusual means of putting men in their place.

Finally, two New Testament women—known by their no-nos but not by their names—give us hope with their stories of being *Bad, but Not Condemned.*

All eight chapters begin with a contemporary, fictional take on our biblical Bad Girls, just to remind us that when it comes to badness, there's nothing new under the sun.

If the first *Bad Girls of the Bible* book was about grace, this second one is all about the sovereignty of God, the unstoppable power of God to accomplish his perfect will, no matter how much we mess up.

Get this: God doesn't work *around* our sin; he works *through* it.

Honey, I can hear you now: "You mean God is waiting for us to sin so he can show his mighty power despite our foolish interference?"

Uh...no. God doesn't have to wait for us to sin in order to act. We're already sinning. No waiting involved. God is also not sitting around wringing his holy hands and saying, "Now look what they've done. How am I gonna manage with *that* mess?"

God is God. He is all-powerful, all-wise. He is omni-everything. My controlling nature, however, chafes at the thought of not being in charge. I suspect our eight Really Bad Girls weren't eager to relinquish control either.

And yet, if we would choose the life of a Future Good Girl over remaining a Forever Bad Girl, there are two truths we need to grasp:

1. God will be sovereign in our lives only if we accept the truth that we are not—and never were—in charge.
2. God will extend his grace to us the minute we admit that we are utterly lost without it.

Dear one, if you've never been in a dark pit, we all rejoice with you. I will, however, offer this gentle reminder: "If you think you are standing firm, be careful that you don't fall!"[2]

If you've been saved from the bottom of the pit as I have, let's celebrate our freedom without forgetting those dear souls we left behind who are waiting desperately to hear the Good News.

And if you're still down in that pit of shame, beloved, remember that Jesus came to earth for *you*. His arms are open, ready, and waiting to carry you home.

Dead Man Talking

'Tis now the very witching time of night,
When churchyards yawn and hell itself breathes out
Contagion to this world.
WILLIAM SHAKESPEARE

D ora smiled out the window at the fading twilight and watched the world surrender itself to the night.

Almost time.

Pouring boiling water over the loose tea with great care, she breathed in the warm, pungent scent, feeling her head clear and her senses sharpen. The teapot lid dropped into place with a musical *clink*.

Dora stole another glance out the window, then settled onto the couch to wait. In the distance a whistle moaned as a freight train passed unseen through the outskirts of town. *Nearly seven.* When the starless sky turned black as ink, the doorbell would ring and business would commence. Her supper dishes were already stacked in the cupboard, her apron folded neatly across the drainer, her kitchen table bare except for a cluster of scented candles and the steaming pot of Ceylon tea.

Dora was ready.

No need to post a sign in her window or run a boldface line in the yellow pages. *Certainly not.* Her customers always found her, however illegal her work might be.

Bending down to stroke the ginger-and-white cat that rubbed along her legs, Dora laughed softly. "Thank the stars we've never been found out, eh, Chelsea?" Purring along with her feline friend, she added in a stage whisper, "Someone rather powerful must be watching out for us."

Years earlier the good citizens of Peoria had voted to abolish all "irregular" businesses like hers. The pastors of the town were behind the ban one hundred percent, Rev. Samuel Clay especially. He kept confusing the hidden arts, calling palm readers "psychics" and astrologers "spiritualists" and the whole lot of them "witches."

Witches! The man was pitifully uninformed.

Since that fateful day, Dora was pleased to point out, not one police car had pulled up to the curb outside her tidy clapboard cottage. Nor had an unwelcome summons appeared in her mailbox. The neighborhood didn't seem to notice the middle-age matrons stumbling through her door after sunset or the curious college students who gathered around the sturdy oak table in her blue-and-white kitchen.

So much the better. Dora didn't need an audience. Those who knocked on her front door were lost souls. Nothing more than friends not met yet, stopping by for tea. If they accidentally left a twenty-dollar bill under their saucer, well, they knew she was a widow who could use the small blessing.

In Peoria, heart of the heartland, mediums were few and far between. No wonder business was brisk. She was needed. A helper, that's what she was. A servant to the forgotten. Hadn't she buried a husband? And a sister? And a child? Dora knew all there was to know about missing loved ones, about longing to hear their voices once more.

She heard something now. The sound of a car drawing near, then the engine abruptly shutting off. *Ah.* Dora's smile broadened. Her first customer of the evening.

It was George Nicholson standing on her dimly lit porch, his soiled herringbone hat crushed between arthritic fingers, his eyes downcast.

She opened the door with a generous sweep. "Welcome, George."

He could barely meet her gaze. "H-hello, Dora."

George usually came on Thursdays—payday. His late wife, Nancy, had been gone for two years, most of which he'd spent trying to contact her, hoping to bring their last conversation to a better conclusion.

That's what most of Dora's work entailed: unfinished business with the dead.

The hour with George went well. He was quite convinced the spirit of Nancy had joined them. Not every word was clear, not every phrase made sense—that was part of what made it appear so authentic—yet George seemed more than satisfied. The additional dollars he slipped into Dora's palm confirmed it. George backed down her porch steps, eyes brimming with grateful tears, and disappeared into the night.

Dora closed the door behind her, exhaled with a deliberate, cleansing breath, then eyed the enormous cat that filled the slipcovered chair like pudding in a cup. "An honest hour's work for us, wouldn't you say, Chelsea girl?"

The cat answered with a slow, silent blink that Dora understood completely, blinking back at her. Chelsea was the only one she could talk to, the only one truly familiar with her work. How could she risk explaining her nocturnal activities to friends and neighbors? The aromatic candles, the soft, tuneless music, the careful, circular arrangement of objects belonging to the dead, the smoky fire on the grate, the groans and murmurs and tortured sighs from here and there, from then and now.

It was exhausting, really. Three visitors a night was her limit. The mental preparation—that was the most demanding part. Total concentration, absolute focus. Then, if all was properly aligned, she would sense words flowing through her and would relax, feeling her customer's clenched hands loosen their grip on hers.

When the spirits were uncooperative or surly, as if she'd rudely disturbed their sound sleep, Dora included a few words of counsel of her own—words of comfort and assurance, to give the living one closure, to give the person hope. Most of the time it felt utterly natural, this talking in a voice that was not wholly hers. Other times it was unnerving, a bit out-of-body, as if perhaps someone else's voice altogether were speaking, though she knew very well how the whole process worked.

Those who might accuse her of "trafficking with the devil"—*honestly, the very idea!*—didn't have the faintest notion of the good she accomplished. She was dealing with departed spirits, not demons. Hers was a sort of white magic, harmless yet powerful.

The response of her customers—their tears of joy and relief—were what kept her going. It was a sacred calling, of that Dora was convinced.

Two more needy souls tapped on her front door that evening. A woman in her twenties wanted nothing more than to hear her mother's voice. Dora squeezed the girl's unlined hands with affection, thinking of her own daughter on the Other Side. Her last customer was an older woman, heartbroken at the loss of her husband two months earlier and desperate for companionship. Weeping throughout their session, the stranger left drained but happy.

Dora felt much the same: emptied yet filled with contentment.

The hour grew late. Nearly midnight, she guessed, stretching her bone-weary limbs, then snapping off the front porch light. The fire had died to scant more than embers, which she poked with listless stabs, yawning all the while. "To bed with us, Chelsea."

The knock on the back door was sharp and sudden.

Dora dropped the iron poker, hearing it clatter on the tile hearth as if it were miles away, her every sense directed toward the kitchen door.

No one ever used that entrance.

It was locked tight. Always.

Bending down to scoop up Chelsea—for support, for protection from who knew what—Dora swallowed an uncomfortable lump in her throat and made her way toward the shadow-bathed kitchen. The candles had been snuffed out some time ago; the cold teapot sat empty in the sink.

Again the curtained door rattled under a series of firm knocks. Voices were raised. Men's voices. Strangers —there was no doubt of it. Her heart was hammering so loud she couldn't discern their ages nor their intent. Only the desperation in their muffled words was certain.

Mustering every ounce of courage in her tired body, Dora called out, projecting her voice across the room. "Who are you? What is it you want?" Her surprisingly firm, authoritative tone reminded her of Carolyn Hutter's dead husband, for whom she'd interceded last Tuesday.

She flicked on the overhead light, and the kitchen instantly looked like home again, the countertops scrubbed clean, all four corners warm and inviting. Until, with a *pop*, the light bulb went out, plunging the room into a shroud of darkness once more.

Not good.

She blinked, willing her eyes to adjust. Her hands, usually warm, felt like ice against the cat's back. Chelsea's furry head was up, eyes and ears pointed toward the door, a low sort of growl stirring in her throat.

Steady, Dora. She clutched the animal tighter to her chest and eased her way across the room, steeling herself. Perhaps it was the police at last, come to put her out of business after all these years.

The men on the porch knocked again, louder and more insistently.

"Coming!" She nearly shouted it, for her own sake more than theirs. Stretching out a trembling hand, Dora pulled aside the gingham curtains that covered the back-door window and assessed the party on the other side of the glass.

Three men formed a broad, human knot on her porch. Two younger ones, their eyes wide with apprehension, and a larger man between them, his face lined with grief, although his direct gaze pierced hers with an uncanny measure of intelligence.

"We've need of your services, ma'am." His rough voice easily cut through the small panes between them. "Don't be afraid. We mean no harm."

Something told her he spoke the truth. Though wise, his eyes also had a haunted look. If anyone was fearful that night, it was this man.

Feeling in control again, her hands no longer shaking, Dora unlocked the door and pulled it open, its seldom-used hinges creaking in protest. "What can I do for you, gentlemen? Made a wrong turn, have you?"

The younger men both offered tentative smiles. "Not at all, ma'am," the taller one on the right said, sounding relieved. "Our boss here wants a...well, he'd like to..."

The older man leaned forward. "I need to speak to my dead father."

"I see." Dora studied the men for a moment. They seemed sincere enough, but she couldn't take any chances—not with strangers, not at this hour. "And what makes you think I could honor such an outrageous request?"

The one on the left piped up. "Everybody knows you're a medium." He pulled out a wallet, thick with bills. "Trust me, we'll pay you well for your services."

She frowned and shook her head. "What you're asking me to do is illegal"—her standard line when an unknown prospect knocked. "If I recall the news story correctly, that kind of business is against the city ordinances—"

"So it is, Dora," their boss barked. "Illegal as sin." The older man stepped across her threshold, towering over her. "Which is why we won't breathe a word of what happens this night, not to a living soul."

"Nor to a dead one?" She swallowed the last of her concerns as a smile tugged at the corners of her mouth.

His laugh was gruff. "Talking to the dead is your department. So, will you help me? I swear on my father's grave, my intentions are honorable."

We'll see about that. With a slight nod, she stepped back and ushered them into her gloomy kitchen. "Kindly give me a moment to get every-thing ready, will you?"

Lighting the candles with a steady hand, she directed the younger men into chairs well away from the table, lest they interfere with her centering efforts. Years of practice showed in her efficient preparation of the proper

setting for a séance. Within minutes, the fire on the grate had sprung back
to life. A heady scent of anise pervaded the room, and deep notes from a
lone cello poured from the hidden stereo speakers, infusing the silence with
a low, hypnotic thrum.

She reached across the table and took the older man's large hands in
hers, not surprised to find his grasp clammy but firm. "Are you ready to tell
me your name?"

"Seth." He lifted his chin, meeting her gaze. "Seth Clay."

"Clay?" Stunned, she drew back, releasing his hands as if she'd been
stung. Why hadn't she seen the resemblance sooner? "The same family as
Samuel Clay, the minister?"

He nodded, his expression grim. "I'm his oldest son. My father died a
few weeks ago. Or didn't you know?"

Of course she knew. Everybody knew. Half the town had attended his
funeral. Dora had not been among them though. She'd celebrated Reverend Clay's passing by buttering an extra scone at breakfast that happy
morning.

Now the wretched man's son was seated at her table, expecting her
to conjure up the spirit of Samuel Clay, a narrow-minded tyrant who'd
labeled her and her friends in the community "wicked witches" and "evil
sorcerers."

Evil? Why, she was nothing of the sort! She *helped* people, made their
lives better, their futures more certain.

She glared across the table at the reverend's fifty-something son, the
lines in his face etched deeper by the flickering candlelight. In his eyes she
saw neither judgment nor reproach. Only sorrow and a great emptiness.

It tore her medium's heart in two. The man desperately needed her
assistance. Samuel Clay was dead and gone, wasn't he? True, with her particular skills, he could still speak from the grave, but he could no longer
hurt her. The curtain between their two worlds was thin but impenetrable.

Let him speak then.

"What is it you want from your father, Seth?"

He gnawed on his lower lip, choosing his words with care. "I'm an attorney, you see."

She merely nodded, remembering some mention of his profession in the obituary. "Go on."

"Tomorrow I face an opponent in the courtroom who knows my every strategy. Without more information, I'm certain to lose the case, if not my entire career." He edged closer. "It's that important."

"I understand." Which she certainly did. "But what of your father?"

"He always counseled me before my trials. He…prayed with me. Helped me see the big picture, how God's hand moved in such situations."

Dora's lips pressed into a thin, hard line. *God deciding court cases?* Samuel Clay had a lot of nerve calling mediums dangerous and fanatical! She'd almost relish conjuring up the loathsome man's ghost, if only to taunt him with his permanently spectral state.

Grasping Seth's hands in hers, more resolutely this time, she closed her eyes and brought to mind an image of Samuel Clay. It was easy enough to picture him, rising to his feet at a city council meeting, his gnarled hand wrapped around a Bible held aloft as if it contained some great truth instead of mere ancient superstitions.

For several moments she did nothing but breathe. The room grew still as death itself.

When she spoke at last, her voice was calm. "I see you, Reverend Clay."

Seth's hands began quivering. His voice was a hoarse whisper. "What do you see?"

So impatient! She saw only what Seth had to be seeing in his own mind's eye: a vivid memory of his father. "I see your father in a gray suit…white shirt…red striped tie with a gold tiepin."

Seth gasped. "Th-that's wh-what he w-was w-wearing when w-we…we *buried* him!"

Dora smiled. The spirits were generous this night. The reverend's limited wardrobe and her lucid memory of the photo in the newspaper helped too. As the vision of Samuel Clay grew in size and clarity, she marveled at how real the image seemed. Why, she would have vowed he was in that very room!

As if lifted by an unseen hand, her eyelids slowly fluttered open, then widened in utter shock.

A bloodcurdling scream filled the air. *Her* scream.

He was there. In her kitchen.

Samuel Clay hovered larger than life behind his son, one ghostly hand still holding a Bible, the other resting on Seth's shoulder.

"Seth!" She swallowed, struggling to speak. "Your…father. He's…here. With us. Now."

Eyes wide with fear, Seth swung around in his chair. "Where? Where is he?" He swiveled back, distraught. "I don't…I don't see a thing, woman! Tell me what you see!"

What Dora saw left her speechless.

She, who many times had mentally reached across the chasm that separates life and death, had never approached such a level of success. It was thrilling. And terrifying.

This much was clear: It wasn't *she* bringing this ghost to life. It wasn't Seth's doing either. *No.* It must be—

Dora suddenly felt her mouth being forced open against her will, her lungs expanding with air, her lips preparing to move.

Rev. Samuel Clay, it seemed, wanted to speak…

⌾

Kings That Go Bump in the Night:
The Medium of En Dor

Somebody please turn the lights on.

Ever since our Girl Scout days, when we circled around a crackling campfire on a black-as-pitch summer night, trembling on our waterproof sit-upons, we've heard and read dozens of ghost stories. Tales of the supernatural are part and parcel of our culture—from Charles Dickens's *A Christmas Carol* to Stephen King's *Bag of Bones*.

Why the appeal? Because such otherworldly journeys are *forbidden*. Our naturally rebellious selves are drawn to things that say "Don't touch!" and "Warning!" Scary stories let us take a (short) walk on the wild side, then run home to a well-lit kitchen.

What's so bad about dabbling on the dark side?

Ask the Lord. You'll find his decree is crystal-ball clear:

> Let no one be found among you who…practices divination or sorcery, interprets omens, engages in witchcraft, or casts spells, or who is a medium or spiritist or who consults the dead. *Deuteronomy 18:10–11*

What a list! Who would ever think of doing all *that*? The Canaanites did. Those nefarious neighbors of Israel filled their religious rites with the entire collection of no-nos listed above.

Three thousand years later such practices are still around—flourishing, in fact—though some go by different names. *Divination* is another word for fortune-telling. Call the psychic hotline for details. A *sorcerer* tries to control people or situations with potions and herbs. Think aromatherapy with a seriously bad attitude. *Interpreting omens* includes analyzing flight patterns of birds, leaves in the bottom of a teacup, or whatever's handy. *Witchcraft*—modern practitioners prefer "wicca"—bewitches us everywhere we turn these days, from movie screens to bookstore shelves.

"Boo" is right.

Which brings us to this chapter's nameless Bad Girl, a *medium* or spiritist who contacted the dead. Label her what you will—"wizard" (KJV), "psychic" (NLT), "necromancer" (RSV), or one who "traffics with ghosts and spirits" (NEB)—the girl was a rock's throw from disaster.

"A man or woman who is a medium or spiritist among you
must be put to death. You are to stone them;…"

Ouch. A zero-tolerance situation, this medium business.

"…their blood will be on their own heads." *Leviticus 20:27*

In other words, by breaking God's laws, they "brought it on themselves" (ICB).

You could say the same thing of King Saul, a man who made himself
miserable by eventually turning his back on God. In the early years of his
reign, though, he sent those necromancer types packing.

Saul had expelled the mediums and spiritists from the land.
1 Samuel 28:3

Don't be impressed. We'll see in a minute how Saul managed to "drive
the devil out of his kingdom, and yet harbour him in his heart."[1] Like so
many of us, he got his outward act together, but inside the dark recesses of
his soul, a rebellious spark still burned.

Lord Byron's take on this biblical story of King Saul and the shady lady
from En Dor catches the spirit of the tale: "It beats all the ghost scenes I
ever read."[2] After all, *this* one was the real thing.

Our ghost story opens—appropriately—at night, on the eve of a battle
with those nasty Philistines.

When Saul saw the Philistine army, he was afraid; terror filled
his heart. *1 Samuel 28:5*

Saul, a scaredy-cat? Saul, the slayer of thousands, terrified?
You bet.

Saul realized he would fight the Philistines alone the next day, without
God's mighty right arm to guarantee the victory. Tough to lift your stan-
dard high with certain death staring you in the face. As a last-ditch effort,
Saul knocked on heaven's door.

He inquired of the LORD, but the LORD did not answer
him…

I know what you're thinking: *What's the deal, Lord? He needs your help!*
True. But Saul had severed his relationship with God by intentionally dis-
obeying the Lord's commands. The prophet Samuel had delivered the bad
news years earlier: "Because you have rejected the word of the LORD, he has
rejected you as king."[3]

Now we find him groping in the dark for answers.

…by dreams or Urim or prophets. *1 Samuel 28:6*

His dreams were nightmares. His trusty Urim and Thummim—two
stones used to determine the will of God by asking yes and no questions—
were dark. Even the prophet Samuel wasn't around anymore, since at age
ninety-eight "the venerable Samuel crossed the boundary line into the
other world."[4]

A desperate Saul decided to bring him back from that "other world"
where only the dead reside.

Crank up the fog machine and cue the eerie music.

Saul then said to his attendants, "Find me a woman who is a
medium, so I may go and inquire of her." *1 Samuel 28:7*

Find him a *what*? You mean one of those people he *expelled*?

At his order, those Bad Girls (and Boys) of the black arts were run out
of town on a rail (okay, a camel), and now he wants one to act as his
"medium [between the living and the dead]" (AMP)?

Desperate wasn't the half of it.

Such women weren't a dime a dozen—honey, you know they charged
more than *that*—but being a medium was a "common occupation among
ancient Near Eastern women."[5]

With little trouble, Saul's men found such a gal.

"There is one in Endor," they said. *1 Samuel 28:7*

Although it's also spelled "En-dor" (NEB), I decided to stick with the old-fashioned "En Dor" (NKJV) since in the original Hebrew it's two separate words: *En* ("well or spring") and *Dor* ("the nearest town").

Just four miles from Mount Tabor[6], this Canaanite stronghold was located in the same general area where we'll discover another Bad Girl—Jael—who nailed that Bad Boy Sisera, "who perished at En Dor, who became as refuse on the earth."[7]

Lovely spot.

For Saul to get to En Dor, he not only had to cross into enemy territory, he had to sneak past the Philistine army. The trip itself was dangerous, never mind what waited for him at the end. In Kipling's words, "And nothing has changed of the sorrow in store for such as go down the road to En-dor."[8] Preach it, brother.

So Saul disguised himself, putting on other clothes…

He skipped the royal robes. Ditto the good jewelry. Saul not only had to keep his identity under wraps for that stealthy stroll past the Philistines, but he couldn't have his own people see him tiptoeing into a medium's abode. The woman herself had to be kept in the dark, lest she panic and refuse to serve the very king who'd put her out of business.

…and at night he and two men went to the woman.
1 Samuel 28:8

In my teenage years, my mother always cautioned me to be home before the stroke of twelve. "Nothing good happens after midnight," she insisted. Mom was right, of course. Did I listen? I did not. Many were the midnight hours of my rebellious youth spent in the backseat of a Camaro or the front row of an R-rated movie or in the middle of a circle of friends passing around some (un)controlled substance.

Hiding from the light.

Hiding from the Lord.

Darkness and disobedience go together. Almost all the scenes of Shakespeare's witchy *Macbeth* take place "either at night or in some dark spot."[9] The apostle John wrote, "Men loved darkness instead of light because their deeds were evil."[10] That night in En Dor even the starless sky couldn't match the darkness of Saul's soul, that night when "death was in the air."[11]

We know not the hour of the night, but we know it was dark indeed. We know nothing of the age or appearance of this unnamed medium, though she was certainly "hedged around with a circle of evil rumors."[12]

Two things we do know: This surely wasn't her first late-night visitor. And the man on the other side of the door wasted no time in stating his intentions.

> "Consult a spirit for me," he said, "and bring up for me the
> one I name." *1 Samuel 28:8*

In ten versions of the Old Testament, this verse is never translated the same way twice. Check out these various phrasings:

"conduct a séance for me" (NKJV)

"perceive for me by the familiar spirit" (AMP)

"tell me my fortunes by consulting the dead" (NEB)

"bring up the ghost of someone" (CEV)

"I have to talk to a man who has died" (NLT)

That last one cuts to the chase, doesn't it?

Reminds me of the advertisement typo I saw for a Christian event where "interpretation for the *dead* will be provided." *Oops.* In Saul's day, however, provisions like that were more than a proofreading problem. They were against the law.

> But the woman said to him, "Surely you know what Saul has
> done. He has cut off the mediums and spiritists from the
> land." *1 Samuel 28:9*

Never mind the fact that talking to dead people broke God's Law. Madam Medium only cared that it broke *Saul's* law. It was clear that her heart did not belong to the Lord God.

Notice she didn't deny being a medium—what, and scare away a potential cash-paying customer? But she, who was "an outlaw, judged worthy of death,"[13] *did* want to find out how this stranger felt about bending the rules.

> "Why have you set a trap for my life to bring about my
> death?" *1 Samuel 28:9*

Was she truly worried…or hoping to raise her fee by pointing out the big risk she was taking?

> Saul swore to her by the LORD, "As surely as the LORD lives,
> you will not be punished for this." *1 Samuel 28:10*

Girls, this is what I call taking the Lord's name in vain. Using his name inappropriately. Blasphemously. Calling on the One whom Saul no longer knew, nor had a right to call his ally.

Sadly, it was also the *last* time Saul uttered the name of the Lord.

> Then the woman asked, "Whom shall I bring up for you?"
> *1 Samuel 28:11*

At this point I want film footage, not a script. Why did she suddenly agree to take the gig? Did he silently press money into her hand when he made that oath? Did the two men with him brandish highly motivating weapons? Or did the obvious desperation on Saul's face prompt her to help this stranger?

She didn't realize he was King Saul—not yet—but she did recognize a beaten man when she saw one. Mediums of her day were older, wiser women, "deeply versed in human nature; acquainted with all the weaknesses, hopes and fears of the human heart."[14]

People came to her as a last resort. Each knock at her door was no doubt followed by the same needy entreaty: "Help me!"

The witches I've met—including the one I almost chose as a roommate when I was nineteen—all had a desire to help people. Misdirected, to be sure, but genuine. They saw their craft as a way of assisting folks who were confused, lost, or discouraged.

Consider this, dear sisters: If you and I don't stand in the gap as holy "mediums"—serving as godly intercessors by sharing the truth of Christ with those who don't know him—our pagan counterparts on the dark side *will.*

Believe it.

Our Girl in En Dor stood ready to serve.

"Bring up Samuel," he said. *1 Samuel 28:11*

Wait. *Samuel?* As prophets go, he was "one of the purest, noblest on any record."[15] You'd think Samuel would be the *last* person Saul would wanna talk to. While Samuel lived, he seldom had good news for Saul. Death would hardly improve matters, would it?

And what of the medium? Wouldn't *she* have been nervous about calling forth a prophet of the Lord?

Aha! Our first clue. She didn't *expect* Samuel—or anyone else—to make an appearance! No wonder she went about her necromancy without hesitation. She wasn't truly calling forth dead spirits. It was nothing but smoke and mirrors and giving people what they wanted.

The next verse, as you'll see, describes the outcome of her efforts…but *not* how she did it. Very wise, Lord. You know us well. If we had a recipe for such conjuring, we'd be tempted to try it.

Records of typical séances in the past reveal a use of something the ancients called "Engastrymysme…or ventriloquism,"[16] which often sounded like "chirping and muttering"[17] to the customers. Probably sounded like gold coins to the medium.

But the woman of En Dor, no doubt gearing up to create this spirit by her own subterfuge, was in for a shock.

> When the woman saw Samuel, she cried out at the top of her voice…

Um…didn't her *customers* usually do the screaming?

What caught her off guard? The importance of the one who appeared? As in, "Wow, it's Samuel! Didn't know my own strength!" Or was she shocked that it occurred at all? Was this in fact the *first* time her mumbo jumbo seemed to work?

That's my vote.

> …and said to Saul, "Why have you deceived me?"
> *1 Samuel 28:12*

Deceived *her*? My, isn't that the cauldron calling the kettle black!

> "You are Saul!" *1 Samuel 28:12*

She saw the ghost of Samuel, screamed, and then identified…*Saul*? That's odd. How did seeing Sam add up to Saul, I wonder. Did Samuel speak Saul's name as he rose? Did the medium reason that Samuel wouldn't have showed up for anyone less than the king himself? In any case, the woman put two and two together and came up with one scary scenario.

Talk about being between a rock and a hard place! A dead prophet on one side, a deranged king on the other. *Eeek.*

> The king said to her, "Don't be afraid. What do you see?"
> *1 Samuel 28:13*

The Hebrew text shows us this isn't a rebuke but a softened form of the words "please don't be afraid." After all, Saul needed her help more than ever because apparently he couldn't see squat.

> The woman said, "I see a spirit coming up out of the
> ground." *1 Samuel 28:13*

No wonder she was frightened at the "ghostly form" (NEB) rising before her eyes. "The ground" didn't mean tilled soil but the region far below it, "the netherworld, the realm of the dead."[18]

Shiver me timbers!

> "What does he look like?" he asked. *1 Samuel 28:14*

Saul still couldn't see anything, but he obviously believed her. Guess the scream did it.

> "An old man wearing a robe is coming up," she said.
> *1 Samuel 28:14*

Honestly, it might have been anybody. "Old man in robe" could describe my own dear father rising from his recliner, wearing the same beige terrycloth bathrobe he loved for ages. But since Saul *requested* Samuel and *expected* Samuel, those two clues were enough to satisfy him.

"Old geezer? Long robe? Yup, that's Sam."

> Then Saul knew it was Samuel, and he bowed down and
> prostrated himself with his face to the ground. *1 Samuel
> 28:14*

It seemed Saul "did homage" (NASB) to the dearly departed. Either that, or he thought putting his ear to the ground might help him hear better.

> Samuel said to Saul, "Why have you disturbed me by bring-
> ing me up?" *1 Samuel 28:15*

I'll bet Sam spoke in sepulchral tones. Dead serious, too. Pointed out Saul's grave errors… (Okay, okay, I'll stop.)

One important question: *Who was doing the talking here?*

The Lord? The devil? Or the Medium of En Dor?

I'm ruling out the medium. She may have been the conduit, but the prophetic words that followed weren't her own.

That old talking snake, Lucifer? Some scholars think it possible, arguing that the devil, by divine permission, could have impersonated Samuel "since he can transform himself into an angel of light."[19]

Yeah, but to what end? Our medium was so scared she probably turned in her crystal ball the minute Saul left, never to consort with the Prince of Darkness again. Besides, Satan has no knowledge of what is to come except that which is revealed in God's Word, meaning the prophecy Samuel shared later would have been beyond Satan's ken.

So was it God himself speaking? Maybe God "miraculously permitted the actual spirit of Samuel to speak."[20] Or maybe it was nothing more than Saul's off-the-deep-end psyche.

Groan. I hate it when I don't have a clear answer.

There are times when I hear a small voice in my own head and heart and find myself wondering who's talking.

Knock, knock. Who's there?

Is that you, Lord? Or old Beelzebub, up to no good?

So how *do* we discern God's voice from the adversary's? Here are three questions I ask myself:

1. What's the message?
2. What's the outcome?
3. Who gets the glory?

We can measure this ghost story with the same yardstick.

The *message* was consistent with God's Word and with Samuel's previous prophecies.

> "The LORD will hand over both Israel and you to the Philistines, and tomorrow you and your sons will be with me." *1 Samuel 28:19*

The *outcome* was Saul being humbled—on the spot, and the next day on the battlefield as well.

> Immediately Saul fell full length on the ground, filled with
> fear because of Samuel's words. *1 Samuel 28:20*

The *glory* went to God alone, since in Samuel's brief speech he mentioned the name of the Lord seven times—the number of perfection or completion.[21]

Saul was undone. Imagine knowing the hour of your own death! Another good reason not to seek knowledge about future events. It literally wiped the man out.

> His strength was gone, for he had eaten nothing all that day
> and night. *1 Samuel 28:20*

No doubt Saul fasted in preparation for his visit with Madam Medium, as was the custom. Add to an empty stomach his wretched emotional and spiritual starvation, his awareness that he stood on the threshold of death, and it's no surprise the man was close to fainting.

> When the woman came to Saul and saw that he was greatly
> shaken, she said, "Look, your maidservant has obeyed you. I
> took my life in my hands and did what you told me to do."
> *1 Samuel 28:21*

Sure wish I could hear her tone of voice here. A gentle reminder…or a sharp rebuke? "Sir, I tried my best to be more than obedient"? Or, "Hey, mister, how 'bout a little applause for the old girl's efforts"?

The medium gets ten points for this: She didn't hand him an invoice.

> "Now please listen to your servant and let me give you some
> food so you may eat and have the strength to go on your
> way." *1 Samuel 28:22*

Like any good hostess, she offered him food. Maybe she harbored a small corner of compassion in her necromancer's heart after all. Samuel had just announced that Saul would be dead the next day, so the king was no longer a threat to her, nor did he indicate any plans to "shoot the messenger"…yet.

She did her best to persuade him to dine. "It will give you strength for your walk back to camp" goes one translation (CEV). Commentators think she was gifted with generosity or honored to find the king under her roof. No question those are strong motivators for any hospitable soul.

Personally, I think she realized the sooner Saul left, the safer she'd be. No wonder she said, "Eat, eat! Go, go!"

> He refused and said, "I will not eat." *1 Samuel 28:23*

Funny how hanging out with ghosts can spirit away your appetite.

> But his men joined the woman in urging him, and he
> listened to them. He got up from the ground and sat on
> the couch. *1 Samuel 28:23*

When a stranger couldn't convince him, his own men did.

> The woman had a fattened calf at the house, which she
> butchered at once. She took some flour, kneaded it and
> baked bread without yeast. *1 Samuel 28:24*

The Medium of En Dor put aside her sorcerer's turban, tied on an apron, and whipped up a late-night feast fit for a…well, you know. It wasn't the sort of thing one finds on the room-service menu at your typical Marriott. Fattened calf was a delicacy, sort of a "free range" thing. The animal was allowed to graze to its heart's content, then sleep safely under her roof—literally, "at the house."

> Then she set it before Saul and his men, and they ate.
> *1 Samuel 28:25*

Think of it as a last supper for King Saul.

That same night they got up and left. *1 Samuel 28:25*

She must have closed the door in utter relief. *Whew. Mission accomplished.*

Wonder what happened the next morning. Did she tell everyone in town about her midnight visitor? Or keep it to herself? With Saul dead, did she resume her former profession or vow never to grab her bell, book, and candle again?

As with our men departing under the cloak of darkness, so the fate of the Medium of En Dor remains shrouded in mystery. She's not mentioned again in Scripture, although folks have been talking about her ever since.

Their opinions boil down to two conflicting views:

1. The Medium of En Dor was a compassionate helper.

Because she "treated a stricken king with kindness,"[22] it would "serve us well to view the woman of Endor with sympathy rather than suspicion,"[23] goes the argument in her favor. She was a thoughtful hostess, a maidservant to the king, and "one of the most attractive exponents of 'the Black Art' in early literature."[24] Give the girl a medal.

2. The Medium of En Dor was a daughter of darkness.

"In spite of her good points, she had sold herself to Satan,"[25] and so "by yielding her soul to spirits, she was abusing herself in the deepest possible way"[26] insist the naysayers. She indulged in the very sin that both God and her government outlawed and used her evil powers for personal gain. Get thee behind us, woman.

Good Girl or Bad Girl?

Listen carefully.

The Medium of En Dor was the worst kind of Bad Girl because she directly opposed God and his Word, yet clothed herself in the guise of a helpful soul. It's easy to be taken in by her caring, generous ways and her servant attitude. Visit a medium today and you'll no doubt find the same warm welcome and desire to please. As a Victorian writer phrased it, "it brings a sigh to think that she was bad."[27]

Sigh away, honey, but the woman was bad, bad, and again I say, *bad*.

Ask yourself these two biggies: (1) Whom did the Medium of En Dor really serve? And (2) how does God view such activities and, as such, reward them?

> Saul died because he was unfaithful to the LORD; he did not
> keep the word of the LORD and even consulted a medium for
> guidance, and did not inquire of the LORD. So the LORD put
> him to death and turned the kingdom over to David son of
> Jesse. *1 Chronicles 10:13–14*

Hear no uncertainty on God's part here.

Sorcery, witchcraft, divination are deadly.

Horoscopes, palm readers, telephone psychics are worse than hoaxes or pleasant diversions—they can cost us our souls.

Modern American spiritualism—according to their very modern Web site—began on March 31, 1848, when a family communicated with a departed spirit. Described as a "common sense religion," the National Spiritualist Association of Churches defines spiritualism as a combination of science, philosophy, and religion that embraces the idea of continuous life, as demonstrated through mediums who "adjust their vibrations to enable communications between the two planes of existence."[28]

In other words, sisters, the Medium of En Dor's descendants are alive and well. And busy.

Their tenets include the belief in one God—called Infinite Intelligence—and one life, endless because there is no death.

How easily a friend who doesn't know Christ as Savior might be drawn to this religion that speaks of "God" and "eternal life." It sounds right... right? Wrong.

Their board of directors is predominantly women—no surprise this. Women historically—and by God's design, I believe—are more spiritually sensitive, drawn to the deeper things, the higher planes. Neither bashing men nor spouting feminist propaganda, I'm talking observable, quantifiable fact: More women than men fill our church pews, Bible studies, and weekend retreats.

Perhaps the spiritualists might agree with the wiccan high priestess who wrote, "We were women seeking a spiritual home, a place where we would be respected and welcomed, where our souls would be healed and empowered, and where our experiences would be honored as a source of spiritual wisdom."[29]

That kind of stuff sells, girls. Look at the words: *home, welcomed, healed, empowered, respected, wisdom.* Some two decades ago I found all that and more at the foot of the cross. But for those around us who are still searching, I fear many voices calling out to them are far more persuasive than ours.

One woman who turned from witchcraft to Christ shared her coven's guidelines for making witchcraft more appealing: "Never frighten anyone. Offer new realms of mystery and excitement. Make it look like natural, innocent adventure. Cover up evil with appealing wrappings."[30] It's easy to see why wicca draws in the curious and disillusioned.

After covering myself with prayer, I studied various books on the occult and found safe-sounding, familiar practices: Prayer and meditation. Ceremonies and sacred days. Music and worship. Sharing of food. Storytelling. Rituals for birth, marriage, and death.

Many similarities. But oh, sisters, *one big difference*!

Our relationship is not with a dead spirit but with a *LIVING CHRIST.*

Our God does not come from within ourselves but from *ON HIGH.*

When people tell me they worship a god "of their own understanding," my heart yearns for them to meet the God of all creation rather than a god you can understand, that you can fit in a box, that you can both define and control. Christ calls us to worship a God we can *never* fully comprehend, let alone control.

Spiritualists, witches, goddess worshipers, and others who beckon us with tempting ways to control our lives are collectively ignoring the Bible and creating their own creeds to suit their selfish desires. No need to give Satan credit for such deceptions, though his evil influence hangs over all of it like a wisp of brimstone. We're plenty capable of deceiving ourselves.

It is the abandonment of self—not the elevation—that draws us closer to the One who knows us better than we know ourselves.

Scary? You bet!

Smoke and mirrors? No way.

One man. One cross. One life-changing God.

What Lessons Can We Learn from the Medium of En Dor?

When God says "I hate this!" pay attention.

We are blessed to live on the other side of Calvary where grace abounds and forgiveness is eternally ours…and where wise women make it their business to know what our loving Lord despises. That list includes the occult practices mentioned in Deuteronomy 18, which are "detestable to the LORD."[31] Though the world encourages a spirit of religious tolerance, God draws the line at the black arts. Shouldn't we?

> A wise man fears the LORD and shuns evil. *Proverbs 14:16*

Dead men tell no tales. The living God does.

The medium depended on the spirits of the dead—and her own talents of illusion—to bring forth Samuel, but it seems the Spirit of God in the form of the prophet Samuel showed up instead. No wonder she screamed! Departed loved ones, however much good counsel they once offered, no longer have the answers we need. God does. Let's turn to his printed Word—the Bible—and his Living Word—the Christ—rather than seeking man's wisdom from ages past or horoscopes present.

> "He is not the God of the dead, but of the living." *Luke 20:38*

The goddess didn't die for your sins...Jesus did.

If goddess worship is "the fastest growing spiritual practice in the United States,"[32] we're dropping the ball, sisters. No one loved, respected, healed, and empowered women more than Jesus did...and still does. Let your love for your heavenly Bridegroom set your face aglow like a candle. Let the fragrant aroma of his sacrifice cling to you like holy incense. While women everywhere are groping about in the dark, longing to find the Light, we who hold it in our hands and hearts must let it shine!

> But the way of the wicked is like deep darkness;
> > they do not know what makes them stumble.
> > *Proverbs 4:19*

Test and see that the Lord is good.

When the spirit of Samuel rose from the ground that dark night in En Dor, even the medium knew something different had happened. We, too, need discernment when it comes to those internal voices that nudge us daily. Is the message consistent with Scripture? Does it draw us toward the Lord... or away from him? Is the tone one of loving concern...or of harsh judgment? And who will get the glory if we obey that inner prodding? With so many voices demanding our attention, these are questions worth asking.

> Dear friends, do not believe every spirit, but test the spirits to
> see whether they are from God, because many false prophets
> have gone out into the world. *1 John 4:1*

Lethal Weapon

*Well-behaved women
rarely make history.*
LAUREL THATCHER ULRICH

Jill pressed her back against the hallway's grass-cloth wallpaper and stared out the door, dumbstruck, vaguely aware of the fluorescent bulbs flickering above her. Despite twelve years of agency training, she felt her chest tighten and her mouth turn into dry desert sand at the sight of a Syrian terrorist strolling along Connecticut Avenue in the muted December light.

As if he had the right to be there.

Watching him, she swore softly through her clenched jaw. *As if he has the right to live.*

Sarsour. The man was a killer. Ruthless. A military strategist and explosives expert.

The terrorist hadn't seen her yet through the long, plate-glass doorway into her office building. Wouldn't know her from Eve even if he did turn in her direction.

But she knew him. The set of his eyes, the slash of his brows, his height and build all matched the computer profile she'd printed out for her boss—what, only four hours ago? On orders from the Directorate of Operations, Barry had steered a dozen of the agency's best officers toward

Dulles International to intercept Sarsour and his deadly Syrian unit, leaving her alone to manage the office.

Jill watched him stop at a pay phone ten yards away, punching in numbers with violent stabs. Even from a distance his anger was palpable.

Sarsour was alone. Did that mean the anonymous tip describing six possible terrorists onboard had proven wrong? That their plans had failed? Or that he had slipped through Barry's fingers at Dulles?

Where *was* Barry anyway? Why was Sarsour in their neighborhood? And what was she supposed to do with this madman while she waited for her coworkers to return?

No way he'd ever peg this building as a situational task force base. The nondescript cluster of rooms buried in the heart of the District was miles away from Langley, Virginia, and CIA headquarters with its baffled interior walls and doubly soundproofed outer ones.

Sarsour looked exasperated, as if no one had answered his phone call, and slammed down the receiver, sending her heart rate soaring. In seconds he'd walk away a free man.

Do something, Jill!

She should approach him, strike up a conversation. Risky, but it might fly. She was a woman, wasn't she? Younger than he and not wholly unattractive. Fact was, the guys in the office teased her unmercifully about her looks.

She had one definite thing going for her: Jill—Jamilah to her family—was Syrian.

Proud to be a first-generation American, she was born to upper middleclass parents and was an honors graduate of George Washington University. Seventh in her class. Even so, the agency had checked her out more thoroughly than most candidates. Trustworthiness was everything with the CIA.

In the end her command of four languages and a detailed knowledge of Arabic customs worked in her favor.

Right now, for example. With Sarsour.

Jill forced herself to breathe, to think logically. Getting him inside the building, sequestered in her office, seemed the best move. She would win his trust, then break away long enough to contact Barry on his cell phone.

But would Sarsour turn the tables? Hold her hostage? Worse?

She exhaled, frustrated at herself for hesitating. Senior departmental secretary or not, she knew her duty here, knew the risks involved. She had to do something, and she had to do it immediately.

Jill squared her shoulders. *Time to get the man's attention.* Assuming the most confident expression she could muster, she moved toward the door, grateful her easily agitated husband, Haddad, wasn't around to see this.

Beneath her outstretched fingers the glass door felt like a sheet of ice as she slowly pushed it open and stepped onto the sidewalk at the precise moment Sarsour turned in her direction.

Hurry, Jill!

Closing the gap between them with purposeful strides, she caught his gaze and held it, then raised her voice just enough for him to hear her say in fluent Arabic, "I've been watching for you, Sarsour. Come inside where it's warm."

He stepped back, every muscle tense, his wary expression not softening one iota at her noncombative tone. His dark gaze raked over her, then settled on her face, his own sharp features etched with a frightening intensity.

Undaunted, Jill tipped her head toward the glass door. "You'll be perfectly safe here, Sarsour." She maintained eye contact, willing herself not to shift her gaze or even blink. "It's much warmer in my office. Trust me."

He paused, his light jacket offering little resistance to the sleet, then sauntered past her, hardly noticing the people bustling around them. Moments later he stood next to her in the stillness of the brightly lit lobby, glaring down at her, entirely too close for comfort.

"Who are you?" The Arabic words sliced the air like knives. "Well? Tell me!"

"Jamilah." It was a common enough woman's name. No real danger in letting him know it. She turned on her heel and strode down the hall toward her office, mentally searching for another familiar name from her morning's labor. "Faruq arranged this." She jammed the key in the door. "You're to remain here until he comes for you."

Sarsour closed in behind her. The heat from his breath warmed the back of her neck. "Faruq said that? Why didn't he tell me so earlier, Jamilah?"

She spun around, momentarily throwing him off balance. "A last-minute decision." Her eyes narrowed, and she made a calculated but risky assumption. "In view of your failure this morning."

His angry expression shifted to guarded resignation. "Asim's miscalculation. He paid with his life."

Shrugging, she turned back toward the door to hide her relief. *It's working! He thinks I'm on his side.* An insider he hadn't met yet. An ally.

Stepping inside the shadowy office, she flicked on her desk lamp. Nothing in the room hinted of government work. Her office might just as easily house an accounting firm, as the sign on the door indicated.

She eyed the right top drawer where her regulation nine-millimeter handgun was hidden from view. As her security clearances and job classification had increased over the years, so had her need to learn how to handle a gun. The joke around the office was that her aim was so true she could nail a terrorist between the eyes from a hundred yards.

Not that anyone ever expected her to try. She had a desk job, right? Right. *Until today.*

Tossing her coat over a hook inside the closet, she grabbed a gray cotton throw, then with her free hand waved Sarsour into a small, dimly lit room next to her office. Sparsely furnished with a couch, a small fridge, an old television, and a sagging, overstuffed chair, it provided nothing more than a place to catch a few winks when the workload got heavy.

A place to sleep—not a holding tank for a terrorist.

Sarsour settled into the couch, still stiff backed and uneasy.

"Your jacket looks damp from the ice." She thrust out her hand, palm up, expectant. *Let him trust me. Please, please let him trust me!* Her carefully accented Arabic flowed like honey. "I'll hang it near the heater for a few minutes. This throw will keep you warm while it dries."

He slipped off his jacket and handed it over, making it abundantly clear that trust had nothing to do with it. She fought the urge to stare at what the flimsy fabric had concealed: a tight, black knit shirt outlining a well-developed set of muscles and a gun harness cinched snugly against his chest. The worn leather cradled a Glock 35 made completely of plastic polymers—undetectable and highly illegal. Though the pistol was safely stuffed inside his holster, the outside snap was undone.

He could kill me without warning. For no reason whatsoever.

The stark reality of it didn't frighten her—it infuriated her.

Jill folded her arms across her suit to keep from doing something foolish, even while additional Syrian names from the man's dossier poured from her lips as naturally as if she chatted with terrorists every day of her life.

"What about Gadiel? Makin? Or Yacoub? What happened to them?"

"Dead. All of them." He ground out the words. "Dabir, too." His eyes sparked, fury mounting in their black depths. "But we took out our share as well. Five of those CIA pigs are dead."

Dead. Her heart squeezed into a hard knot.

Not pigs. My friends. Jill fought for control and forced herself to say the words: "Very good. What of their leader, Barry King?" Holding her breath, trying to look disinterested, she waited for news of her superior.

Sarsour shook his head, dejected. "Missed him. Then they split up, started hunting us down, drove us apart. He tried to keep up with me, but I lost him on the Beltway."

His smile was anything but friendly. "This is the last place he'll look for me. In the District. In a pretty woman's office. Alone." He leaned forward to brush a long, dark-skinned finger along her own. "Lucky me. Isn't that so, Jamilah?"

"Perhaps not. I'm married." She straightened, sending a message she knew he couldn't miss: *Don't touch.* "Might I get you something to drink? You must be thirsty."

He shrugged. "Water is fine."

"I can do better than that." Turning to open the fridge behind her, Jill pulled out a fresh carton of holiday eggnog and poured him a generous glassful. "Drink up." She offered him the beverage. "There's no rum in it," she added, knowing a good Muslim wouldn't touch liquor.

Not that Sarsour was a good anything.

Tamping down her anger, Jill watched him polish off the eggnog in one greedy gulp, then wipe his mouth with the back of his hand. She glanced at the door, praying her emotions wouldn't show on her face.

His bark caught her off guard. "Who are you looking for?"

"Uh...Faruq," she stammered, adding another lie to her growing collection.

Seemingly satisfied, he handed her his empty glass.

She reached for the carton, surprised to see how steady her hands were, then tipped her head. "More?"

Waving his left hand dismissively, he fell back against the couch cushions, exhaustion written all over his face. "Look, I haven't slept in two days. Leave me alone for a few minutes, will you? But watch that door. If Faruq comes, let him in. Anybody else, I'm not here. Got that?"

She merely nodded, then hurried into her own office, pulling the connecting door closed behind her. Silently exhaling a breath she'd held for five endless minutes, Jill tiptoed to the door and opened it only long enough to check the hallway and foyer. *Empty.* No sign of Barry or anyone else.

Quietly pushing the door shut again, she slid into the worn, cloth-and-vinyl chair behind her desk and rolled up to her computer. Since a phone call might easily be overheard, could she risk trying e-mail? The security of the line wasn't her concern—the man in the next room was. If he heard her PC keys clicking, he'd be sure to check on her, ask questions, demand to read the message on her screen, something.

Jill stared at her right desk drawer, picturing the nine-millimeter pistol inside. Would it bring her freedom? Or certain death? The minutes ticked by as she swallowed her fears and prayed.

A sudden rumbling from the next room stopped her heart until she realized what it was. *Snoring.* The brute was snoring! A deep well of anger boiled up inside her. How dare he sleep so soundly after killing five of her friends! *Five.* Men with whom she'd worked, trained, studied. Even men she'd bested in target practice.

Well, she had a target now.

The bile rising in her throat threatened to choke her. Her friends were gone. *Gone forever.* Was there no way to avenge their deaths, make everything that went wrong turn out right?

A faint picture ran through her mind. Of her—Jill, the gutsy secretary—being named the hero of her department. The one woman who took down the man who took down five agents and untold civilians.

Easing the desk drawer open, her hands visibly trembling, Jill lifted out her weapon. She had a license to carry a concealed weapon…but not a license to kill. In self-defense, yes. Not a sleeping, defenseless man.

He's not defenseless, Jamilah; he's armed.

Furthermore, he was wanted by the CIA. And the NSC. A threat to domestic security. A threat to world peace.

A murderer.

She rose and walked around to the front of her desk, her footsteps soundless on the thick carpet. Holding the slender pistol safely out of sight behind her right hip, Jill slowly pulled open the door that separated her from Sarsour.

He hadn't budged, though his head slumped awkwardly to the side, and his mouth hung slack.

Incredible. The man was sound asleep. Dead to the world. Which meant he wouldn't hear her lift the gun to his head. Wouldn't feel the bullet penetrate his skull until it was too late.

No! She shook her head, disgusted with herself.

Such a plan was illegal, and she knew it, chapter and verse. Executive Order #12333 of 1981 explicitly prohibited the agency from engaging, either directly or indirectly, in an assassination.

Never mind Hollywood. In real life it was against congressional law.

She *could* threaten him, though, when he woke up. Maybe it was his turn to feel vulnerable. So what if she couldn't legally pull the trigger? He didn't know that.

Let him beg me for mercy.

A slight grimace of satisfaction moved across her features as Jill silently crept into the room and eased down onto the chair across from her sleeping enemy, training the pistol on his exposed right temple.

Ten minutes dragged by, and still he slept. Drooled, even. It was revolting.

Jill shifted soundlessly in her seat, her forearm aching from holding her pistol just so. She stared at the sleeping giant. Though his features were those of her own lineage, there was nothing attractive about this man Sarsour. His appearance didn't mirror that of her handsome Haddad, nor her two brothers, nor her dear father.

For many, Sarsour was the face of death itself, the last eyes they looked into before their lives were snatched from them by this…this *scum.* Jill stood, not making a sound, and leaned over the sleeping form. *Sarsour.* The name suited him. Arabic for *bug.*

Sarsour had been responsible for the deaths of dozens, even hundreds of innocent people over the last decade. An entire classroom of Israeli children in 1998. Two American families on holiday in the Holy Land last summer. Even several of his own countrymen had died at his command.

He was evil itself, slipperier than the Potomac in January and high on the CIA's short list.

From her tenth-floor apartment along Route 50, she had a bird's-eye view of Arlington Cemetery—row upon row of white grave markers rolling across the green, grassy expanse. Thousands of soldiers rested beneath those stones, soldiers who had given their lives to make America a safe place to live while this creature Sarsour delighted in shattering that dream.

She looked back at him again, her thoughts reeling.

Five of her friends lay dead because of him. Five women would learn today that they were widows, that their children no longer had fathers.

Her grip on the gun tightened.

Sarsour deserved to die.

He deserved the same mercy he gave his victims: none.

He deserved a bullet through his brain, clean and neat, over in a matter of seconds.

She slipped off the safety and tightened the distance from barrel to temple. Her heart was pounding so loudly in her chest she feared he might hear it even in his sleep.

Could she pull the trigger? *Yes.* She could.

Sweat poured down her back, plastering her silk blouse to the skin between her shoulder blades.

And still Sarsour slept.

Could she kill a man? And live with the consequences?

Yes, she could kill Sarsour. But *should* she?

It was more than illegal; it was immoral. *But so is he, Jill.*

A sound in the hallway stopped her thoughts cold. Footsteps drew closer, then just as quickly receded.

Sarsour never moved.

Another option presented itself. She could wait for Barry to return. Surely he would do so and soon.

Or she could wait for Sarsour to awaken, reach for his Glock 35, and put a bullet through her own brain, clean and neat. Or not so neat.

Jill pushed down the lump in her throat. This was no time for tears.

Gripping the gun with both hands to keep it from shaking, she pointed it once more at his temple and began to pray with all her might…

⟋

Floats like a Butterfly, Stings like a Bee:
Jael

So…does she nail him? Keep reading, babe.

Our ancient sister Jael from the book of Judges was faced with this same dicey dilemma—does the end justify the means?—not with a deadly gun in her hand, but with a seemingly harmless tent peg.

We get two heroines for the price of one in this story: (1) Jael, our Bad-for-a-Good-Reason Girl, whose agility and strength fit her Hebrew name, "mountain goat," and (2) Deborah, a Good Girl of the first order, whose name meant "bee." Deb was a busy woman, all right, but not the least bit flighty.

Deborah, a prophetess,…

A *what*? "Prophet*ess*," as in female prophet? Write that down, honey. It's more rare than a decent dress on the 75-percent-discount rack—in your size.

Seems there was a Mr. Deborah, too.

…the wife of Lappidoth…

Lappidoth isn't mentioned anywhere else in the Bible. His only gig here is being the husband of a famous woman. (I must admit finding a certain justice in that.)

There were at least three other women who prophesied in the Old Testament—Miriam, Huldah, and Noadiah. But only one woman was named judge of all the land: Deborah.

…[she] was leading Israel at that time. *Judges 4:4*

The woman was flat *in charge.* Big medicine. The head kahuna. People from far and wide gathered beneath Deborah's palm tree to receive her wise counsel.

To give us a sense of this time period (in case, like me, you sometimes get lost in the Old Testament and need a dateline to figure out where you are), Deborah and Jael's story falls around 1125 B.C.[1] We're talking *after* Moses and Joshua, *before* David and Saul. Scholars call these the "Settlement" years, when clans or tribes were all the rage and leadership was anything but an inherited right.

The Israelites and the Canaanites were hostile neighbors—Israel worshiped the one true God, Jehovah, and Canaan worshiped the false god Baal. Since both camps were convinced they were right, the two were constantly at each other's throats. Even within their own circles, bickering was a way of life. Without a king to lead them, the people looked for a natural leader among their ranks.

> She held court under the Palm of Deborah…and the
> Israelites came to her to have their disputes decided.
> *Judges 4:5*

Make no mistake, a judge was powerful. But the job came with zero guarantees. Judge today, jilted tomorrow. Not too different from today's politics: Do the work and watch your back. Deborah, leader that she was, preferred to look forward. And give orders.

> She sent for Barak son of Abinoam…

Barak was her military leader, but his marching orders came straight from God.

> …and said to him, "The LORD, the God of Israel, commands
> you:…"

This gives me chills. A woman— one of *us!*—delivering a message that began, in essence, "Thus says the Lord." Glory be! If the question ever comes up, "Does the Lord use women in a mighty way?" Deborah stands as our witness that *yes,* God most certainly does.

With those few words, Deborah established that the battle of Taanach she was about to describe belonged to God, the "first warrior of the people."[2] The army was helpful, Barak was a bonus, but the battle was God's alone.

> "'Go, take with you ten thousand men of Naphtali and
> Zebulun and lead the way to Mount Tabor.'" *Judges 4:6*

Check out the tight sentence structure found in the Bible. No wasted verbiage here! In eighteen words (thirteen in Hebrew), Deborah told Barak where to go, whom to take along, and where to find them. Imagine our own paper-logged government moving ten thousand troops with a single sentence! As Margaret Thatcher said, "In politics, if you want anything said, ask a man. If you want anything done, ask a woman."[3] Ooo-eee, Maggie!

In-charge Deborah outlined God's war plans for Barak:

> "'I will lure Sisera, the commander of Jabin's army, with his
> chariots and his troops to the Kishon River and give him into
> your hands.'" *Judges 4:7*

The Hebrew word translated *lure* means "to lead along"—in this case, with hostile purpose. In other words, "Sweateth not, Barak." With God in control, victory was a done deal.

But Barak pulled a Moses…

> Barak said to her, "If you go with me, I will go; but if you
> don't go with me, I won't go." *Judges 4:8*

You remember Moses at the burning bush? God commissioned him, and Moses whined, "Who am I?" and "What if they do not…listen to me?" and "O Lord, please send someone else to do it."[4]

Wimpy, wimpy, wimpy.

No wonder the Lord's anger burned against Moses! One wonders if Deborah had to cool her jets to keep from feeling the same way about Barak. Was he a "weak-kneed character that needed continual encouragement,"[5] or did his Debbie-go-with-me speech mean he "trusted more in the woman than in her God"?[6]

Either way, not too smart, buddy.

You can almost hear this Good Girl heaving a big sigh of resignation.

> "Very well," Deborah said, "I will go with you." *Judges 4:9*

The queen bee herself, then, would go into battle. Joan of Arc springs to mind, clad in her armor, leading her troops to victory in Orléans. Think what she might have accomplished in Paris if she'd had ten thousand men at her command!

Deborah, Joan of Arc's ancient role model—and ours—shifted into prophetic language again, a disgruntled ruler smacking the fingers of her hesitant general.

> "But because of the way you are going about this, the honor will not be yours, for the LORD will hand Sisera over to a woman." *Judges 4:9*

Major bad guy, that Sisera. As head of the Canaanite army, he'd made life miserable for the Israelites for twenty years. Not anymore. Sisera's hours were numbered, and his end would come via the worst humiliation for a man: death at the hands of a woman.

You go, Deb.

Just to show you how guys *hated* that, several chapters later a mortally wounded Abimelech begged his armorbearer, "Draw your sword and kill me, so that they can't say, 'A woman killed him.'"[7]

Oh, brother.

Despite his wishes, the crushing of Abimelech's head by a woman remains in the pages of Scripture as historical fact. As we'll soon see, Sisera's head bashing gets even more ink.

Barak no doubt assumed the woman slated to put down Sisera would be Deborah herself since she'd agreed to go into battle with him. But the Bible provides a single-verse aside in the midst of those battle plans, a clue to the mysterious woman's identity, something writers call "foreshadowing."

> Now Heber the Kenite had left the other Kenites, the descen-
> dants of Hobab, Moses' brother-in-law, and pitched his tent
> by the great tree in Zaanannim near Kedesh. *Judges 4:11*

The Kenites were a dark-skinned, seminomadic desert tribe of farmers and metalworkers who sided with the Canaanites.[8] However, Jael's husband, Heber—meaning "ally"—had physically separated himself from his clansmen. And that "great tree" just happened to grow along a certain road that would serve as an escape route for Sisera.

But first, the battle.

Two armies assembled: the ruthless Sisera with his nine hundred iron chariots and untold numbers of men, and Barak with his ten thousand foot soldiers yet not a chariot to his name.

One suspects Barak might have hesitated there on Mount Tabor, gazing down at the myriad foes who waited below to slaughter his outnumbered troops. Time for Judge Deborah to bang her gavel and command his attention with a short motivational speech.

> Then Deborah said to Barak, "Go! This is the day the LORD
> has given Sisera into your hands. Has not the LORD gone
> ahead of you?" *Judges 4:14*

Deborah commanded. Barak obeyed. God won.

> All the troops of Sisera fell by the sword; not a man was left.
> *Judges 4:16*

Of course, there's always *one* lone survivor who manages to get away unscathed.

Sisera, however, fled on foot…

Sisera was the kind of man "who in a perilous emergency thinks with his legs."[9] Sisera hoofed it north, pursued by Barak under Deborah's command, hoping to reach Hazor safely but running out of steam.

Little did Sisera realize he was escaping one woman's grasp only to land in the hands of another.

…to the tent of Jael, the wife of Heber the Kenite…

Ah, but "the stillness of this tent and the hand of this one woman were to be more dangerous to him than the noise of the battle and the weapons of the ten thousand men."[10]

Sisera didn't know that yet. This tent, pitched apart from the others, seemed isolated enough, and the wife of Heber was alone. Besides, the Kenites were allies of the Canaanites, right? How dangerous a stopping place could it be?

…because there were friendly relations between Jabin king of
Hazor and the clan of Heber the Kenite. *Judges 4:17*

In other words, they had a peace treaty. That and the strict rules of hospitality of that age convinced Sisera he'd found a safe haven from Barak. Not only that, the woman of the house—well, tent—was strolling out to greet him.

Jael went out to meet Sisera…

Ooh, a gutsy girl that Jael! She faced this ruthless military leader head-on. Note that her actions were intentional. She wasn't hurrying outdoors to hang laundry, accidentally stumbling over the fleeing Sisera en route. She stepped out on faith, on purpose, and without fear.

I wonder if she knew Sisera was coming. Did the God of Israel whisper in her ear what surprises the hours ahead might hold?

Or did she have designs of her own, created the moment this enemy of Israel came into view? If so, was her plan one of overt hospitality…or covert hostility? Was she "decisive and courageous"[11] or "brave but treacherous"?[12]

You decide.

> …and [she] said to him, "Come, my lord, come right in."
> *Judges 4:18*

An invitation, then. The hostess with the mostest. Calling him "my Lord" showed respect—or cunning—on Jael's part. Makes me think of that line from *Hamlet* describing one who "may smile, and smile, and be a villain."[13]

At this point in the story, Jael's words seem more friendly than fiendish.

> "Don't be afraid." *Judges 4:18*

Hmm. Maybe Jael knew something we don't. Otherwise, why would *she*—a woman with a "plain, quiet, harmless way of living"[14]—need to comfort *him,* a bloodthirsty general fresh from the battlefield?

Perhaps, after twenty years of watching the merciless general crush his opponents, Jael realized that peace would reign over the land only when Sisera's body resided underneath it.

> So he entered her tent, and she put a covering over him.
> *Judges 4:18*

That covering was probably a camel's-hair cloak or rug. Was the point to hide him from Barak? Keep him warm? Help him fall asleep with his blankie? Jael was prepared to make her guest feel at home and cozy, despite her meager furnishings: a coarse straw mat for a bed, a piece of leather spread on the floor for a table, a hole in the ground for a stove.[15] Plenty for Sisera's temporary needs.

"I'm thirsty," he said. "Please give me some water." *Judges 4:19*

A simple request. When I'm visiting a friend's kitchen and ask for a glass of water, I'm always delighted if she offers something more flavorful. That was precisely what Jael did.

> She opened a skin of milk, gave him a drink, and covered
> him up. *Judges 4:19*

The supple skin bottles made of animal hide were reused without being adequately washed clean, such that the fresh goat's milk quickly curdled, creating a drink called *leben,* still used by the Arabs today.[16] Deborah would later sing of this "fermented and intoxicating drink"[17] that Jael offered: "In a bowl fit for nobles she brought him curdled milk."[18]

Got (bad) milk? *Mmm-mmm.* How tasty.

> "Stand in the doorway of the tent," he told her. "If someone
> comes by and asks you, 'Is anyone here?' say 'No.'" *Judges 4:20*

To Jael's credit, she didn't *agree* to tell such a lie. Although she may have stood in the doorway—for a minute or an hour, we'll never know—no conversations with passersby were recorded. Instead she probably thought through her options and the potential repercussions. It's entirely possible that Jael's welcome was genuine and that it wasn't until she saw the man slumbering at her feet, alone and vulnerable, that the idea struck her: She could bring down the mighty Sisera.

Would her actions please or anger Heber? Buy her a ticket to fame or a death sentence for putting asunder those "friendly relations" with the Canaanites?

Unlike Barak, Jael was not under the direct command of Deborah. If she took Sisera's life, she couldn't claim, "Deborah made me do it!" She alone would bear the burden of her drastic measure.

Sisera's last words were a request for protection.

Jael, however, provided just the opposite.

But Jael, Heber's wife, picked up a tent peg and a hammer…

A tent peg. A hammer.

Common household items for tent dwellers. "Who would ever have thought of that device but a woman?"[19] Indeed. Among nomads, the woman of the household pitched the tents, so Jael would have stored these basic necessities close at hand—the hammer kept tight and sound, the pegs sharpened for ease in driving them into the ground. Though wooden pegs were common in that era, trees were scarce in the northern part of the country. For metalsmiths like the Kenites, bronze tent pegs were easier to come by and might explain the ease she had in carrying out her plan.

Perhaps her intent was to catch a bit of his tunic on the sharp point of her tent peg and pin him to the earth, hoping against hope that Barak or one of his soldiers would appear moments later to finish the grisly deed.

…and went quietly to him while he lay fast asleep, exhausted.
Judges 4:21

Sisera may have gone without sleep for days, waging a losing battle, watching his troops diminish until they littered the battlefield with their fallen bodies.

In Jael's tent, underneath the warm camel's-hair covering, his stomach full of soothing, fermented milk, Sisera succumbed to the irresistible allure of sleep.

Zzz…

Whether he slept on his back, his side, or his stomach, he was clearly counting sheep instead of Jael's stealthy footsteps. Nor did he hear the swish of the peg and hammer as her arms lifted over him.

She drove the peg through his temple into the ground…

The word *temple* indicates a weak, thin place, specifically that soft, indented spot on the side of the head. Touch your hand there for a minute, next to your eye, and imagine…never mind.

Too gruesome.

Rather than penetrating a tent fabric made of handwoven goat's hair, Jael's sharpened peg traveled through flesh, blood, and bone before the point pierced the earth.

>   …and he died. *Judges 4:21*

No kidding.

The *New English Bible* fairly revels in its graphic translation: "His brains oozed out on the ground, his limbs twitched, and he died."

Ugh. Too much information.

Though treachery and violence were as common in those days as goat's milk in skin bottles, pinning the man's head to the ground does strike one as an over-the-top method for cutting his visit short. Maybe Sisera snored like a pro wrestler with sinusitis. Or drooled on his straw pillow.

He was her guest, yes, but the enemy of Yahweh as well.

Did Jael harbor "murder in her heart"?[20] Was it self-defense? Or an act of guerilla warfare? Is she a heroine? Or a criminal?

That's the question at the crux of this story. Jael's motives for killing Sisera will tell us if she was a Bad Girl gone mad or a Good Girl who was momentarily Bad for a Good Reason.

Here are a half-dozen legitimate reasons that might explain why Jael raised her lethal weapon:

1. She wanted to assure her own safety.
Though he hadn't brandished them, surely Sisera was armed with a weapon or two of his own. When the general awoke, energy renewed, he might have raped or killed her on the spot, especially if he figured out her true loyalties rested with the Israelites.

2. During times of warfare, all bets are off.
He was the enemy, and as such was a marked man, a walking target. What is considered murder during peacetime is called victory during war. As one writer astutely asked, "Would a man in her position have done any less?"[21]

3. After two decades of bloodshed, he deserved to die.
Sisera was not a nice guy. He'd slaughtered and oppressed those with whom Jael had ancient ties, their current tribal truce notwithstanding. Bloodlines ran deep. It was time for his blood to run.

4. Sisera's dead body would serve as the ideal peace offering when the Israelites showed up.
Since it was clear Israel was the victor, better they should find the enemy dead in her tent than alive and hiding behind her skirts. One commentator suggested Jael killed Sisera to "cement a friendship with Deborah."[22] In a political sense, perhaps, but not a personal one. (I can't picture these two strong women yelling across the battlefield, "Hey, girlfriend!")

5. She hoped to spare others from being killed under Sisera's violent command.
That's the selfless, heroic, courageous reason, the one that "makes her a genuine war hero."[23] A self-defense motive would have branded her only as a frightened woman. To bravely kill one man so others might live requires a sacrifice of self.

6. The Lord, God of Israel, ordained his death.
Deborah made it very clear to Barak that "the LORD will hand Sisera over to a woman."[24] Jael was that woman. It was the fulfillment of divine prophecy, consecrated by a God who empowered a brave woman with a tent peg to strike a blow for righteousness. "Even God lends a hand to honest boldness."[25]

   This, then, was the true reason: It was the Lord's will. Sisera was such a slime bag that "God intended that Jael should slay him."[26]

How like God to use someone weak—a woman alone—to vanquish someone strong—an army general accustomed to leading thousands.

How like God to see that she didn't bludgeon him to death with multiple blows, seeking revenge with each angry swing. Instead, she wielded "just the right amount of power at just the right time."[27] One strike, hammer to peg, while the man mercifully slept, and Jael's work was finished. Sisera never knew what hit him.

And how like God's timing—to bring Sisera to her tent at the most fortuitous moment, with Barak following neither too soon nor too late.

> Barak came by in pursuit of Sisera…

Surely he wasn't far behind. This wasn't a long passage of time. A fleeing general doesn't take off unnoticed. The whole of this scene in the tent lasted as little as thirty minutes, at most an hour or two.

Once Jael was certain Sisera was dead (you'd hardly need a coroner for that one), she no doubt watched from the doorway to see who might happen along next. When she spied Barak approaching, her heart must have leaped with joy…and relief.

> …and Jael went out to meet him. "Come," she said, "I will
> show you the man you're looking for." *Judges 4:22*

Attagirl, Jael! Can't you hear the triumph in her voice? Even before Barak had a chance to reveal his mission, Jael assured him of victory. Funny how she did exactly what Sisera had asked her *not* to do. "Don't tell anyone I'm here," he'd begged. What was the first thing Jael told Barak? "He's here!"

> So he went in with her, and there lay Sisera with the tent peg
> through his temple—dead. *Judges 4:22*

Still dead. No changes there.

> On that day God subdued Jabin, the Canaanite king, before
> the Israelites. *Judges 4:23*

If there was any doubt who masterminded the Israelite victory that day long ago, this verse makes it clear: "God subdued," that is to say, "put down, oppressed, thwarted." God did it—not that busy-bee Deborah, not hesitant Barak, not even courageous Jael and her trusty tent peg. It was the Lord God who brought down the proud Canaanites in the presence of their enemies, his chosen people, Israel.

By the time the postvictory party ensued, Deborah had composed a song befitting the occasion, giving God the glory and Jael the praise. Known as the "Song of Deborah," and in literary type, a victory song, this "oldest remaining fragment of Hebrew literature"[28] must have been written very soon after the incident, so vivid and accurate was the description of Sisera's demise.

Planning on ordering the CD? Be forewarned that it will carry the labels "explicit lyrics" and "extreme violence," especially when Jael's big tent peg number kicks in during the last third of the song:

> "Most blessed of women be Jael,
> the wife of Heber the Kenite,
> most blessed of tent-dwelling women." *Judges 5:24*

If that "most blessed of women" phrase sounds familiar, it should. Those words were recorded in Scripture on one other, quieter occasion, spoken by the angel Gabriel when he announced to the young virgin Mary, "Blessed are you among women!"[29]

Ooh, baby.

This parallel has made scholars hot under the ecclesiastical collar for centuries. "No, the blessedness of woman is not for Jael," argued one. "It was reserved for another—the mother of Him who was to teach men a grander recompense for injury than hatred and murder."[30]

An early feminist from the 1890s, Elizabeth Cady Stanton, declared "the deception and the cruelty practiced on Sisera by Jael" to be "revolting," calling it "more like the work of a fiend than of a woman."[31] Don't get your bloomers in a twist, Ms. Stanton. It was God's idea all along.

Deborah herself is judged and found wanting by modern critics for elevating the status of Jael. "Patriotism has made her cruel," wrote one,[32] while another insisted Deborah "sings with rapture the praises of a dastardly deed. I will not join in the chorus."[33]

Easy, fellas. No one's asking you to sing along.

If the men who wrote those words in the first half of the twentieth century were still alive today, I would point them toward the words of David, who sang with delight, "It is God who arms me with strength" and "trains my hands for battle." David said of his enemies, "I crushed them so that they could not rise" and "I beat them as fine as dust borne on the wind."[34]

Would those same scholars accuse King David of being patriotic to the point of cruelty? I think not.

Perhaps what makes this business with Jael distasteful to some readers, and Deborah's praise that followed even more so, is that *women*, rather than men, were God's instruments. I'd have to agree that it *is* rare, scandalous, unexplainable…and so like our heavenly Father.

The truth is loud and clear in this story: The Lord will use whom he will, how he will.

Let me say it again. God will use a woman, if he chooses, to see that his victory is won. Unusual in military history, yes. Impossible, no. "For nothing is impossible with God."[35] Not even nailing a man to the ground with the lowliest of weapons.

Deborah sang her Jael jingle with joy.

> "At her feet he sank,
>   he fell; there he lay.
> At her feet he sank, he fell;
>   where he sank, there he fell—dead." *Judges 5:27*

As in any good song lyric today, the main point—the memorable "hook"—was repeated to drive home the message. Literary scholars called this verse of Deborah's song an "outstanding example of climactic parallelism."[36] Goodness! Lizzie simply adds up those lines to equal three *sank*s, two *feet*, and one very *dead* Sisera.

Deborah decided such a fate should smite all who oppose God.

> "So may all your enemies perish, O LORD!" *Judges 5:31*

Another translation gives her words more bite: "May all your enemies die as Sisera did!" (NLT).

What a curse! And what a blessing follows it.

> "But may they who love you be like the sun
> when it rises in its strength." *Judges 5:31*

Deborah loved God and was his woman, start to finish.

Jael, despite her husband's previous alliance with the enemy, was God's servant as well and decisively finished what Deborah started.

The last line of the chapter isn't part of the song, written while the victory shouts still rang through the Israelite camps. It is a mere historical footnote, yet one that could not have been possible without the leadership of Deborah and the courage of that envelope-pushing, quasi–Good Girl, Jael:

> Then the land had peace forty years. *Judges 5:31*

Forty was a significant number. In forty years one could be born, mature, marry, have children, and then grandchildren. Thanks to these two women, an entire generation lived in peace.

Jael's story gives me hope that the Lord's promise of "Vengeance is Mine"[37] will be fulfilled. When I see the sickness and violence, bloodshed and tears that fill our world, I find myself crying out, "Do something, God. Quick!"

History demonstrates that he has. He is. And he will. In his perfect timing, not ours.

Did the Lord God use Jael that day in her tent pitched near the great tree? You decide.

What Lessons Can We Learn from Jael?

God is in charge. Deal with it.

Stories like Jael's are difficult to grasp in light of our New Testament understanding of grace and mercy. Yet remember the plagues that descended upon Egypt from God's hand. Consider the destruction of Sodom and Gomorrah. Think of God's only Son, hanging from a wooden cross. The Lord is infinitely patient...and ultimately just. We aren't expected to understand all his ways. We are called to trust them as part of his grand design and realize that "though the mills of God grind slowly, yet they grind exceedingly small."[38]

> "As the heavens are higher than the earth,
>
> so are my ways higher than your ways
>
> and my thoughts than your thoughts." *Isaiah 55:9*

Check your motives.

The Talmud says, "A transgression with good intent is more meritorious than the performance of a commandment with no intent."[39] We can't be certain of Jael's motives, but we can certainly examine our own. We might never pierce a man's head with a sharp instrument, but we've pierced many a heart with sharp words. We need to ask ourselves why. For the other person's benefit? Probably not. For spite. For revenge. In anger. Because of hormones. Just because. Let's go for godly motives and pray for methods that match them.

> Test me, O LORD, and try me,
>
> examine my heart and my mind. *Psalm 26:2*

Learn from Jael but don't imitate her.

It's said that Jael's gory tale "reflects an earlier stage of ethical development and as such offers little for emulation."[40] In other words we're not to reenact her story—luring Satanists into our homes on Halloween with promises of candy, then bashing them over the head with candlesticks. Not hardly. What we *can* imitate is her wise decision to align herself with God and not the enemy camp.

> Discretion will protect you,
> and understanding will guard you. *Proverbs 2:11*

Leaders do more than command—they do.

When Barak refused to march out alone, Deborah said, "I will go with you." When Jael saw the opportunity to subdue Sisera, she didn't run and get someone else to do it; she did what needed to be done. Leaders don't just point; they shoot. How often I'm guilty of seeing a need, then praying another person will handle it. "Somebody ought to do something," I often grumble. Oh that I might have the courage of my ancient sisters and step forward!

> Then I heard the voice of the Lord saying, "Whom shall I send?
> And who will go for us?"
> And I said, "Here am I. Send me!" *Isaiah 6:8*

Peculiar Grace

There is something in a face,
An air, and a peculiar grace,
Which boldest painters cannot trace.
WILLIAM SOMERVILLE

T he day was barely born, but Grace's mind was already made up: She
would spend her free afternoon as an expressionist painting.

Squinting at the alarm clock, she sat up in bed with a lazy, catlike
stretch and rolled the stiffness out of her shoulders, smiling into the shadowy darkness of her dorm room.

Yes. At two o'clock she would stake her claim on a bit of bare wall space
facing Quincy Street and plant herself among the likes of Klee, Beckmann,
and Kandinsky, creating a human *objet d'art.*

It seemed the perfect pastime for an artist's model. After sitting utterly
still for hours while Boston-area art majors reproduced her on canvas or
sketch pads, it was her turn to become the artist, using her own body as
modeling clay.

People gawked at her, of course, and giggled behind her back. So?
Being watched by others felt completely natural to her. Last Thursday she'd
assumed a surreal pose in the vicinity of her favorite Picasso until the Fogg
Art Museum curator pointed a sharply raised eyebrow in her direction.
Grinning, she'd scampered out the front door into the late spring sunshine,
anonymous once again.

Today, then, she would join the expressionist collection.

She glanced at the mirror mounted on her closet door, imagining a live action van Gogh. *Hmm.* A suitably primitive posture would be easy enough. She'd arrange her features in an intense, emotional display as well. But what color in her closet was bold enough to please the masters?

Swinging her long legs over the side of her sagging mattress, Grace eyed the fiery slash of fabric draped across the chair, a reminder of last night's hasty undressing when the spark of passion flared. *Good choice, Grace.* The red dress would do nicely.

The other remnant from last night lay snoring beneath her quilt. She smoothed a hand over the double-wedding-ring pattern that wrapped itself around his broad shoulders. The cotton was faded, the edges frayed from too many trips through the campus laundry, yet the male body beneath the fabric felt solid and warm with sleep.

He barely stirred at her touch. What was his name again? John. No, *Jon*—minus the *h.* Jon Something-or-Other. They'd met at Widener Library a few nights back. A first-year instructor in the philosophy department, he'd told her.

Not particularly handsome. Not exceptionally bright.

But the man made her laugh. Called her bodacious. Kissed her thoroughly when he caught her in the art history section shelving her favorite volume on Monet. Yes, he'd made quite an impression—both that night and last.

A predawn stillness hung over the small space crammed with books and drawings piled in an artless heap. While she showered in the bathroom down the hall, Jon would no doubt slip out. A note would be a nice touch, though she wouldn't get her hopes up. He'd probably walk out of her life when he walked out the door.

Moving across the room, a thin cotton towel in one hand, shampoo in the other, she jumped when an angry fist suddenly pounded on her door and a male voice barked, "Grace Fallon, are you in there?"

"Wh-who is it?" All at once she felt exposed, vulnerable. Her body was covered with nothing but a nervous scattering of goose bumps. "Who's there?" she asked again.

"Who's *there* is the question, Grace." A second male voice. "Got a fellow named Jon in your bed?"

On cue, Jon sat up with an exaggerated yawn. "What's with all the noise, babe?" He combed his hair with his fingers, then reached for his jeans. "Some jealous boyfriend out there?"

Grace stared at him, then at the door, eyes wide with shock. How could those men out there—whoever they were—possibly know about Jon? Forcing herself to sound calm, she called out, "What's it matter to you who's in here?"

"To me? Nothing." The stranger's gruff laugh was humorless. "To his wife, though, I'd say it'll matter quite a bit."

His *wife*! Grace clutched the towel against her and stared at the man searching for his shoes. Jon hadn't mentioned being married. Then again, they usually didn't.

She kept her voice as steady as possible. "I'm…afraid you've got the wrong room."

"No, Grace." A different voice this time. A woman. "You've got the wrong *man* it seems. In the wrong place."

Grace stifled a groan. *Lynne. The Head Resident.* A humorless older woman with a penchant for enforcing rules few people cared about anymore.

"We're coming in, Grace."

A key connected with the lock and began to turn. Startled, Grace yanked the red dress off the chair and over her head, barely covering the essentials before the door swung open and three pairs of eyes stared at her in joint disapproval: unsmiling Lynne and two men Grace vaguely recalled as faculty types.

It was obvious from his expression Jon knew them. Maybe even expected them. Scratching his stubbly chin, Jon ignored Grace, addressing instead the older of the two men while nodding in Lynne's direction. "Why'd you drag her into this, Jim?"

The man, bearded and balding, merely shrugged. "She was the one with the key."

"Right." Jon looked a tad flustered as he buttoned his shirt. "So…uh, am I in any trouble here?"

The second man, beanpole thin with bleak, gray eyes hidden behind thick glasses, lifted his shoulders in a careless shrug. "Not if you keep your mouth shut, just as Lynne has assured us she will."

Grace watched them exchange knowing glances and felt a spark of anger ignite. "Would someone get to the point?" She jerked her chin up, doing her best to take charge of the situation, knowing her clingy red dress worked against her.

The older man, no taller than she, sobered quickly. "The *point* is, your days on this campus have come to a close, Miss Fallon." He met her belligerent stare without blinking. "Adultery is a moral issue, one best left to a higher authority. But a man, a faculty member at that, spending the night in your freshman dorm room…well, there are rules, Miss Fallon."

Grace shook her head, her anger turning to confusion. "I figured they were nothing but words in a student handbook. Since when did anyone make them stick?"

Lynne snorted. "Since two minutes ago, I'd say."

Grace felt the heat rising to her face, no doubt staining her cheeks the color of her dress. "Listen, I know my rights." And she did, despite her second-term status. "If you're thinking about expelling me, you'll have to take it up with the Student Affairs Ethics Committee."

She eyed the twenty-something man sitting on the edge of her bed, looping his tie around his neck at a leisurely pace, not even pretending to look concerned. Her suspicions aroused, she baited him. "Jon, I assume that committee doesn't include you."

"Oh, but it does. I'm the newest member." He inclined his head toward the door. "Appointed to a four-year term by Law and Order there."

She studied the older men's faces, recognition dawning at last like the faint daybreak outlining her window curtains. *Of course.* Dr. James Lowe and Dr. Kenneth Oehrter. *Lowe and Oehrter.* Two philosophy professors who rode herd on their department—if not the whole school. They'd served on the ethics committee for years, exhilarated by the sense of power it gave them. At least that was the rumor.

If Jon had cast his lot with them, then obviously the whole thing was a scam. *So much for my "irresistible body," you jerk.* Their motive wasn't clear, but their method was—disgustingly so. Grace sighed, the bitter taste of defeat in her mouth.

Law and Order, my foot. "Now what, gentlemen?"

Dr. Lowe, the bearded, balding one, stepped to the side and flapped his hand toward the hallway. "Jon, suppose you pull yourself together for your first class and let us press on with this morning's...uh, activities."

Jon protested as he rose. "But don't you need—"

"No." Dr. Lowe held up his palm, silencing him. "Better not involve yourself any further on this one. You've done enough."

Without a word or a glance in her direction, Jon strode out the door and down the narrow, tiled hall until an exit door at the top of the steps banged shut behind him.

In the awkward silence Grace found her voice again. "What sort of 'activities' are you talking about?"

Dr. Lowe slipped a cool, firm hand around her wrist. "You wanted to stand in front of the ethics committee, yes? Consider it done. Minutes from now we'll have the three votes necessary to send you back to Bangor, Miss Fallon." He pulled her toward the door, causing her to stub her bare toe on the battered leg of her desk in the process.

"Ouch!" She wrenched her arm out of his grasp. "Let go of me, you...you..." Swallowing a throat full of tears, she jammed her feet into a pair of black flats, wincing when her sore toe pressed against the leather. "I'd like to get dressed first, if you don't mind."

"But I do mind." He snagged her elbow this time and held on tight. "Your present attire is...more than appropriate."

Grace caught a final glimpse of herself in the mirror—wild hair tangled from a night too long on lovemaking and too short on sleep, makeup reduced to dark circles beneath her eyes, and nothing to cover her nakedness but a short, half-buttoned dress that, without anything underneath it, revealed more than it concealed. "No!" she whispered through dry lips as they eased her through the doorway. "Not like this."

"Exactly like this." Dr. Oehrter wrapped his gnarled hand around her other arm, and together the men directed her down the hall, leaving Lynne to lock the door, her minor role finished.

Grace hated being manhandled, and she chafed under their firm control. "Wh-where are we going?" Unwelcome tears filled her eyes as the trio made their way down the stairwell with halting steps, then stumbled out the back door into the pale daylight.

Help! It was all she could think of, over and over. *Help me. Somebody. Help!*

"We're making a surprise visit to the head of our committee," Dr. Lowe explained, steering her along as cheerfully as if he were escorting her to freshman orientation. Their steps were aimed across the Yard toward the art department classrooms, her home away from home. She knew the building well. Maybe she could untangle herself and duck out a side entrance. When she wiggled ever so slightly, their grip on her tightened. *Maybe not.*

Numb with embarrassment, Grace staggered forward, avoiding the curious gazes of her peers hurrying toward their eight o'clock classes. None of it made any sense. Who were they taking her to see? And why did the casual morals of one freshman matter to anyone, let alone these two?

Easy answer, Grace: It doesn't matter. Something else was going on.

She would pay for her mistake, no question—but she wasn't the one they were really after. *Who then?* They kept talking about the head of their committee in disparaging terms. Maybe he was another stiff-necked, know-it-all prof who'd crossed Law and Order one time too many. That's what it sounded like to her, at any rate.

"Lookin' fine there, Grace." The taunting words and roguish wink from a male student passing by started a fresh wave of heat climbing up her bare neck. She didn't even have a free hand to button her dress, gaping halfway to her waist.

When she'd climbed into bed—last night with Jon, last week with Kevin, last month with Richard—she'd never imagined it coming to this. Lots of girls slept around, didn't they? Was it really so bad? Not just against dorm policy, but truly *wrong*?

She didn't like the answer that stirred in her conscience.

A wolfish whistle made her snap up her head, then wish she hadn't. It was Kevin. *Speak of the devil.* What was he leering at? He'd seen it all before.

"Good morning, gentlemen." He nodded at the profs with some measure of respect. "Caught her red-handed I see…up to her usual tricks. Red-faced, too." Kevin's dark, laughing eyes and cruel smirk cut her to the quick. "Been nice knowing you, Grace."

She refused to meet his gaze and instead stared straight ahead, lengthening her stride. Several agonizing minutes later they reached the double doors into the building.

"You first, Miss Fallon." The men shoved her ahead of them, pinning back her elbows, piloting her down the busy hallway like the prow of a ship. Thrust amid her classmates, she was mortified to find men brushing against her on purpose, bold eyes drinking their fill of her barely covered body. Their murmured comments were crude and suggestive, their expressions more so.

You deserve this, Grace. The thought sickened her.

Could she change her ways? *Would* she change, given the chance to start over? *Moot point, babe.* It was simply too late.

Classes were in session and the hallways nearly deserted by the time they reached their third-floor destination. Pausing in front of a frosted glass-and-oak door, Dr. Lowe jerked her to attention and rapped two sharp taps on the glass before pushing the door open without waiting for an invitation.

Teetering on the edge of emotional shock, her vision blurred, her thoughts more so, Grace slowly lifted her chin to survey the crowded art room. Within seconds her eyes snapped into focus, and she gasped. *So he's the one!* Absorbed in his work, the tall, muscular art professor sat perched on his favorite chair in the front of the classroom. *Dr. C!*

As if he'd heard his nickname spoken aloud, Dr. Frank Consuelo looked up from his easel and met her gaze. For the first time that morning, she took a complete breath. All was not lost. Professor Consuelo was straight as an arrow, but at least he was fair.

"Sorry to interrupt things, Frank," Dr. Oehrter mumbled, shoving her toward the front. "I'm afraid we have a serious ethics committee issue that can't wait until the monthly meeting."

The classroom full of students craned their necks, taking in the proceedings with wide-eyed fascination. Naturally they all knew her. This was where she did most of her modeling; they'd sketched her many times. *But not like this.*

Dr. C always made certain she was modestly dressed and carefully positioned, never asking her to strike a provocative pose. *"It's your lovely face, Grace. That's what I want them to draw."*

His words had warmed her soul, made her want to be a woman worth studying, worth capturing in charcoal or paint. He made her feel special, even though she knew it wasn't true.

Particularly not now—standing in front of his classroom, shamelessly exposed, the too-bright morning light pouring through the open blinds, the candid stares of her peers turning her skin the same blatant shade as her dress.

Right now Grace felt anything but special.

Mere feet away Dr. Consuelo remained seated, barely nodding in acknowledgment of their presence, saying nothing. He seemed to know why they were there and that he was the real reason, not her.

Dr. C was too honest for them; that was obvious. Too righteous. *Too good.* Control freaks like Lowe probably wanted him off the committee. Maybe even off the faculty, considering Dr. Consuelo wasn't tenured and was a rebel besides, one who put student needs first and always challenged the status quo.

A chill ran across her bare arms as the whole ugly picture came into view: Frank Consuelo's number was up. She was nothing more than a fly in their tackle box; he was the prize trout they were after. He'd always made his own rules. The students loved him for it; the faculty did not, since it invariably made them look bad.

Jon had been used. *She,* even more so.

This much was clear: Frank Consuelo's silent welcome was making Law and Order nervous and fidgety. *Good for you, Dr. C.*

Dr. Lowe finally cleared his throat. "Uh…it's like this, Frank. We found one of our new faculty members in this woman's dorm room this morning. A *married* faculty member, I might add. As you know, freshmen are not permitted to have members of the opposite sex in their dorms between the hours of ten and eight. Totally against school policy. Isn't that right, Dr. Consuelo?"

She watched as Dr. C listened, neither agreeing nor disagreeing with the man's caustic accusation. Just listening.

Dr. Oehrter coughed once, then chimed in. "It's right there in the student handbook, spelled out in black and white. No men in the dorm overnight. Grounds for expulsion. No warnings, no second chances, no grace."

No grace. She closed her eyes, overcome with the truth of it. Her carefree artistic life was over. She would be expelled by day's end. No one could save her now, not even Frank Consuelo. They had him over a barrel. He couldn't argue with the printed word. Dr. C knew she'd broken the rules. Even *she* knew that. Everyone did.

"So, Frank…what's your verdict?"

Her lids fluttered open in time to see Dr. Oehrter pull a folded sheaf of papers from his suit pocket. *Here we go.*

"Will you sign the committee's statement to expel her? Dr. Lowe and I are prepared to do so. Now it's up to you. Yes or no?"

No. Please. Grace bit her lip, fighting tears. Getting away with it—

until today—hadn't made it legal. It'd just made it easy to forget what was right. If Dr. C was head of the ethics committee, his choice was clear: her neck or his. She clutched her stomach and prepared herself for his decision.

He wasn't deciding though. He was painting. *Painting!* Brush in hand, the back of his easel facing them, Dr. Consuelo busied himself covering the canvas with strong broad strokes, studying his efforts intently. Ignoring the men completely.

Stunned, she looked around the room as others shrugged and then began dipping their brushes into various paints—*red* appeared to be their favorite—working with quiet, concentrated movements. From the corner of her eye, she noticed that their brushes, driven by carnal imaginations run amuck, revealed even more curves than her short dress promised.

While Lowe and Oehrter stood there, fuming in silence, the students eyed her at length, then returned to their canvases. Their unguarded expressions told her exactly what they thought of her.

Whore.

She was dressed like one, wasn't she?

She'd acted like one, hadn't she?

The lust on their faces as their gazes undressed her further made her feel sick to her stomach and dizzy with shame. Even some of her female classmates seemed overly interested. It was too much to bear. *Way too much. Get it over with, Dr. C.*

As though reading her mind, he looked up from his painting. His eyes met hers with honest warmth and not a hint of desire. In all the weeks she'd posed in his classroom, he had never looked at her with anything but the kindest regard. She felt her skin cooling at the faint whisper of an unseen breeze, sensed her heart slowing to a more peaceful cadence.

When Dr. C finally spoke, every head turned, every ear listened.

"If you've never done a single thing you're ashamed of, gentlemen, then by all means, sign the paper."

At that, he returned to his painting.

Without another word.

Grace, however, heard an unspoken word fill the hollow spaces inside her. It was growing louder by the minute, set to music by the rhythm of her heart: *Hope.*

Somehow—was he a miracle worker or what?—Dr. C had managed to accuse the men of nothing yet put them on trial at the same time. *Never done a single thing they were ashamed of?* Who would dare confess such a foolish lie!

She bit back a smile and watched his partners in campus ethics try to handle *this* one. A word she'd learned in Comp 101 suited their situation perfectly: Law and Order were *flummoxed.* The men looked at each other for an answer and found none. They looked at the students busily paint-ing and came up empty-handed. They looked at her, then quickly looked away. *Now whose turn is it to blush, fellas?*

Mesmerized by the graceful strokes of his brush, she focused on Dr. Consuelo instead, marveling at the ease and speed of his movements. Was there anyone better in all the world? Absolutely no one else came to mind.

Putting his brush aside, he straightened and exhaled with some mea-sure of satisfaction. "So, Grace. Where are your accusers?"

"They're…" She whirled around and found to her amazement that Drs. Lowe and Oehrter had quietly disappeared, leaving the classroom door wide open. "Oh! They're…gone."

Dr. Consuelo gathered the legal-looking papers they'd left behind, tore them in half, and tossed them in a nearby wastebasket. "Then I certainly won't be the one to sign your life away."

She faced the man who'd given her back her future. "You…" Tears that had threatened earlier returned as a tight knot in her throat. "Y-you won't?"

"No, Grace." He lifted his painting off the wooden easel and turned it around for her—and the entire class—to see.

It was a portrait of her. Of Grace.

Fully swathed in white from her neck to her toes with only her face in fine detail, she was radiant and innocent as a young girl, shining forth from the canvas as if lit from within.

"This is how I see you, Grace."

Her tears began spilling over their banks. "But I'm...I'm..."

"Forgiven." Propping the still-wet painting on the floor, he slipped his jacket off and tucked it around her shoulders. "Now go home, Grace. Wash your face. Get dressed. Start over."

Forgiven!

That single word filled the bare walls of her heart like a timeless masterpiece. Overwhelmed, Grace turned toward the open door that awaited her. Walking past her classmates, she hardly noticed as, one by one, they cleaned their brushes and began covering their scarlet images of her with pure, fresh white...

☙

Caught in the Act: The Adulteress

Good morning, beloved.

I mean *really* good, before everything was said and done.

> At dawn [Jesus] appeared again in the temple courts, where all the people gathered around him, and he sat down to teach them. *John 8:2*

How lovely to begin the day with the Lord, to watch the sun rise over the shoulders of the One who said, "I am the light of the world."[1]

Our woman of the hour wasn't on the scene quite yet, but you can be sure she was already wide awake that morning.

In true rabbinical tradition, Jesus "sat down" to teach, even with a sizable crowd. How eagerly they must have waited to hear his words! No microphone, no blackboard, no PowerPoint software. He commanded their attention with his presence and his wisdom, period. *Wow.*

Into this large but orderly assembly came a well-timed disturbance by men who should have known better than to rudely interrupt the rabbi's open-air classroom.

The teachers of the law and the Pharisees...

In their time these were supposed to be the Good Boys, the "custodians of public morality."[2] In our time, though, we think of them as the Bad Guys, the men who made life miserable for Jesus and his followers. How'd they earn such a shady rep? From pulling shenanigans like this one.

...brought in a woman caught in adultery. *John 8:3*

Or to be more precise, she was "caught in bed with a man who wasn't her husband" (CEV). Uh-oh. A sin in any time and any culture. No doubt they had some euphemistic expressions for adultery just as we do today: He has a "wandering eye"; she's having an "affair"; he's "stepping out on her"; she's enjoying a "fling"; he's "sowing his wild oats"; she's "fooling around."

Adultery, no matter how you dress it up with fancy lingo, breaks the law of God and the law of man. She was clearly a Really Bad Girl.

But those rabbis and Pharisees weren't very virtuous either. The whole thing feels like a setup to me. How could a group of men "catch" a couple copulating without some sort of prearrangement with the man involved? "Come by at first light, fellas. I promise you'll find her in a compromising position." Perish the thought, but he may have been part of the gang who dragged her into the temple, knowing his buddies wouldn't give him away.

Then again, she might have been 100 percent guilty of having a long-term sexual relationship with her unidentified partner. The Pharisees might have trailed her to their love nest and waited for an opportune moment to knock on their door.

Whatever the case, their treatment of her was reprehensible.

> They made her stand before the group... *John 8:3*

They needed witnesses, you see, to carry out their dastardly plan. Although they needed only two of them—male, of course—since "no one shall be put to death on the testimony of only one witness,"[3] it was even juicier to have the whole community see this little melodrama played out.

No name is mentioned for this woman, yet I feel her utter broken-ness and shame. Embarrassing enough to have *one* person discover you're an adulteress—but a whole town? As Nathaniel Hawthorne wrote of Hester Prynne's morning journey from the darkness of her jail cell to the unforgiving light of day, "Iniquity is dragged out into the sunshine. Come along, Madam Hester, and show your scarlet letter in the marketplace!"[4]

I knew a young woman once who slept with a married man and woke to find herself two hours from home but only one hour away from the start of her workday. Bad enough to show up with her hair standing on end and her makeup a mess. Walking into the office wearing the same dress two days in a row would've been very much like wearing that scarlet *A*.

What did she do?

She waited outside a department store until the doors opened at eight thirty, ran in and bought the first thing that fit (you can bet it wasn't bright red), and changed in the dressing room, assuring the cashier as she handed her the tags, "If you don't mind, I'll just wear it home, thanks."

How well I remember the humiliation of that morning long ago. The dress wasn't scarlet, but my cheeks were.

This nameless woman was silent. The rabbi was quieter still.

The Pharisees kept talking.

> ...and said to Jesus, "Teacher, this woman was caught in the act of adultery." *John 8:4*

Hold it. "This woman"? Not only did it take two to commit adultery, they were *equally guilty* under Mosaic Law: "both the adulterer and the adulteress must be put to death."[5]

Where, oh where, was the man? Sleeping in, having breakfast, reading the *Mount Olives Times*? Who knows? Meanwhile, our accused woman stood alone.

To be caught "in the very act" (NASB) meant...well, just that. The men didn't nab her slipping out the door after the fact; they found her in the man's arms, no doubt in a state of at least partial undress.

To expose her sin they no doubt exposed her *skin,* dragging her out of bed "probably naked, through the streets"[6] or at the very least with her hair down (major faux pas in those days), her tunic disheveled, her face red as a beet. Possibly they claimed for themselves the words of the prophet Hosea: "So now I will expose her lewdness before the eyes of her lovers."[7] Certainly these men dishonored her to the core.

She wasn't a human being, an individual, to them; she was an object, a pawn in their hands, a means to an end. They wanted to draw a crowd, did they not? Then as now, nefarious men often exploit women's partially clad bodies, especially when going about the business of selling lies. Beware the ad campaigns filled with half-dressed women. Beneath them rests what lay at the bottom of these men's souls: "a graceless, pitiless, barbarous brutality of heart and conscience."[8]

They saw no guilt in themselves, of course.

Only in the woman.

"In the Law Moses commanded us to stone such women."
John 8:5

What blasphemy, hiding their cruel intentions behind the words of God! As teachers of the Law, they knew every jot and tittle of the command to "take the man or woman who has done this evil deed to your city gate and stone that person to death."[9] Never mind that such capital punishment was seldom enforced. The law still remained on the books, as it were. Once again, the man's part in this episode was left out of the discussion.

But stoning the woman wasn't their ultimate goal. No, it was creating a stumbling block for this false (to their way of thinking) teacher.

> "Now what do you say?" *John 8:5*

Jesus was being squeezed into a no-win situation. If he agreed with the Law of Moses, as expected of a rabbi, he would condemn the woman to death, and all his teachings about grace would go down the drain—well, aqueduct. If he disagreed with the Law of Moses, then he would be in direct opposition to the religious leaders of his day—in other words, *this* merciless bunch—and brand himself a heretic.

What a mess!

Not only that, Jesus couldn't legally judge or condemn her actions anyway. Protocol dictated that she be brought before a whole group of rabbis—not one man, and certainly not *this* man, whom the Pharisees saw as having zero authority to begin with.

Can you say "sting operation"?

> They were using this question as a trap, in order to have a
> basis for accusing him. *John 8:6*

The woman was merely bait to catch a bigger fish. Well-chosen bait too, since Jesus had a reputation among the scribes and Pharisees as a "champion of women."[10] What they hadn't counted on was a man more concerned with *people* than with *practices*. After all, the Bible doesn't say "*law* one another"—it says "*love* one another."

Imagine the pin-drop silence in the temple as the Pharisees waited, the Adulteress wept, and the crowd watched—all straining to hear how this man would respond.

> But Jesus bent down...

Bent down? *Psst.* Uh…Lord? Didn't you forget something? They're waiting for you to answer them.

Ohhh. That *was* your answer.

He stooped down, "but not to pick up a stone."[11] Perhaps—how I love the very thought of it!—he crouched down out of respect for the woman. Bless you, Lord, for not gawking at her as the others did.

While down there, you and I might tighten a loose shoelace or scoop up a stray coin. Jesus, however, continued his teaching in silence.

…and started to write on the ground with his finger. *John 8:6*

Writing what? "Don't go away mad, just go away"? This is the only record of Jesus doing any writing,[12] yet we're clueless about what he "wrote in the dust" (NLT).

Maybe the better question isn't "what?" but "why?"

Was he buying time—for himself or for her? Was he contemplating his response while he doodled in the dust? Some translations add "as though He did not hear" (NKJV), but the majority don't show that additional comment. Maybe he was trying to "relieve the tension of the moment" or to "get the piercing eyes of the critics off of the terrified woman."[13]

Maybe this business about playing with dust on the temple's earthen floor pointed to an old tradition recorded in the book of Numbers. God outlined a specific (and grisly) test for an unfaithful wife that included putting holy water in a clay jar and mixing it with dust from the tabernacle floor and forcing her to drink it. If she was innocent, nothing happened. If she was guilty, her thigh would waste away, her abdomen would swell, and the woman would "bear the consequences of her sin."[14] Ugh. We're not talking about Alka-Seltzer here.

You can count on one thing: Everybody was craning their necks to read over Jesus' shoulder that day. Did he write out the Law that stated the *man* was to be stoned as well? How about a quick rundown of the Ten

Commandments, forcing the onlookers to examine their own hearts? Or did he, who "not only heard their words, but knew their thoughts,"[15] tally the Pharisees' specific sins and name them one by one?

Whatever Jesus wrote in silence, it didn't keep them from speaking out.

When they kept on questioning him, he straightened up...

I'll bet *that* move put an end to their yapping!

So Jesus "raised Himself up" (NKJV), did he? What a portent of things to come! And what a bold, dramatic statement, to rise and meet them eye to eye. In a scene filled with tense moments, this exceeds them all. What a hero. What a Savior!

> ...and said to them, "If any one of you is without sin, let him
> be the first to throw a stone at her." *John 8:7*

Remember, they wanted Jesus to make the final decision. Instead, he wisely put the choice back in their hands. I love the challenging tone of the *New Living Translation:* "All right, stone her."

Risky? Nope. Jewish law dictated that the witnesses themselves had to throw the opening pitch. "The hands of the witnesses must be the first in putting him to death, and then the hands of all the people."[16] Jesus added one simple requirement: innocence. "Is there anyone here who has never sinned? The person without sin can throw the first stone at this woman" (ICB).

Think about this: Jesus is the *only one in history* "without sin," the only man who could have tossed that rock in her direction...but he didn't. *He didn't!*

Dear one, do you see that when you hear an accusing voice taunting you with a litany of your mistakes or shaming you with a review of your weaknesses or belittling you with your failures, it could never be the voice of Jesus? "For God did not send his Son into the world to condemn the world, but to save the world through him."[17]

At this point he did not stone nor stand nor speak. He stooped to conquer their foolish pride with his silent witness.

Again he stooped down and wrote on the ground. *John 8:8*

More enigmatic writing! We can only imagine what his words encompassed.

A few Sundays ago our worship leader at church added an unusual twist to our meditation time during Holy Communion. On a large screen he projected a list of the Seven Deadly Sins, a spiritual accounting that doesn't appear in Scripture as such but has been around at least since Pope Gregory the Great—A.D. 600, give or take. In their traditional order, those seven killer crimes are

1. Pride
2. Greed
3. Envy
4. Anger
5. Lust
6. Gluttony
7. Sloth

The minister suggested we pray through the familiar list of sins (by no means exhaustive!) and ask the Lord to show us where we might need to repent and seek forgiveness.

I sat there with my mouth hanging open, stunned by what God revealed to me. On any given day—in any given *hour*—I've seen every one of these sins at work in my flesh. *Ouch!* times seven.

When, for example, I discover another writer has received a big book contract, am I thrilled for that person, eager to send along my heartfelt congratulations? Oh, sure…eventually. But first I sink to new depths of spiritual shallowness and commit the first *four* of the seven cardinal sins *simultaneously.* My pride says, "My proposal was better." My greed says, "We really needed that money." My envy says, "How can I get a contract like that?" My anger says, "Who can I complain to in the meantime?"

Given a few more minutes, I could easily fit in the other three deadly deeds, no problem.

It was a humbling experience that day in church, one I obviously needed. "If we claim to be without sin, we deceive ourselves and the truth is not in us."[18] Oh, I see the sin all right, Lord, and boy is it *ugly*.

I wonder if that wasn't precisely the kind of truth Jesus was drawing in the temple dust: a grocery list of personal sins for his onlookers to consider. Whether it was his mysterious messages in the dust, his bent body, or his sheer holiness that spoke to them, the Lord's challenge to "throw the first stone" found no takers.

At this, those who heard began to go away…

Jesus once said, "He who has ears, let him hear."[19] It seems the "conscience-stricken" (AMP) men had heard enough and started slinking off, their plan to trap Jesus left behind in the dust.

…one at a time, the older ones first…

"One at a time" points to *personal* conviction of sin. The men arrived as an angry mob bent on challenging the authority of Jesus, yet departed one by one when he challenged them individually instead. The older, wiser ones left first—maybe they had a longer list of sins and more guilt to go with 'em. The younger men followed suit.

…until only Jesus was left, with the woman still standing there. *John 8:9*

With no one left to hold her prisoner, to force back her arms or shackle her wrists, the woman stood there alone awaiting her sentence as you and I will someday: "For we will all stand before God's judgment seat."[20]

Though her accusers were gone, the rest of the crowd hung around, curious to see what would happen to this woman "standing in the midst" (NKJV), pinned in place by her fear, her guilt, her shame, her…hope? *Yes!* With her detractors out of the picture, things were looking up. She who'd sought love in the arms of the wrong man—whether one time or a hundred—now found herself in front of a man who seemed genuinely concerned about her welfare.

Might he be merciful? Did he truly care?

Fact is, Jesus cared about *all* those who gathered in the temple that morning. They were all sinners—not just the accused woman. Though she was the one whose skin was bared, the patient Christ had stripped bare the souls of everyone present, that they might come to repentance.

> Jesus straightened up and asked her, "Woman, where are they?" *John 8:10*

Rising again to meet her. Eye to eye, heart to heart.

"Woman," he called her. Not "slut." Not "sleazebag," but "woman." A term of respect.

"Where are they?" he asks. I hear a smile in his voice, don't you? After all, his question was rhetorical: "They" were *history*! Perhaps Jesus wanted to give her time to comprehend what had just happened and savor the freedom that was only a heartbeat away.

This story in John isn't found in some of the early manuscripts, perhaps because it was so scandalous: Jesus standing in the gap for an adulteress? Preposterous! Some theologians rejected it, including Erasmus and Calvin.[21] The *New English Bible* includes it at the *end* of the book of John with the notation that it "has no fixed place in our witnesses.... Some place it after Luke 21:38, others after John 7:36" and so forth.[22]

Hey, girls, it's in my Bible! And as the *Amplified Bible* puts it, "it sounds so like Christ that we accept it as authentic, and feel that to omit it would be most unfortunate."[23]

Yeah, especially for that half naked woman in the temple.

She wanted her story told. And we need to hear it.

Jesus asked her a second question, a more pointed one this time. That first inquiry had been about the disappearing men. This second was about her.

"Has no one condemned you?" *John 8:10*

Ah. They had *accused* but not condemned. Satan is the "accuser of our brothers, who accuses them before our God day and night,"[24] but even that wily serpent can't condemn us to death. Christ alone has the power and authority to condemn us. "Fear him who…has power to throw you into hell."[25] If he chose to exercise that power, Jesus could send her there with a pummeling of rocks against her soft skin.

Uh-oh.

Were her knees trembling? Was her stomach in a knot? Did she silently curse her partner? Her accusers? Herself?

How bravely she faced certain death as she stated the obvious.

"No one, sir," she said. *John 8:11*

Notice she speaks only the truth. She doesn't deny her wrongdoing nor beg his forgiveness nor blame the Pharisees for setting her up or her lover for letting her down.

Eve blamed the serpent.

Potiphar's wife blamed Joseph.

The Adulteress blamed no one—except perhaps herself.

Yet this man Jesus didn't join her in that refrain.

"Then neither do I condemn you," Jesus declared. *John 8:11*

Good heavens! Did that mean she wasn't guilty? Not at all. It simply meant that she wouldn't pay for her sins. There would be no penalty, no punishment for her.

Say what? How can that be considered justice?

If she was guilty—and all evidence indicates she was—the Law said stoning was the appropriate penalty. Meaning the woman deserved to die, right? By law.

Even at the start of the twenty-first century, there are nearly forty states in our democracy where the death penalty is enforced. Electric chairs, lethal injections, gas chambers, even firing squads stretch from Texas to Tennessee, Utah to Florida, Virginia to Wyoming, New Hampshire to Nebraska.

But not in the state called *Grace*.

In that sacred place, there is but one means of capital punishment—a wooden cross—where Jesus bore the death penalty on this woman's behalf. "By refusing to punish her, he has gathered her guilt to himself."[26]

Oh, Lord.

That's what you've done for us, isn't it? Transferred onto your spotless garment the stains of our sins. The scarlet letters we've worn over the years like badges—*A* for adultery and *B* for blasphemy and *C* for cowardice and *D* for denial and *E* for envy and all the rest of our bitter alphabet soup of disobedience—are stitched onto your pure white robe in letters red as blood.

Why, Lord?

It isn't logical to die for people who barely live for you. That adulteress twenty centuries ago, did she even know your name? How could you look past her sexual sin and see her broken, empty heart? She didn't even *ask* to be forgiven, Lord! Didn't even say the words *I'm guilty* or *I'm sorry.*

She didn't deserve your favor, Jesus.

I don't either.

The truth? *None* of us deserves your gift of grace, Lord.

What we deserve is fire and brimstone. Look what you offer us instead! "There is now no condemnation for those who are in Christ Jesus, because through Christ Jesus the law of the Spirit of life set me free from the law of sin and death."[27]

Grace instead of condemnation.

Life instead of law.

Freedom instead of bondage.

Go, go, go, girl!

"Go now..."

His command was a gentle release, not a rebuke. "Jesus was not send-ing her away. He was setting her free!"[28] Free to make her own choices. Free to live a new, clean life. By doing so publicly, he restored this adulteress to the community and spared her further humiliation.

"…and leave your life of sin." *John 8:11*

My scholarly Bill tells me this is one of those awkward phrases in the Greek that defies simple translation. Various versions have rendered it "do not sin again" (NEB), "don't sin anymore" (CEV), and perhaps the most familiar to our ear, "go, and sin no more" (KJV).

Any way you phrase it, it's clear she *had* sinned. Definitely guilty as charged then. But we knew that. We're all guilty of something.

The past—hers and ours—isn't the point. The Lord is more inter-ested in our future. "Go," he says. "Now. Do it. Move forward, putting your past behind you. You're a free woman. Stay out of bondage. Don't go there again."

The question is *not,* did she in fact go and sin no more? The question is, will *we*?

What Lessons Can We Learn from the Adulteress?

Exposure is painful but often necessary.
Public confession is one thing. It's usually done willingly with grateful tears of relief. Public humiliation is something else again. It's done without our consent, and the only tears are those heated by anger or shame. We've seen examples of both in the media over the last decade. Which would you rather watch: a contrite confession or an angry admission? Wise is the woman who brings her dark deeds out into the light of God's love and grace privately, willingly, rather than waiting for someone less sympathetic to force the issue in a public forum.

> But everything exposed by the light becomes visible, for it is
> light that makes everything visible. *Ephesians 5:13–14*

Adultery is no more (or less) a sin than any other transgression.

Ooh, this is tough to swallow! Adultery means a broken marriage vow, a severe breach of trust, a risk of disease or pregnancy, a shattered relationship, a sacred act made profane. Surely, with all those awful repercussions, Jesus would have considered adultery to be one of the deadliest sins. Yet nowhere in Scripture are the sins numbered in severity, ranked from least offensive to most abhorrent. There *are* lists of those the Lord finds particularly odious—Proverbs 6:16–19 comes to mind—but not a complete catalog of "The Top 500 Sins." Why not? Perhaps because the danger in categorizing sins is that we might compare ourselves to others we deem "worse" in the sin department and ignore our own failures. Write this down: *All* sin breaks the heart of God, and *none* of us are without sin.

> "You judge by human standards; I pass judgment on no one."
> *John 8:15*

> For all have sinned and fall short of the glory of God.
> *Romans 3:23*

Silence is golden.

In this story from John, the teachers of the Law and the Pharisees did most of the talking. Making accusations, setting traps, asking questions. The woman spoke only once when spoken to, and even Jesus spent more time drawing in the sand than he did talking. Yet those who would have punished her walked away, themselves convicted. Amazing! Next time we feel the urge to point out someone else's shortcomings, let's remember the example of Jesus and let the truth speak for us.

> Now we know that whatever the law says, it says to
> those who are under the law, so that every mouth may be

silenced and the whole world held accountable to God.
Romans 3:19

Obedience and freedom walk hand in hand.

Now that his words are written—not in the dust, but in millions of Bibles
and on the tablets of millions of hearts—we need only turn there to discover his will for our lives. When we stand in his holy presence, when we
read his holy words, we are changed, released from sin's stranglehold…but
only if we leave behind our sin and walk in true freedom. That means not
just listening to his words but also acting on them.

> But the man who looks intently into the perfect law that
> gives freedom, and continues to do this, not forgetting what
> he has heard, but doing it—he will be blessed in what he
> does. *James 1:25*

Blood Will Tell

There is no animal more invincible
than a woman…
nor any wildcat so ruthless.
ARISTOPHANES

I'm their best choice. Regina pinched back a wicked smile. *Their only choice.*

Squaring her shoulders, she arranged her features to their most striking advantage—chin up, eyes alert, smile faint but pleasing—and surveyed the boardroom like a queen perusing her subjects. A dozen men sat at attention, silhouetted against the backdrop of a late spring rainstorm that turned the skies over Buckhead into a gray shroud.

The neutral color matched their expensive business attire. "The suits" their employees called them. The men who managed the biggest corporation by far in greater Atlanta, and one of the largest in the world. Mostly younger men, they flanked Regina on either side of the long oval table, papers stacked neatly before them, untouched.

At the far end of the table stood the CEO, commanding every eye in the room, including hers.

The men were not ready for Alan's retirement announcement.

Regina Banks was more than ready.

She was the veteran among the senior VPs—second only to Alan on the corporate ladder—and the lone woman on the management team. It had always been thus. She'd arrived on the tidal wave of affirmative action during the booming eighties, a season of swift, unparalleled growth. Over the years she'd watched one young Turk after another come and go, threatening her silent authority but never usurping it.

The current batch of business-school grads tolerated her second-in-command status but no doubt wrote her off as the least likely to move up to CEO. After all, she was a…she.

Barely listening to Alan drone on about new acquisitions in the Far East, Regina let her imagination soar at the thought of those three significant letters printed after her name on her next batch of business cards: "Regina Banks, CEO." Alan probably had a supply of them already waiting on her desk, wrapped in a box with a bright red bow. *Clever man.* Regina let her restrained smile broaden. *Woman, you are about to make history!*

From Regina's viewpoint, Alan had timed things perfectly, even if he was being forced to retire due to illness rather than age. Her seniority and expertise made her promotion to CEO the most obvious—and least popular—choice Alan could make. Hadn't he slipped her a note at the start of the meeting? "Prepare yourself" was all the note said. All it needed to say.

Ever the eccentric, Alan kept major announcements to himself. When confidentiality was called for, he typed his own memos. And news such as *this*…well, no wonder he hadn't breathed a word.

Except to her. *Prepare yourself.*

Never in the company's ninety illustrious years had they seen fit to put a woman at the helm. Alan's choice of successor would knock the corporate world back on its heels. Tomorrow's banner headline would cover the front page of the *Atlanta Journal-Constitution,* the *Wall Street Journal,* and the *Financial Times,* not to mention the business pages of most major newspapers around the globe.

Here in Atlanta, Regina's adopted city, she would ascend to the very highest social stratum. Her name would appear at the top of every gala guest roster. Come October, she'd no doubt be asked to serve as honorary chair for the governor's Charity Ball.

How unfortunate that her late husband wouldn't be around to escort her to such events. Jerry had always worn his evening clothes with particular style. She glanced at the slight indentation on her ring finger where a gold band had once dominated her hand. A loss, to be sure, but such a man wouldn't be difficult to replace. *If* she found it necessary to do so.

At the other end of the boardroom, Alan stretched a shaky hand in her direction. "As I've already alerted Regina, the time has come for me to…" The CEO's voice faltered, and he gripped the edge of the table. "That is to say, I've chosen my…" A sudden grimace twisted his face, and raw pain filled his eyes as he struggled to breathe.

"Alan?" Regina leaped to her feet and moved toward him, genuinely concerned. *The announcement hasn't been made yet!* Her peers needed to know absolutely whom Alan intended for his successor. It had to come from his lips. She couldn't risk them turning wholly against her. Not now, not when she was so close.

Regina reached his side just as her superior slumped down into his leather chair, his face white with the strain. "Alan, what is it? What's wrong?" She leaned closer and lowered her voice. "Should I call your doctor?"

He nodded slightly, although she'd already pressed the intercom on the nearby boardroom phone to reach his private office. "Get Dr. Kline," she barked into the speaker, then punched the off button and turned to find Alan sweating profusely.

"Kathryn!" She snapped her fingers at her wide-eyed assistant. "Find the man a glass of water!" Bending over him, Regina made a concerted effort to appear worried about his health, even while issues of a more pressing nature—corporate issues—filled her thoughts. He seemed so weak, disoriented. Dare she ask him to voice his plans?

Moistening her lips that had gone dry in the tension of the moment, she murmured, "Alan, is there something you were about to tell everyone? Something important?"

He clutched the narrow lapel of her linen suit and pulled her close enough to reach her ear with his ragged whisper. "It's all in my top folder there." He bobbed his head toward the tidy pile. "I'm…I'm sorry, Regina. There'll be another time for you."

With a heavy moan he slumped over the arm of his chair, his knuckles brushing the carpet. Everyone in the room gasped in unison, horrified. The man was obviously dead. Dead, without naming who in the room would fill his shoes.

While the men around her sprang into action—righting his body, attempting CPR, calling 911, alerting the office staff—Regina reached a steady hand toward the top folder, sliding it along with several others under her arm, hoping its absence would go unnoticed in the hysteria of the hour.

Alan's last hour as CEO.

But not Regina's first hour as his successor after all.

Perhaps she'd misunderstood. The man was dying as he said it. Said he was "sorry." *Sorry for what?* He was confused. *That's it.* She patted the files for assurance, stepping back as the EMS crew rolled into the room, gear in tow.

No one noticed her slip out into the hallway, elbowing her way past the rubbernecking staff. The farther she walked from the boardroom, the quieter things got until she heard nothing but the echo of her high heels on the Italian marble floors. Relieved, she ducked into her office unseen and closed the door behind her with a lengthy sigh.

Without the afternoon sun to warm the bank of west-facing windows, her private office was gloomy. Regina shivered as she settled into her desk chair and adjusted the computer monitor. The antique brass lamps on her oak credenza took a bit of the chill off the room, as did the familiar whir of her hard drive.

"Prepare yourself," Alan had said. Even so, her hands shook with nervous anticipation as she spread open the slim manila file folder and scanned the first memo, looking for her name.

At the second line, her heart thudded to a stop.

It can't be true. Not him!

She fought for control, resisting the instinctive desire to sweep everything off her desk, tear the priceless artwork off her walls, smash her heavy desk chair through the window and send it plummeting down twelve stories.

She stared at the paper, swallowing hard.

The black-and-white truth was undeniable.

Had he lived, Alan would have named Bruce Tyler—*Bruce, that dimwitted bean counter!*—as the new CEO, with faithful Regina serving as Bruce's right-hand woman.

That was not how it was going to work.

Using a few simple keystrokes, she reset the clock on her computer to two hours earlier—*before* their disastrous management meeting had begun—then accessed Alan's desktop PC through their shared network.

Sorting his files by date, she quickly located the last one he'd worked on today and smiled when it came up on the screen: *successor.txt*. Alan had never been one for clever file names. The more obvious, the more likely he was to remember them, he'd explained.

Her fingers flew across the keys, altering the memorandum to suit her intentions. *She* would be CEO. Surely no one would question her right to the position. Resent it, no doubt, but not question it.

She was groomed to take over. She was *born* to run this company. Her father and her grandfather both had been CEOs in their time and place, hadn't they?

It was her turn. Her *destiny.*

Regina clicked on Save, then printed the page to proofread it. Surely there were other files, additional memos that required fixing. She took a deep breath, noting the actual time and reminding herself she had precious little left before someone came looking for her. Immersing herself in her work, she scanned Alan's recent documents. With minor difficulty she located similar references to Bruce's being chosen as Alan's successor and made the needed corrections.

Any mentions older than those files could be chalked up to the old man changing his mind.

After thumbing through his file folders and printing off new documents to replace the old, she shoved the discarded ones into her paper shredder and changed back the clock on her computer.

Her diamond-studded Rolex, the century-old Seth Thomas on the wall, and her Pentium processor all agreed: It was 3:11 p.m.

Time to take charge.

Regina hardly noticed the windshield wipers slapping back and forth, momentarily blocking her view of West Paces Ferry Road as she pointed her Lexus toward home. She was too engrossed in the scene that had played over and over in her head for the last hour.

A scene in which she'd been the star player and the other actors had taken second billing. *A distant second at that.* Ripples of pent-up laughter cascaded from her freshly lined lips. Her mother insisted top management skills for a woman included keeping one's makeup as presentable as one's desk.

Regina smiled in the rearview mirror. *You'd have been proud of me today, Mother.*

Her swift ascent to CEO began with an emergency executive meeting she'd arranged for four o'clock, ushering the same dozen men back into the boardroom. They were a subdued group, finding their seats but talking little among themselves.

"I want to share the last thing Alan said to me," she began, knowing they'd seen the CEO pull her close for a whispered good-bye. "His final words were 'It's all in the top folder.'"

So far, nothing but the truth. Amazing how easily the words fell from her lips.

Opening the file, she lifted out a piece of paper. "Copies of this memorandum are being distributed to you now." She nodded at Kathryn, who hurried to hand out the single sheets. Then Regina continued, projecting her voice across the room, "As you can see, Alan spelled out very carefully his recommendations for the future leadership of this company. I hope you will honor his years of dedicated service to our organization by giving me your complete support."

She sat, allowing the unexpected news to take root. *Look at Bruce Tyler's face, will you!* Regina kept her own expression in check as she watched each man react, swallow his dismay, then look up to meet her gaze. To a man, their eyes reflected a desperate plea for mercy.

Most of them had made her life miserable, one way or the other. *Payback time.*

Regina chose her words with care. "There are other changes outlined in a private memo from Alan to me." If these men had any brains at all, they'd know what was coming next. She cleared her throat for effect. "Bruce, Kenneth, Lyle, if you'll follow me."

Standing again, she zipped up her leather briefcase and tucked it under her arm, savoring the heady pleasure of their stunned silence. "As for the rest of you, it's business as usual. I'll be in my office all day tomorrow should you have individual questions."

Moments later she met with the three stooges one at a time, handed each a generous severance check, and waved them out the door. *Good riddance.* Word would quickly travel through the ranks that she was not to be trifled with. More heads would roll unless she received the utter loyalty she demanded.

Regina knew what they called her behind her back: *Queen B.* And not the sort that buzzed. *Too bad.* Her goal in life had never been to be popular nor to be loved. She wanted to be in charge.

Thanks to Alan's timely death this afternoon, now she was.

Regina swung the Lexus onto the long drive that led to her front door, winding through a quarter mile of verdant parklands before she pulled to a stop. Turning off the engine, she gazed up at the house she'd called home for the last ten years. A sprawling Tudor Revival built at the turn of the last century, it positively reeked of old money.

Jerry had never cared for it. Too showy, he said.

She adored every half-timbered inch.

The lights were on. *Good.* Portia was home. No after-school activities for a change. Regina questioned whether most of those "activities" weren't in fact one-on-one sessions at a friend's house with a certain loser named Theodore.

"Teddy," Portia had announced when she'd introduced him a few months back. A name suitable for a stuffed animal, Regina decided, but not good enough for her only daughter's beau. Teddy's car was *not* in the drive, she noted with satisfaction. It would be just the two of them for supper.

Maneuvering her way around the puddles, Regina ducked inside the massive doorway, shaking her umbrella out before shoving it into the marble stand. "Por-tia! I'm home."

No answer.

Regina strolled through the dim house, flicking on lights as she went. No sign of her daughter in the kitchen, not even crumbs on the counter from an afternoon snack. The study was dark, the media room deserted, although the large-screen television flickered, filling the room with the latest news from CNN.

Odd. Where *was* the girl?

It wasn't until Regina started up the steps that she heard a stereo jump to life behind her daughter's bedroom door. Screaming guitars and pounding drums polluted the air.

"Portia? Open up." Regina knocked on her door, softly at first, then louder when it seemed she wasn't being heard. Or obeyed. Frustrated, she called out, "Like it or not, I'm coming in."

She found her fifteen-year-old daughter stretched facedown across her four-poster bed. Discarded clothes, CDs without their cases, battered books, dirty plates, and crumpled candy wrappers were strewn everywhere.

Regina groaned and aimed her voice above the din. "Would you kindly explain this mess?" Shaking her head, she bit back the bitterness that always surfaced in her dealings with Portia. The child was so ungrateful! A perfect home, an exclusive academy, the best friends money could buy, and a wardrobe to rival any runway model's.

And still she lived like a sow in a pigpen.

Regina stopped the deafening music with an impatient jab at her daughter's new JVC stereo. "Portia Banks, this room is a disgrace."

The girl regarded her with thinly veiled contempt. "I didn't invite you in here, you know." Portia rolled onto her back and sat up with one fluid movement as only the young can, then reached toward the stereo.

"I won't begin to guess what's troubling you, Portia." Regina wrapped a cool hand around her daughter's wrist in midreach and held it, resisting the urge to squeeze tighter. "Suppose you tell me over supper."

"Supper?" The girl snatched her hand free and backed up, eyes glaring. "Food is the last thing on my mind, Mother."

"Fine." *Must she always be so dramatic?* "I won't bother to fix you a plate of your favorite seafood salad I picked up on the way home." Regina held up a cautionary finger. "But I expect you in the dining room promptly at seven. Dressed decently, if you don't mind."

Regina swept out the door, realizing yet again how much easier life would be without a teenager under her roof. When Jerry had been around to handle her, life with Portia had gone much more smoothly. Now the girl did nothing but whine and refuse to cooperate at every turn.

Thirty minutes later Portia appeared—on time for a change—and slumped into one of the side chairs. She'd managed to wash her face and comb her hair into some semblance of order, but her mood was still sullen.

Regina stabbed at her salad with more force than necessary and stated the obvious. "Something is wrong. Are you going to tell me what it is?"

Portia's lips curled into a practiced sneer. "*Everything* is wrong, Mom. I turned on the six o'clock news and found out my own mother is the new CEO of the biggest company in the world."

"Not the whole world, dear," Regina murmured. *Not yet.* "I'm sorry you had to hear about it from CNN. I would've called and told you myself, but things were in such an uproar with Alan's unexpected death."

"Was it really unexpected, Mother?" Portia's chin jutted forward as her bravado rose. "Or did you help him along on the road to his great reward?"

Regina gasped in midswallow, nearly choking on her crabmeat. "Did I…did I *what?*" She flung her napkin aside in disgust. "How dare you accuse me of such a vile thing!"

The teenager shrugged. "You've wanted the job since before I was born, Mother. The way it all came together today, I assumed you were behind it."

"You assumed incorrectly." Regina's eyes narrowed to slits. "Portia, you are one heartless young woman."

"Like mother, like daughter, eh?" Portia's laugh was brittle ice dropping into an empty glass. "Well, I intend to do a much better job of raising *my* little girl."

Regina retrieved her napkin, spreading it across her lap with exaggerated care. "Someday, when you're a mother, you'll regret those words."

Portia leaned forward until their noses were mere inches apart. "I don't regret anything, least of all motherhood."

Regina blinked, uncomfortable with the knowing gleam in her daughter's eyes. "You're years away from being a mother."

"Nope. Months away." Portia's smile was triumphant. "Six months, to be exact."

Regina felt her hands begin to shake and clasped them in her lap. "Wh-what are you talking about?"

"I'm pregnant, Mother." She leaned back and patted her still-flat tummy. "You know. Expecting."

"It isn't possible!" Regina stood, almost knocking over her chair, denial rushing through her like a river overflowing its banks. "*Pregnant?* You're only fifteen! A mere baby yourself. Who… Who is…"

"C'mon, Mom, who else?" Portia was positively beaming now. "Teddy is the father, I'm the happy mother-to-be, and you'll be a grandmother in December, near Chr—"

"*Grandmother?*" Regina closed the gap between them with one stride and slapped her daughter's smile clean off her face. "How could you? *How could you!*" She shoved her chair in place and paced the dining room, waving her arms for emphasis, ignoring the pain reflected in Portia's brown eyes.

"Do you realize how this is going to look?" Regina fumed. "The new CEO and her pregnant-out-of-wedlock daughter paraded across the tabloids." The knot in her stomach drew tighter. "Don't think it won't happen, Portia. They'll be searching for weaknesses in my résumé, proof that a woman can't run this company. You've just handed those vultures their lead story: 'Terrific Chief Exec—Terrible Mother.'"

"But *I'm* the one who's pregnant," Portia whined. "Why does that make you terrible?"

"Oh, grow up, child!" Regina stopped pacing long enough to collect her thoughts. Something would have to be done and soon. *Send her away?* Too many questions. *Put the baby up for adoption?* Too many strings attached. She sighed heavily, resting her hands on the table for support. "Portia, Portia," she muttered, shaking her bent head. "How could you be so selfish?"

"*Me* selfish?" The pain in her eyes sparked to anger. "What about you?" The girl's tone was sharp, her words sharper still. "You never have any time for me, Mom. No wonder I got pregnant, with you gone twelve hours a day."

Regina's head snapped up. "Don't you dare blame this on me, young lady!"

"So it's *my* fault. So what else is new?" Portia exhaled, losing some of her head of steam. "Everything around here is my fault."

There's your opening, Regina.

"That's not true. *Everything* isn't your fault, Portia." Regina pulled her chair out again and eased into it, forcing herself to soften her features, tone down her voice. This would take a certain amount of finesse. "I've erred as well. For instance, I should have asked why you've been moodier than usual lately." Regina watched her daughter's face relax a bit and added as warmly as she could, "You're not so far along that we can't correct this problem."

Portia wrinkled her brow. "Correct it?"

Regina nodded reassuringly. "One phone call to the clinic on Piedmont Road, and your worries are over."

"Mother!" Her eyes widened. "You aren't saying—"

"That's exactly what I'm saying." Regina patted her hand, noticing how much warmer it was than her own. "Trust me, you're far too young to handle childbirth, much less mothering an infant."

Portia's pink face crumpled for the first time that evening, making her look even younger than her fifteen years. Her voice was high and pleading. "But I *want* this baby!"

"Now, now. We can't always have what we want, can we? Listen, your sixteenth birthday is right around the corner. Suppose we take a trip together, just the two of us. London. Or Paris." She pushed the corners of her smile out further. "Now *there's* something you can't manage with a baby."

It took more than an hour of coaxing to convince Portia to let her call the clinic and make an appointment. "It's for the best," Regina assured the girl for the umpteenth time. "The sooner the better."

Tomorrow afternoon, if they'll take you.

*   *   *

Two phone calls after breakfast the next morning and the whole unpleasant matter was settled. "I'll send a car by the house for you at 3:30—"

"Mo-ther!" Portia threw her arms in the air, clearly put out. "You mean you aren't even going with me?"

Regina shook her head firmly. "You know that's not smart. Not with my face plastered all over the media today. I've given my verbal consent. I'll fax them a signed document later this morning. Besides, Marc's a good driver and very discreet." She handed her daughter a neatly handwritten list of instructions. "The clinic is expecting you at four o'clock. By suppertime you'll be home again, and all this will be behind us." She brushed a stray wisp of hair from the girl's eyes. "Then we can talk about Europe."

Portia shrank from her touch. "I don't care about Europe."

Regina resisted the urge to reprimand her and just nodded, hoping to appear sympathetic. It truly was for the best. Portia was much too young and irresponsible to raise the child—as if she knew the first thing about being a mother!

Watching the girl gather her school things and head for the front door, her shoulders sagging, Regina reminded herself that had the child been born, *she* and not her daughter would have carried the burden—and the expense—of raising this unwanted grandchild. Someday that child would have inherited her considerable wealth as well.

Bad enough that *Portia* would be handed such a fortune on a silver platter, the ungrateful girl.

Never mind. At least the grandchild problem was solved.

As Regina expected, reporters were waiting outside her office when she arrived. Patting her already smooth hair, she settled into her seat like a queen assuming the throne and proceeded to outline her plans for the company in breathtaking detail.

"Visionary," the *News at Noon* called her agenda. "Cutting edge," reported the *Atlanta Journal-Constitution*. "A much-needed housecleaning," declared the *Washington Post*. The day was filled with impromptu meetings, lunch on the run, and several more abrupt VP dismissals.

"A bloodbath," the rank and file complained, though none too loudly and not to her face.

"It's for the good of the company," Regina explained to the shell-shocked staff that jumped to do her bidding.

She found the whole thing exhilarating and couldn't believe her watch said 4:19 when she reached for the phone buzzing insistently on her crowded desk. "What is it, Kathryn?"

Her assistant's voice was shaking. "Line two is for you. West Paces Ferry Medical Center. Personal, they said."

Something about Alan's collapse yesterday perhaps? Curious, Regina punched the button for the second line. "This is Mrs. Banks."

"Mrs. Regina Banks?"

A male voice. Young, unfamiliar. Nervous, it seemed. "I'm calling from the ER of West Paces Ferry Medical Center. On Howell Mill Road? It's about your daughter, Portia Banks."

She gripped the phone. *Impossible.* Portia was at the clinic. On Piedmont Road. "The ER, you say? Is there some problem?"

Regina heard the man pause.

"Yes ma'am. Your daughter was in an automobile accident this afternoon. A man named Marc Dillard was driving."

"Yes, go on." Regina stared hard through the window, the hospital barely visible on the distant horizon. "Never mind Dillard. What about my daughter? Is she hurt?"

"I'm sorry to be the one to tell you this, ma'am. Your daughter was critically injured—"

Regina shot to her feet. "*What!* Why wasn't I notified immediately? From the ambulance?"

"We *have* been calling, Mrs. Banks. Apparently the phone lines to your office have been so tied up we couldn't get a call through."

She swallowed a bitter taste in her mouth. *Tied up in knots.* "So then, what are her injuries?"

"They…" He coughed, stalling. "They were fatal, ma'am. Two separate head injuries, a broken neck, a crushed abdomen. I'm sorry, ma'am. Very sorry."

Regina fell in her chair, overwhelmed. "She's…dead?"

"Yes. Along with…the babies."

Her mind was reeling. "*Babies,* did you say?"

"Twin boys. A tragedy to lose all three of them, for certain." He coughed again. "Look, Mrs. Banks, we need you to come to the Medical Center ER immediately. Identify your daughter, fill out the… Well, anyway, I'm very sorry to burden you with such terrible news."

Without a word, Regina hung up the phone.

Portia is gone.

Just like that, and her whole world had changed.

No grandchildren, thank goodness, but no daughter either.

No Portia. No one to inherit her hard-earned fortune.

Her house would be exceedingly quiet. Her life would be filled with nothing but work. Day after day, nothing to do except stand at the helm of one of the biggest corporations in the world.

Regina sat in utter stillness for several minutes, letting the truth sink in.

She was surprised to find her breathing normal, her hands warm, her mind clear. *So be it then.*

"It's for the best," she murmured, standing once more and smoothing her suit jacket across her hips. "Kathryn?" She raised her voice and called toward the next room. "Come here, please."

Her assistant stuck her head around the door, eyes wary.

"I need you to handle things here for an hour or so," Regina explained, collecting her cell phone and car keys. "I'll be back shortly. If anyone calls, I'm in an important meeting and can't be disturbed. Is that understood?"

"Whatever you say, ma'am. You're the boss…"

⌇

Mommy (Not So) Dearest:
Athaliah

I don't like this woman one bit. Don't connect with her, don't identify with her, don't want anything to do with her bad self.

And no wonder.

Her excessive drive toward success steps on my toes, and I feel the painful pressure of the truth. This strong-willed woman and I *do* have something in common: selfish ambition.

Ouch.

We grew up, you and I, in an era when women were told to head straight for the corner office, the one in the penthouse, the slot at the top of the corporate food chain.

Not all of us bought that line. Some of us pursued creative endeavors where titles mattered little and talent alone counted for something. Others among us poured our energies into raising the next generation. Still others found outlets for our abilities and never longed to climb an elusive ladder of success, wisely knowing most of those ladders leaned against abandoned, empty buildings.

Oh, but some of us went for it, honey.

And in doing so we discovered that lurking deep inside us was a woman like modern Regina—like ancient Athaliah—a woman who would sacrifice anything to be the queen of her universe.

Prepare yourself. This is not a pretty story, but it *is* one that can teach us some valuable lessons if we're willing to let God shine a light on that dark, queen-at-all-costs spirit many of us harbor deep in our hearts.

Among the Really Bad Girls, Athaliah—pronounced "ath-uh-LIE-uh"—the daughter of Ahab and Jezebel, qualifies as "a class-A rotter."[1] Amen to that! The woman was abhorrent, accursed, antagonistic, appalling, arrogant, audacious, avaricious, and just plain awful.

And speaking of the letter *A*, I'll do my best to help you sort through all the players in this story whose names start with *A* or *J*. Let's just say that monogrammed towels would *not* have made life easier in Athaliah's household!

Athaliah and her husband, Jehoram, met under the wedding canopy for much the same reason her ungodly parents, Ahab and Jezebel, joined forces: political maneuvering. In this case it was the bad King Ahab and the good King Jehoshaphat building a bridge between their lands through the arranged marriage of their children.

Jehoram brought his bride to Jerusalem—a woman with "evil flowing through her veins."[2] It was soon clear Athaliah had a stronger influence on him than did his godly father, King Jehoshaphat.

Some daughters reject everything that reminds them of Mom. Not our Athaliah, daughter of Phoenician princess Jezebel, the Baal worshiper. She "inherited, to the full, the bigotry and almost insane cruelty of her mother."[3]

Maybe that's why folks dropped dead all around Athaliah's dangerous self.

Her father was pierced with an arrow in battle and died in his chariot, from which the blood was licked clean by dogs.

Her mother was trampled by horses and also eaten by dogs.

And her husband was stricken with a nasty bowel disorder, as prophesied by Elijah in a letter.

> The LORD afflicted Jehoram with an incurable disease.
> *2 Chronicles 21:18*

Trust me, you don't want the medical details.

Jehoram's illness came not from an improper diet or too many free radicals in his system but straight from the hand of the Lord.

He died in great pain. His people made no fire in his honor,
as they had for his fathers. *2 Chronicles 21:19*

A double disgrace for this man—afflicted by God and snubbed by his
people, even in death.

He passed away, to no one's regret...

Or, as elsewhere translated, "without being wanted" (AMP). Ouch! You
almost feel sorry for Athaliah's hubby, dead at forty, until you realize that
he summarily executed all his brothers when he ascended to the throne[4]
and flaunted his flagrant disrespect for God by marrying a daughter of
Ahab[5] and worshiping her god, Baal.

Stunts like that are what planted him in an ignoble grave.

...and was buried in the City of David, but not in the tombs
of the kings. *2 Chronicles 21:20*

No fancy ceremonial funeral pyre, no costly marble headstone.
Next king, please.

The people of Jerusalem made Ahaziah, Jehoram's youngest
son, king in his place, since the raiders, who came with the
Arabs into the camp, had killed all the older sons.
2 Chronicles 22:1

Good grief, another generation of dead sons. Athaliah's sons, at that.
Did she mourn their loss? Did her heart ache as she put away their belong-
ings for the last time? Even a truly evil woman would surely have a spark
of compassion struck in her heart upon the birth of her own children...
wouldn't she?

Ahaziah was twenty-two years old when he became king,
and he reigned in Jerusalem one year. His mother's name
was Athaliah, a granddaughter of Omri king of Israel.
2 Kings 8:26

Here's everything you need to know about her Opa Omri: "But Omri did evil in the eyes of the LORD and sinned more than all those before him."[6] The fact that Athaliah's roots are mentioned here is a blinking red light: bad past, bad present, bad future.

The nefarious bloodline ran straight through Omri to Ahab to Athaliah to the young King Ahaziah.

> He too walked in the ways of the house of Ahab, for his
> mother encouraged him in doing wrong. *2 Chronicles 22:3*

Odd choice of words there. Encouragement conjures a picture of lifting people up, inspiring them to new heights, not driving them downward to new depths of deprivation. Athaliah's brand of motherly motivation promoted the worship of the false god Baal, using her sons to do her dirty work.

> Now the sons of that wicked woman Athaliah had broken
> into the temple of God and had used even its sacred objects
> for the Baals. *2 Chronicles 24:7*

Breaking and entering was crime enough, but desecrating the holy temple of the Lord was inviting disaster on their misguided heads.

The boys' dead father, Jehoram, was certainly no prize, but Athaliah is the one singled out as the source of depravity in her sons. Once they were killed—save Ahaziah, who took the throne—Mommy dearest was his "counselor in doing wickedly,"[7] with a little help from her friends back home.

> He did evil in the eyes of the LORD, as the house of Ahab had
> done, for after his father's death they became his advisers, to
> his undoing. *2 Chronicles 22:4*

To put it another way, "they led him to ruin" (NLT). Literally. The boy picked the wrong King to tangle with and was soon as dead as his dad.

Another funeral in the family. Another empty throne.

> So there was no one in the house of Ahaziah powerful
> enough to retain the kingdom. *2 Chronicles 22:9*

Back at the palace, the widowed Athaliah had a major problem on her hands. Her husband and father-in-law, the previous kings, were already history. Now her son had joined them, meaning her legal status, her claim to fame and fortune, was kaput. She was no longer the daughter of a king, the wife of a king, *or* a queen mother.

She was a widow. A soon-to-be pauper.

Worst of all for Athaliah, she was no longer *in charge*.

Rather than stepping in as regent until one of her offspring was prepared to rule, Mrs. A became "a self-styled queen."[8]

> When Athaliah the mother of Ahaziah saw that her son was dead, she proceeded to destroy the whole royal family of the house of Judah. *2 Chronicles 22:10*

Even another translation, "destroyed all the seed royal,"[9] doesn't communicate what really happened here. She intended to slaughter the lineage through which the promised Messiah was to come, "rubbing out anyone with DNA from the House of David."[10] To do so, Athaliah had to kill her own grandchildren.

Her *grandchildren*!

Grandmothers, can you fathom such an unspeakable act? Can you ever envision yourself, on your worst menopausal day, ordering hit men to gather up your precious grandbabies… Of course not.

Three thousand years ago the execution of relatives was business as usual around the palace. But to our twenty-first century sensibilities, the pattern of sin and slaughter is beyond belief, almost numbing.

Although rulers before her had protected their right to the throne with an equal show of violence, there's something chilling about a *mother*, a *grandmother* doing such a thing. Such disregard for human life breaks my heart in two, to think that "the tender sex could be so barbarous."[11]

Athaliah was concerned only with becoming the first (and last) queen of Judah. Not by birth, marriage, or motherhood but by removing the competition. Talk about selfish! This "wholesale, merciless, cruel-hearted murderess"[12] was worse than any corporate cutthroat we've seen in modern times.

I'm delighted to report she didn't get away with her coup. Like baby Moses safely hidden from Pharaoh's deadly grip, the lone surviving grandchild of Athaliah, a mere infant, was spirited away by his doting Aunt Jehosheba.

> But Jehosheba...took Joash son of Ahaziah and stole him
> away from among the royal princes, who were about to be
> murdered. She put him and his nurse in a bedroom to hide
> him from Athaliah; so he was not killed. *2 Kings 11:2*

Smart girl! That bedroom—in truth, a storage room where mattresses were kept—was located inside the temple of Jehovah, the "one place the idolatrous queen could be counted upon not to visit."[13]

Way to go, Aunt Jehosheba! As wife of Jehoiada the high priest (yet another *J* name), Aunt J would have had easy access to the temple, coming and going without raising an eyebrow, no doubt humming the hymn of David under her breath: "For in the day of trouble he will keep me safe in his dwelling; he will hide me in the shelter of his tabernacle."[14]

Between his nanny and his auntie, young Joash was in good hands.

> He remained hidden with his nurse at the temple of the
> LORD for six years...

As a mother who couldn't keep a child quiet even for a one-hour church service, I consider Aunt J's ability to keep little Joash safely tucked away for half a dozen years to be a minor miracle!

> ...while Athaliah ruled the land. *2 Kings 11:3*

That's the only thing said about this female monarch's six-year reign. Since some kings were lucky to last a week, let alone a year, Athaliah's half-dozen years in power were a "tribute to her cold-blooded competence"[15]...but that doesn't mean we have to like her.

I see Queen A as merely a Bad Girl bookmark holding a place for Joash—the remnant in the lineage of David, God's true, anointed king. When the child reached his seventh year, he was ready to take his rightful throne, and the priest Jehoiada was prepared to make it happen.

Summoning both commanders and guards, he showed them the would-be king, then gave them assignments in various locations. Even those men normally off-duty were pressed into service.

> "Station yourselves around the king, each man with his weapon in his hand. Anyone who approaches your ranks must be put to death. Stay close to the king wherever he goes." *2 Kings 11:8*

Any priest worth his robe knew how to inspire others to greater service, and Jehoiada had just the thing on hand to remind the men of their divine calling.

> Then he gave the commanders the spears and shields that had belonged to King David and that were in the temple of the LORD. *2 Kings 11:10*

Impressive, Uncle J. By calling to mind the strength and honor of King David, Jehoiada quickly won their allegiance for the new boy-king. Joash's coronation followed with great celebration.

> Jehoiada brought out the king's son and put the crown on him; he presented him with a copy of the covenant...

That "covenant," or "testimony" (NASB), was a copy of the Mosaic Law. *Finally!* After six years of Judah's citizens being forced to worship Baal to please Queen Athaliah, the throne belonged to a follower of Yahweh, and the Lord's commandments would be revered once again.

> ...and proclaimed him king. They anointed him, and the people clapped their hands and shouted, "Long live the king!" *2 Kings 11:12*

This was a serious jam session, y'all. Another account tells us, "Singers with musical instruments were leading the people in a great celebration."[16] Can you say, "Par-tay!"

However, not everybody was thrilled to discover the festivities had started without them.

> When Athaliah heard the noise made by the guards and the
> people, she went to the people at the temple of the LORD.
> *2 Kings 11:13*

Curiosity got the best of the queen and drew her out of the palace and down the street to the temple. *Alone.* Not smart, Queen A. Bet Athaliah wasn't ready for the sight that greeted her when she strolled inside the very temple she loathed.

> She looked and there was the king, standing by the pillar, as
> the custom was. The officers and the trumpeters were beside
> the king, and all the people of the land were rejoicing and
> blowing trumpets. *2 Kings 11:14*

Shock. Denial. Realization. Anger. You name it, the woman's emotions no doubt traveled the gamut in a blinding rush.

> Then Athaliah tore her robes…

The woman wasn't planning on taking a shower. Tearing one's robes was done as an act of grieving.

> …and called out, "Treason! Treason!" *2 Kings 11:14*

This translation nails the sentiment perfectly: "You betrayed me, you traitors!" (CEV). What irony, when *she* was the traitor to the throne and Joash was the rightful king!

Jehoiada took charge of the situation and gave orders to his commanders, who were in charge of the troops.

"Bring her out between the ranks and put to the sword
anyone who follows her." For the priest had said, "She
must not be put to death in the temple of the LORD."
2 Kings 11:15

If she had any supporters, they no doubt shrank back at Uncle J's
promise of sudden death. Alone and undefended, the ruthless queen
Athaliah met her gruesome end.

So they seized her as she reached the place where the horses
enter the palace grounds, and there she was put to death.
2 Kings 11:16

Though she was not trampled by horses like Mama Jezebel before her,
Athaliah's unceremonious death by sword point at the Horse Gate[17] was
anything but coincidence.

Did she die with her head held high, regal to the end? Did she, who
never extended mercy to others—not even her own grandchildren—beg
for mercy from her executioner? With her last breath, did she curse Yahweh…or blame Baal for not protecting her?

The false god Baal had his own problems, since Jezebel and Athaliah's
mother-daughter religion received a fatal blow as well.

All the people of the land went to the temple of Baal and tore it
down. They smashed the altars and idols to pieces and killed
Mattan the priest of Baal in front of the altars.

Then Jehoiada the priest posted guards at the temple of the
LORD. *2 Kings 11:18*

Jehoiada's precaution of posting guards was "so that no one who was
in any way unclean might enter."[18] The most unclean among them—
ex-Queen Athaliah—was no longer a concern.

And the city was quiet, because Athaliah had been slain with
the sword at the palace. *2 Kings 11:20*

Jerusalem was quiet once more, not unlike Israel enjoying forty years of peace after Jael's victory over Sisera. "When the righteous prosper, the city rejoices; when the wicked perish, there are shouts of joy."[19]

I'm rejoicing myself now that Athaliah's story is behind us. Ugh. Of all the Bad Girls and Really Bad Girls I've studied, Queen A takes the prize for Least Sympathetic and Most Despicable.

When I focus on the bloodshed surrounding her, I'm relieved to find nothing in my own life that resonates with Athaliah. *Whew.*

But if I consider her take-charge-at-all-costs personality, I have to admit an uneasy shiver of understanding ripples across my soul. How many social situations have I dominated by insisting on having the last word? In how many business meetings have I ended up calling the shots or making sure things were done *right* (which means to *my* specifications)? How many family dinners have ended on a not-so-sweet note because Mom copped a my-way-or-the-highway attitude?

One family mealtime in particular comes to mind. Bill and I were discussing business at the dinner table—not good manners in any century—when suddenly Lillian (age eight at the time) cut through our conversation with a pointed pronouncement: "Mom, do you realize you haven't even *looked* at Matthew and me this whole meal? It's like we're not even here. Like we're invisible. Don't we matter, Mom?"

My heart was cut to the quick. My own children, doubting their mother's love!

"You are the most important people in the world to me," I said, my voice catching. I meant every word, even though my actions at the moment didn't back it up.

Lilly said as much. "We sure don't *feel* important. Can we please talk about family stuff when we're together?"

I swallowed hard and nodded. "You bet. Help me remember, okay?"

That's a task she is only too happy to perform. At mealtime, in the car, sitting around the family room—when Bill and I fall into an after-hours discussion of business details, Lilly pipes up, "Family first, Mom."

Gulp. She's right, of course.

Then the Lord whispers a holy postscript: "Me first above family, Liz."
Right again.

Priorities were a serious problem for Athaliah, but some days I don't do
much better. I can't blame an evil mother or a sick husband or a weak god,
though Athaliah had all three.

Instead, I had a moral upbringing, married a godly man, and serve a
mighty God. Which means I'd better not miss the message in Athaliah's
gory life story: The Lord alone belongs on the throne.

What Lessons Can We Learn from Athaliah?

A leader succeeds only when surrendered to God.
The difference between powerful-but-good Deborah and powerful-but-bad
Athaliah boils down to one thing: the One whom they served. Deborah
served the God of Israel and gave him glory for the victory. Athaliah served
Baal and lost her life for it—though in truth, she served mostly herself.
When it comes to serving—and succeeding—we all have a choice. Choose
wisely, sisters!

> "Now then," said Joshua, "throw away the foreign gods that
> are among you and yield your hearts to the LORD, the God of
> Israel." *Joshua 24:23*

Never confuse what is socially acceptable with what is right.
Though killing family members was the norm in the dark days of Athaliah, it was despicable to God, then and now. We fool ourselves if we think
that because man's law declares something legal—abortion, euthanasia,
capital punishment—it will automatically be acceptable in God's eyes as
well.

> There is a way that seems right to a man,
> but in the end it leads to death. *Proverbs 16:25*

***Ambition* is a nice word for covetousness.**

Athaliah wanted that throne so desperately that her "paranoia and lust for power formed a toxic mixture."[20] Toxic is right! It not only killed her family, but it also eventually killed her. Ambitious people are often described in the most positive of terms—"driven," "motivated," "determined," "hard-working," and "goal-oriented." When the goal is only to please self, the Lord has another word for it: *sin.*

> For where you have envy and selfish ambition, there you find disorder and every evil practice....
> You kill and covet, but you cannot have what you want.
> *James 3:16; 4:2*

Wicked plans fail. God's plans prevail.

Athaliah did her best to wipe out the line of David, God's anointed. Though she was not privy to Isaiah's Messianic prophecies a century away, she was determined to promote Baal and demote Jehovah God. Foolish woman. Through David's "royal seed" would come the One who would bring salvation to the world. Did she really think her hatred could stop God's love? Thank goodness "no one can thwart God's purposes of grace,"[21] not even one of the baddest girls in God's Book.

> But the plans of the LORD stand firm forever,
> the purposes of his heart through all generations.
> *Psalm 33:11*

Bathing Beauty

*A woman takes off her claim to respect
along with her garments.*
HERODOTUS

M rs. Lam-bert!"

Putting her book aside, Bethany Lambert turned toward the sliding glass doors that opened into the kitchen. "What is it, Lois?"

The housekeeper poked her head out, weariness lining her face. "I'm done in the house, ma'am. Mind if I go?"

Bethany waved her off with a gentle laugh. "You look like you could use a tall glass of iced tea."

"Yes ma'am. Already had two." Lois wiped her brow with the back of her hand. "Mighty hot for April. I'll see you next Thursday then. Give the mister a hello for me."

Nodding as the housekeeper disappeared inside the house, Bethany shifted back into a comfortable position on the chaise lounge, the open book beside her forgotten. *The mister.* Sure, she'd tell him hello sometime. When he called. *If* he called. Huey hadn't touched home base in two days. Not unusual for him this early in the season, but she already missed the sound of his voice.

Right fielder Huey Lambert lived for one thing: opening day of base-ball season. After weeks of spring training, he was wired, revved up, and major-league ready for life on the road.

Next up to bat: St. Louis. Houston. Pittsburgh.

Maybe later tonight she'd watch the game on ESPN. He expected her to keep up with things, know his stats, follow the team standings. "I'll stay on top of it this year," she'd promised when he left for the opener in New York earlier that month.

It wasn't like she hated the game or anything.

Liar. Bethany smiled to herself and stretched out her long legs. Curling her pink-tinged toes, she leaned back into the cushions, letting the heat of the sun bake every inch of her to a toasty glow.

Face it, girl. You loathe baseball.

That was the truth of it. She loved Huey, loved seeing the pride on his face when he introduced her to his friends, loved making a nest for him to come home to for the off-season. Problem was, they didn't see enough of each other, and when they did, it was nonstop sports—on the tube, on the phone, on his mind constantly.

She wouldn't see him until the weekend after next when they played the Braves in town. The next ten days on her calendar looked like a deserted beach.

Squinting at her watch, she checked the time—three o'clock—then settled back into tanning mode. Several of the wives were having an early dinner tonight at the Chart House. It was walking-distance close. She might go. *Might not.* The main topic of conversation would be either who was on the injured list—the utmost concern for every player in pro sports, especially injury-prone Huey—or their various off spring. After a round of pointed questions like "When are you and Huey gonna settle down and have a baby?" Bethany usually looked for an easy exit line.

She'd have a hard time explaining even to them how seriously Huey took his conditioning program. How he had time to lift weights but no time to sweep her off her feet. How he was convinced any effort expended in their bedroom would cost him dearly in the outfield.

So. No dinner at the Chart House tonight. The broiled seafood was outstanding, but the sun on her skin felt even better. Bethany pressed farther back into the lounge chair and smiled, drifting in and out of consciousness. A flutter of wings soared overhead. The midafternoon rays poured down on her, lulling her to sleep with a steady wave of warmth.

Two hours later she woke to the sounds of the sea. Beyond her white stucco walls, on the other side of Ocean Boulevard, the salty waters of the Pacific rushed closer then drew back, heading toward high tide. Maybe she'd go for a beach walk later. *Maybe not.*

Bethany grinned and extended her arms in a wide arc. *Pure laziness.* Well, so what? She didn't have to do anything she didn't want to do. She squinted at the pale blue depths of her swimming pool. Small, elegant, meant for personal pleasure rather than athletic endeavors, the crescent-shaped pool was her gift to herself last summer. The maintenance man had left mere hours ago, so the water was pristine, cool, and inviting.

Maybe later.

Maybe now.

Her shorts and halter top, almost glued to her skin with a faint sheen of sweat, made her feel sticky and uncomfortable. She stared at the water, suddenly more interested. Where was her favorite Speedo? Had she tucked it in the top drawer after last month's trip to Florida?

Bethany eyed the shimmering surface. *I'll just stick my feet in. That'll cool me off.* Sliding off the lounge chair, she eased down onto the custom Mexican tiles surrounding the pool. Toes, ankles, calves, then knees sank into the water.

"Ahh…" She couldn't resist sighing as she swished her legs back and forth. The water wasn't as chilly as she'd expected. *Hmm.* Where was that bathing suit? Maybe she could find it before the setting sun sent temperatures plummeting to normal for an April evening.

The thought came out of nowhere. *Who says you need a bathing suit?*

The answer followed just as quickly. *Don't even think it, Bethany!*

She laughed softly, gazing up at the ten-foot-high stucco walls that enclosed her courtyard. The walls were, after all, topped with huge urns full of palms and blooming plants she'd picked up at Coronado's annual flower show last weekend.

Not a soul could see inside her cozy courtyard.

Still, it was so…so *not* her style. So daring.

So…why not, Bethany?

Feeling giddy, she stood, looking around as if someone *could* see her yet knowing they couldn't. The nearby houses were single story, and besides, hers was a corner house. Maybe the sea gulls would get an eyeful, but other than that, she was utterly alone—the front door safely locked, the cover of impending twilight beckoning, a cellular phone by her side if she needed something.

Right now, all she needed was to get in that water.

Her top and shorts peeled off in an instant. Undies, too? *Oh, why not?* Discarding the last of her clothes, she took a deep breath then walked down the steep corner steps, slipping at last under the glassy surface with a graceful slap of water against skin.

The refreshing water awakened her senses instantly, sending a flush of goose bumps along her arms when she rose to her feet. Pushing off the bottom of the pool, she did a lazy backstroke—her eyes closed, her smile at half-mast—and enjoyed the sensation of gliding along under her own steam, the water surrounding and supporting her completely.

Had she ever felt this relaxed, this free from worry, this *good*, from head to toe? *Not in a long time, Mrs. Lambert.* She turned and started back across the pool, grinning broadly up at the blue sky. *Not in a very long time.*

Rex Davis couldn't believe what he was seeing.

A woman, unabashedly naked, swimming in her courtyard pool.

He gulped down another swallow of Merlot and glanced at his watch, determined not to stare out the window any longer. Wasn't he supposed to be somewhere right now? Dinner? A meeting? Somewhere?

St. Louis.

Rex put down the crystal stemware with an impatient *clink*. All right, okay, so he should have gone with the team. But what did they need him for? His general manager was the best in the game. Team owners just got in the way, right?

He glanced through the curtained windows of the Hotel Del Coronado and, despite his best intentions, found himself watching the brazen young woman swimming back and forth in a carefree design, oblivious to his gaze.

The sight was far headier than the wine. From this height and distance, he couldn't make out her face, but if it matched her body and the waist-length hair floating around her, she'd be worth seeing up close.

Enough, Rex!

He was a married man. Not always happily, but always married.

Never mind that men in his position invariably found other women—younger women—to bolster their egos. A winning team was sufficient to keep his ego pumped. Anyway, he'd always held himself to a higher standard than most.

Still, a man could *look,* right? He found himself moving closer to the window, holding the curtain aside. *She* was the one showing off her best assets, right?

Not showing off, Rex. Swimming—alone—in her private pool. Not against the law.

There were penalties for what *he* was doing though. Groaning, he dropped the curtain. *Get to work, buddy. Do something useful.* He crossed the finely appointed room with long strides, then flipped open his briefcase and paused, hand in midreach. There, on top of his papers, sat a pair of binoculars, the ones he used at the ballpark to get a better look at the out-field action.

Binoculars, of all things. *Not good, not now.*

He fought the urge to pick them up and step back over to the window, knowing it was beneath him to do such a thing.

Still, her hair swirling around her, her long legs in motion…

Seconds later he was standing by the window, binoculars in hand, adjusting the knobs until the brunette swam into focus. His mouth went dry at the sight of her lush curves moving across the water.

Oh, man.

Out of the corner of his eye, he caught a glimpse of himself in the mirror and tossed the binoculars on the bed in disgust. *Pervert!* It was rude and shameful and a bunch of other stuff that didn't fit his image.

He was leaning on fifty. She was probably half that age. And anyway, he wasn't the Peeping Tom type. In the circles he traveled, he had women swimming around him all the time. Over the years he'd married several of them. Most of the younger women were piranhas, hungry for his substantial trough of cash. There were a few pretty angelfish in the bunch though.

Call one of 'em. Now. Just for dinner, just for a distraction, nothing more.

He fished a cell phone out of his pocket and flipped it open, intending to track down Suzan or Connie until his eyes were drawn again to the tantalizing swimmer below. The woman probably felt safe down there, knowing her neighbors would never see her, forgetting about The Del rising behind its tall ivy hedge across the street.

Mesmerized, Rex reached for his binoculars again in time to catch her standing waist-deep in the pool, water sluicing down her narrow shoulders. *Not fair, sweetheart.* He swallowed hard, then abruptly shifted his focus toward the house, desperately trying to keep her out of sight and out of mind.

The place looked vaguely familiar. White stucco, red tile roof, nice landscaping. Had he ever been inside? He'd stayed at The Del often enough. More than a few of his better players lived in Coronado. "The Crowned One," the Spaniards had called it.

Had he met this woman perhaps? *One way to find out.* Picking up the bedside phone with his free hand, Rex punched in a set of numbers he knew by heart and waited for a familiar growl at the other end.

Click. "Rodriguez."

"Just the guy I need. Ty, you know anything about an oceanfront house in Coronado? White stucco? Across from The Del?"

"You wanna buy the place, boss?"

Rex chuckled. "Not exactly. I wanna know if we've got a player who lives there."

He could hear the man's mental gears grinding until they meshed. "Yeah. You're probably talkin' about Huey Lambert's place. Got a pretty courtyard in the back."

It sure does. Rex nodded, his binoculars glued to the spot. "That's the place, Ty. What's his wife's name again?"

"His *wife*? You mean Bethany the Beautiful? Good thing you're a trustworthy guy, boss. If you so much as knocked on her door, Huey would—"

"Would what?" Rex cut him off as an unwanted stab of guilt pierced his chest. "Huey would be smart to keep his eyes on the ball and his ankle out of a stabilizing boot this season."

"You're right there." Ty coughed, obviously waiting for some instructions. "Look, you want Bethany's phone number?"

"No, I want *you* to call her." Rex hated the longing he heard in his voice. "Ask her to join me for dinner."

Ty snorted. "Just dinner, right, boss?"

Rex felt his face growing hot. Was it that obvious? "Ty, I…"

"Hey, I'm only kidding, Mr. Davis. She's a nice girl; you're a nice guy. Huey's got nothing to worry about."

That was true, wasn't it? Dinner, nothing more?

Rex kept talking, as if he needed to convince Ty. Or himself. "I figured with Huey out of town and me right next door, a fancy dinner on the boss's AmEx might be welcome." Rex gave him the number for his suite. "Tell her I'll be expecting her at eight. Wait…make it seven thirty. Got that?"

Rex hung up the phone, surprised to find his hand shaking. He gripped the binoculars and willed his thudding heart to slow down, even

as the sight of her sent it into overdrive. Bethany was swimming again, slic-
ing through the water with graceful, sure strokes, more beautiful than ever.
She'd be standing in this room in one hour.

Enough time for a shower and a shave.

Enough time to do a little research on Huey Lambert.

Enough time to ask himself what in the world he was doing.

Fresh from a lengthy dive to the bottom, Bethany surfaced in time to hear
the chirp of her cell phone next to her brightly covered chaise lounge.

Drat. Easily pulling herself out of the water, she ran across the mani-
cured grass, noticing how much cooler the air had become. She punched
the phone on, still breathless from swimming. "H-hello?"

It was Ty Rodriguez. Worked in the team office in some capacity or
another, she recalled. Gruff talker but a nice enough guy.

Yanking the dry halter top over her shivering arms while she juggled
the phone, she listened to his small talk wind down before she cut to the
chase. "What can I do for you, Ty?"

"Rex Davis would like a…meeting with you this evening. If that's convenient."

Rex Davis! The owner of the team wanted to meet with *her*? Rattled, she
tucked a long strand of wet hair behind her ear. "What's this about, Ty?"

"Beats me, missy. Probably something about Huey."

Her eyes widened. *His injury!* Huey was being taken out of the lineup.
Or traded. *Or worse.* Maybe he'd been hurt in St. Louis, taken out of the
park on a stretcher.

"Uh…okay, Ty. Sure, I'll be happy to meet with Mr. Davis. Where
should I—"

"The Del."

She gulped and looked up, the red-roofed turrets and graceful ivory
lines of the century-old hotel looming beyond her garden walls. "Right
next door? How convenient." *A little too convenient.* Surely Rex didn't see…

Nah. She wouldn't even consider the possibility. "Tell me when and where, Ty, and I'll be there."

Fifty minutes later, her lightning-fast shower behind her, she stood in the ornate lobby of Hotel Del Coronado, a mammoth, historic resort squeezed along Orange Avenue between the Pacific Ocean and Glorietta Bay. The Del held happy memories for her. She and Huey were married there in the Crown Room. Celebrated their honeymoon with a sweeping ocean view and a spectacular California sunset bathing their high-ceilinged Victorian room in golden splendor.

Dinner at The Del? *No problem.* They had three restaurants to choose from. No doubt he was waiting for her in the Prince of Wales, voted San Diego's "Most Romantic Restaurant" or some such thing.

She smiled as the desk clerk hurried over to assist her. *Not that Rex has anything like that in mind!* It was just a bit quieter, classier, more suited to Rex's good taste. The restaurant also featured a dynamite jazz pianist, and everybody knew Rex loved music. Even if he had bad news to tell her, Rex would do his best to soften the blow.

"May I help you, madam?"

Bethany asked the bright-eyed clerk to ring the room number, then almost swallowed her tongue when she heard the clerk say, "Yes, Mr. Davis, I'll send Mrs. Lambert right up."

The clerk disconnected the line, then beamed at her. "He's expecting you. You'll want to take that elevator. Yes, the one that looks like a bird-cage. Have a nice evening."

Bethany turned on wobbly knees and headed for the elevator. She didn't intend to have a nice *anything* in Rex Davis's private suite! Climbing into the elevator, she punched the button harder than necessary, then forced herself to breathe. *Calm down.* He was probably finishing some business and didn't want to leave her standing around in the lobby. *Very thoughtful.*

Relieved, she smoothed the lines of her black linen dress and wondered again if it was appropriate for a serious business meeting. The design was nicely tailored and not at all revealing, but it was rather…well, *short.* "Too short," Huey had said the last time she wore it, then kissed her soundly. It was that kind of dress.

She knocked on the door of Rex's suite, surprised to feel her cheeks warming. Nerves probably. He could have very bad news, she reminded herself, running her hands over the fabric again.

The door opened wide, and there stood Rex, wearing a golf shirt and a crooked smile, his hair still wet from the shower. Or a swim. He motioned her inside, quickly closing the door behind her.

"Have a seat, Miss…uh…Mrs.…um…"

She offered a tentative smile. "Bethany."

That's odd. Now *he* was the one who seemed nervous. Almost embarrassed. He poured a generous glass of wine and held it out to her, an unspoken invitation.

"Thank you, Mr.… "

"Rex, okay?" He shrugged and offered a boyish wink. "It's only fair…Bethany."

She held the glass in one hand, running her finger around the rim in a shaky circle. "Uh…is my husband…is Huey okay? I mean, has he been injured again, or…"

"No!" Rex coughed and waved his hand dismissively. "No, nothing like that. Huey is fine. Great player. Arizona's loss was our gain. We're glad to have him on the team this year." He nodded toward a love seat upholstered in fine, polished chintz, then joined her when she eased into it. "Glad to have *you* on the team, for that matter, Bethany."

Rex sliced a thin sliver of cheese and dropped it on a cracker, then lightly placed it in her open palm. "Hungry?"

She was, in fact, famished. Had she even eaten lunch?

They chatted over their glasses of wine, soon drinking a second. Or was it a third? Rex Davis had always been cordial to her the few times they'd met since the trade, but she hadn't noticed how friendly, even funny, the man could be.

The longer she looked at him, the less he looked like her husband's boss and the more he looked like what he was—a strikingly handsome, late-forty-something, wealthy-beyond-measure man. He'd kept his body in excellent shape and his bank account more so. She found herself smiling back, even laughing, enjoying his company. If he was working up to bad news, he sure was taking his time.

Their dinner arrived at eight, a feast fit for a king. And his queen. And the rest of his court, for that matter. They sampled one dish after another for nearly an hour, carrying on like good friends, telling bad jokes and trading worse puns. She never knew he was such a nice, regular kind of guy.

With a dramatic groan, she leaned back from the table. "Rex, who's going to eat all this?"

He shrugged, a faint redness washing over his rugged features as they considered the array of desserts before them. "I wanted to make sure there was something here to please you."

She looked at him—really drank her fill of him for the first time that night—and finally understood what he was trying to say. His darkening eyes confirmed it. The pace of her heart quickened in response.

So this was what tonight's "meeting" was all about. She'd pretended not to notice what was happening between them, but there was no denying the attraction—it was mutual and it was powerful. Frighteningly so.

Not to mention that Rex was in a position to make her life—their lives, hers and Huey's—miserable if she refused him.

Not that she wanted to. Not that she could.

"I'm more than pleased," she whispered. "But I'm…married."

He nodded, the blush replaced by a steady, serious gaze. "I know. And I'm sorry." He slowly moved toward her, edging around the table to brush a tentative hand across her cheek, lifting her hair ever so slightly, splaying his fingers underneath the dark strands. "Do you want to leave now, Bethany?"

I do. I don't. "I'm…not sure."

His other hand slid around her neck, pulling her closer. "You're not sure if you can stay?" His words were a caress.

"No." Her voice dropped lower. "I'm not sure if I can leave."

Rex bent toward her. "Because I won't let you?"

"No." Her gaze met his and held it. "Because *I* won't let me…"

∽

In Her Case, Cleanliness Was *Not* Next to Godliness: Bathsheba

Never have the words "wrong place, wrong time" fit a situation so snugly. Toss in "wrong person, wrong reason," and you've summed up the David-and-Bathsheba fiasco in a nutshell. It's a story replete with "seduction, intrigue, and murder,"[1] starring the most unlikely of players: David, king of the Good Guys.

The setting was Jerusalem, the season was spring, a time when—as Tennyson put it—"a young man's fancy turns lightly to thoughts of love."[2] And other stuff.

> In the spring, at the time when kings go off to war, David
> sent Joab out with the king's men and the whole Israelite
> army. They destroyed the Ammonites and besieged Rabbah.
> *2 Samuel 11:1*

What do war and springtime have in common? Good weather. At the end of the rainy season in the Middle East, the roads were in decent shape for traveling, and the troops found plenty of fodder in the fields for their war horses.[3]

Off they went, destroying and besieging.

> But David remained in Jerusalem. *2 Samuel 11:1*

Wait. If all the king's horses and all the king's men went off to war, how come Humpty Dumpty stayed home?

There's our first clue that trouble was brewing. Since military leadership was one of his most important duties as king of Israel, David belonged with his troops. We're not told why he stayed home—but we can guess.

David was about fifty years of age, no longer a young man. Sleeping on the ground, eating army grub, wearing fatigues—war just wasn't much fun anymore. Why not let Joab handle things?

Warning! Putting aside critical responsibilities because of laziness, weariness, or boredom is the first step toward disaster. "When we are out of the way of our duty we are in the way of temptation."[4]

At least, that's how things shook down for David.

> One evening David got up from his bed…

The sky was still streaked with light. Since evening officially began at three o'clock,[5] the translation "late one afternoon" (CEV) gives us a clearer picture. And he wasn't necessarily sleeping the day away but rather was waking up from a short siesta on his "couch" (NEB).

> …and walked around on the roof of the palace. *2 Samuel 11:2*

In Jerusalem the roofs were flat and served as an extra room of the house, utilized for worship, sleeping, or drying things like fruit and flax[6]— remember Rahab's flax-covered roof?

David, however, wasn't doing any of the above. He was restless, pacing to and fro without any destination in mind—after all, roof walking gets you nowhere fast. Unfortunately our Walking David turned into a Peeping Tom.

> From the roof he saw a woman bathing. *2 Samuel 11:2*

Note that David was on *his* roof, but she wasn't necessarily on *hers*. As one translation describes the scene, "A beautiful young woman was down below in her courtyard, bathing as her religion required" (CEV). Whether she was washing indoors near a curtainless window or splashing in a well-concealed courtyard or—it *is* a possibility—flashing on her own flat roof, Bathsheba was *not* soaking in a bath full of bubbles up to her chin like those bathing beauties in the movies. This was the desert, remember?

Water was at a premium, and heated water, a luxury. Her tub would have been a small basin of water from which she sponged herself clean, then rinsed her body by pouring fresh water from a pitcher.

In other words, she was exposing more than her shoulders. Even if the details were fuzzy, David got an eyeful.

Commentators—male and female—have scolded Bathsheba for her bathing ritual. One insisted that "had she been a careful, modest woman, surely she would have looked around the easily seen adjacent roofs."[7] Complained another, "David may be a voyeur, but Bathsheba is an exhibitionist."[8]

Listen, folks, you can guess all you want, but *we simply don't know* whether Bathsheba was innocently bathing or shamelessly baiting her neighbor. True, she knew that her husband was away at war and the king was not. Jerusalem's rumor mills were no doubt churning with that bit of unusual news. But if she had disrobed on purpose, hoping David would take a peek, wouldn't she have risked other men on other rooftops drinking their fill of her as well?

Besides, the Bible states that David saw *her*—but it doesn't ever say that she saw *him*!

For me, the enticement argument just doesn't hold water. A well-bred lady at home alone, with only her maidservants to protect her, would never have risked bathing in full view of her neighbors. Especially not a married woman who was well aware of the ability she had to attract male attention.

The woman was very beautiful. *2 Samuel 11:2*

The Hebrew literally means "exceedingly good of appearance." You'll find it translated "very lovely to behold" (AMP) and "unusual beauty" (NLT), while the LRV (Lizzie Revised Version) is "Ooh, honey chile!" It's a phrase reserved for those who were exceptionally easy on the eyes—Vashti, Rebekah, and, yes, David himself. Truth is, these two must have made a striking couple. The word suggests a certain amount of "sensual appeal."[9] A feast for the eyes, as it were.

Considering he didn't have binoculars or bifocals at his disposal, David's vision clearly wasn't undergoing a midlife crisis. From some distance he saw not only that she was bathing but that she was beautiful.

If only he'd taken Job's vow—"I made a covenant with my eyes not to look lustfully at a girl"[10]—or heard the words of his descendant Jesus, spoken a thousand years after David was dust: "Anyone who looks at a woman lustfully has already committed adultery with her in his heart."[11]

Alas, like Eve in the garden reaching toward the beautiful fruit with her hands outstretched, David let his eyes and his active male imagination lead him astray. "Ruled entirely by his passions,"[12] he took the next fatal step.

> David sent someone to find out about her. *2 Samuel 11:3*

Odd. Here she was, a neighbor and a knockout, yet he didn't know her name or marital status. Let's cut him some slack and assume he was in the dark about her hubby, Uriah, and was considering adding this comely bather to his long list of wives and concubines. That seems innocent enough. Except it also went against God's strong advice to any man who would rule Israel as king: "He must not take many wives, or his heart will be led astray."[13]

David's eyes had already gone astray. His spy brought him news, however, that should have put a stop to David's wayward thinking.

> The man said, "Isn't this Bathsheba, the daughter of Eliam
> and the wife of Uriah the Hittite?" *2 Samuel 11:3*

Lots of information here. Her name, for starters. Her lineage as the daughter of an upper-class warrior and righteous man; in Hebrew, *Eliam* means "God is kinsman." The messenger saved the most important tidbit for last: Bathsheba was married to Uriah, one of David's loyal servants on the battlefield, a soldier and a saint among men.

Uh-oh. Look at all those red flags!

The fact that the messenger worded it as a question—"isn't she so-and-so?"—sounds like a gentle attempt on his part to convey, "Can't you see she's off-limits, David?" The biblical command is firm: "You shall not commit adultery"[14] and, more specifically, "Do not have sexual relations with your neighbor's wife."[15]

The messenger did everything except quote these verses to his king, but to no avail. If you've ever tried to stop someone from dating the wrong person, from cheating on his or her beloved, from going too far sexually, then you know what it's like to fight a losing battle with raging hormonal urges.

David was no longer thinking with his kingly head or his godly heart. Another part of his anatomy had seized control.

> Then David sent messengers to get her. *2 Samuel 11:4*

Two or more messengers to bring back one woman? Boy, he wasn't taking any chances on her responding, "Not tonight, I've got a headache." The literal translation is "take" her, or "fetch" her (NEB), like a dog. Doesn't sound like she had much choice.

Did David's men, in effect, kidnap her, saying nothing about where they were taking her? Or woo her with "The king requests your presence," then treat her like royalty as well? Or did they fib for David, hinting that the king had news from the battlefront about her husband Uriah—maybe even tragic news?

The how of it matters not.

We already know the why, which without question made this "one of the most cruel deeds of David's life."[16] He already had a dozen or more women under his roof who would gladly have cooled the heat of his ardor.

But no. He had to have the beautiful, untouchable Bathsheba.

Sisters, this wasn't just about sex.

It was about control. It was about power. It was about asserting his kingly rights—and ignoring his godly calling.

And every time I insist on opposing God's Word to appease my fleshly appetites and my longing to control my own destiny, *I make the same fatal mistake David did.* How dare we sit in judgment of a man who is nothing more than a mirror for our own sinful nature!

Oh, Lord, now I understand why I've avoided studying this story for so long. Bathsheba's shadowy sins aren't the issue, nor David's blatant ones. It's my own sins that cry out for confession. "For I know my transgressions, and my sin is always before me."[17]

Groan.

Had I been David, I would have commanded Bathsheba to come and relished the authority to do so.

Had I been Bathsheba, I would have convinced myself I had no choice in the matter and bowed to David's royal decree, secretly grateful to submit to such a powerful man.

We don't know how she felt, but we know what she did.

> She came to him... *2 Samuel 11:4*

Climb inside Bathsheba's heart for a moment.

The king—the *king*—has brought you into the inner chamber of his fine palace in the cool breeze of a moon-kissed spring evening. You are freshly bathed, a flush of anticipation warming your skin. You've been alone for days, weeks—a beautiful young woman without a husband to share your bed or gladden your heart.

The king—*your* king—stands before you, older but still handsome. A brilliant musician, a mighty warrior, a capable ruler, a wealthy man able to grant favors, bestow riches, and provide for you if your husband is killed in battle. This prince among men gazes at you with longing, frank desire widening the irises of his dark eyes. He slowly extends his hand to you with an invitation that is unmistakable...

Okay, girls.

You are Bathsheba. Do you refuse to follow the man into his bedchambers on the grounds that you are married and for you this is an act of adultery, king or no king? Do you scream? Faint? Beg for mercy? Remind him of his commitment to Jehovah God? Quote Leviticus? Pray for miraculous intervention? Scratch his eyes out? Run for the door?

I will never fault Bathsheba for going with the messengers to the palace. The king requested to see her. As his subject, she responded with proper obedience.

But once his motives were clear—and her future was cloudy—Bathsheba might have stood her ground, reminded him of her marital status, and bravely said no, begging for his righteousness to prevail. Wasn't David a good, honorable, godly man, at least most of the time? The Scriptures assure us he was.

> For David had done what was right in the eyes of the LORD
> and had not failed to keep any of the LORD's commands all
> the days of his life—except in the case of Uriah the Hittite.
> *1 Kings 15:5*

Why is it "the case of Uriah the Hittite," not "the case of Bathsheba the Hit-On"?

Because David took Uriah's wife and *then* took Uriah's life. According to Hebrew tradition, "adultery was a sin against the husband,"[18] so it was the *man* who was wronged when adultery was afoot—never mind if the woman was dumped on as well.

Did Bathsheba even *try* to refuse David? If she did (big *if*), her refusal was ignored.

> ...and he slept with her. *2 Samuel 11:4*

Fight the temptation to romanticize this scene with candlelight and soft music. Nowhere does love factor into the equation. "They were not in love. They simply chose to behave in a dishonorable and destructive way."[19]

How much was Bathsheba to blame for all this? Was she a virtuous victim? Or a villainous vamp?

Her name doesn't tell us much. Depending on whom you listen to, *Bath-sheba* either means "daughter of abundance," "seventh daughter," or "daughter of an oath." Too bad it didn't mean "daughter who talks a lot," because the girl barely spoke! If only she'd been more of a yakker like two of David's other wives—gracious, chatty Abigail or that sharp-tongued talker Michal—then we might have our answer.

By giving us the silent treatment, Bathsheba forces us to assemble the puzzle pieces of her character based on her actions alone. No wonder no one can agree on whether she was Really Bad—or Really *Had*. Opinions fall into two distinct camps:

1. Bad to the Bone
Some say she was an "adulterous wife" who "schemed to gain prominence for herself and her child."[20] Rather than resisting, she caved. As such, Bathsheba has been painted as a latter-century Eve, solely responsible for David's demise—"the woman you put here with me" kind of thing.[21] There are those who conclude "Bathsheba knew what was right but she did not do it."[22] Hang your head in shame, Sister B. Obviously that night of illicit passion was all your fault.

2. Had by the Throne.
Other scholars insist Bathsheba doesn't "fit the wicked woman image."[23] Instead of being a temptress, she was nothing more than an "innocent victim of his lust,"[24] at the mercy of a king who could have any woman he wanted, no questions asked. The text suggests that David's men "did not ask her if she wanted to go; they simply took her."[25] Lift your head with pride, Sister B, since David was to blame and none of it was your fault.

See the problem? If you choose the "Bad to the Bone" viewpoint, she's both tempter and adulteress. But the "Had by the Throne" version turns her into a victim and means that her one-night stand with David "was in essence rape."[26]

Oh, dear. Do we have to go there?

The fact is, whether she was bad or good, Bathsheba's actions and motives cannot be changed. *But ours can.* That's why we're here, girls. Not to figure out "was *she* bad?" Rather, we need to decide "have *we* been—or might we be—bad in a similar situation?" If the answer is yes, then what should we do about it? That's the real deal.

There's no question that David started this skin game, but there's also not a word in the text that suggests Bathsheba put up a fight. We know only that she arrived tip-to-toe clean, fresh from her bath.

> (She had purified herself from her uncleanness.)
> *2 Samuel 11:4*

Why the parenthetical addition? It's a heads-up for some startling news soon to follow. The Law was very forthright about women and hygiene: "When she is cleansed from her discharge, she must count off seven days, and after that she will be ceremonially clean."[27]

Get your calendars out, girls, and follow along. Bathsheba's "uncleanness"—her monthly period—had already come and gone, lasting perhaps four to seven days, so clearly she was not pregnant. She'd waited all seven required days *after* the bleeding stopped and then performed her ritual bath, which is when David saw her. That would have been at the midpoint in her monthly cycle, the time when a woman usually ovulates. Like, I mean, you know...*fertility central*!

There's also the possibility the verse means she cleansed herself *after* their night of passion, which was also required by Mosaic Law and would have served a dual purpose since "washing is an Old Testament metaphor for cleansing from sin."[28]

But that past-perfect tense phrase—"she *had* purified herself"—says "old news" to me. Especially considering what happened next.

> Then she went back home. *2 Samuel 11:4*

If Bathsheba had been less than godly herself, she might have tried to track down the 1000 B.C. version of those nasty morning-after pills. Instead, she waited, counting the days and watching the subtle but significant changes that occur in a woman's body from the very moment a fertile egg and a healthy sperm are touched by the hand of God.

The woman conceived…

Though it takes two to get things rolling, the fact is, the man is usually taking a hot shower by the time conception occurs. That sacred, silent moment is between God and the woman. Days or weeks later, when she realizes what has occurred—whether it is the best news or the worst news of her life—it is her secret alone. Hers and God's, that is, until she spills the beans.

Many of us know the joy of sharing that incredibly good news with a husband. When I discovered I was expecting our firstborn, I was nearly thirty-fours years old and beyond ecstatic. Bill and I kept it to ourselves for a few weeks, wanting to be sure, but also longing to savor our husband-wife secret, giggling and winking our way through Toys"R"Us, hoping we didn't see anyone who might recognize us.

Others know what it's like when a pregnancy is anything *but* good news. Although I never conceived out of wedlock (a miracle, considering my B.C. lifestyle), there were several times I *thought* I was pregnant and had to wrestle with how I would tell the unsuspecting father the dreaded news. Been there, sis? Then you know the fear, the apprehension, the knot in your gut that's nothing like morning sickness and everything like shame: *What will I say to him?*

Bathsheba went for the mince-no-words approach.

> …and [she] sent word to David, saying, "I am pregnant."
> *2 Samuel 11:5*

She finally spoke. Even then, it wasn't face to face; it was a message delivered verbally or by written note. Crucial words though. Life changing. Think how many movie plots and novels have hinged on a woman announcing, "I'm pregnant." We get this, honey. We really do.

Your turn, David.

So David sent this word to Joab: "Send me Uriah the Hittite." And Joab sent him to David. *2 Samuel 11:6*

Good heavens, no word to Bathsheba? *Hmm.* Sure does *look* like David
was more concerned with his men than with his unborn child and its
unwed-to-him mother.

David knew his royal neck needed protecting, that his reputation was at
stake. What soldier would willingly serve a king who might sleep with his
wife while he was waging war for him? Nip it in the bud—that was David's
philosophy.

Just as he'd sent for Bathsheba, now he sent for Uriah.

Just as she'd obeyed, so did her husband.

> When Uriah came to him, David asked him how Joab
> was, how the soldiers were and how the war was going.
> *2 Samuel 11:7*

Oh, for heaven's sake. David made *small talk* with the man!

If David had been a class act, he would have confessed his sin to Uriah
on the spot, begged his forgiveness, and agreed to support the child in
whatever way Uriah chose. Risky, yes, but righteous.

But he was the king. He didn't do any of that stuff.

Meanwhile, the poor cuckolded husband must have thought he was
coming up in the world, summoned by the king—the *king*—simply to
share the latest news from the front. If only Uriah had known the sad truth
that David's troops were the last thing on the ruler's mind.

> Then David said to Uriah, "Go down to your house and
> wash your feet." *2 Samuel 11:8*

This is an Old Testament euphemism. David was really telling Uriah
to go home and enjoy his wife, not take a footbath. Please, no more
bathing scenes, David. Wash your mind out with soap.

> So Uriah left the palace, and a gift from the king was sent
> after him. *2 Samuel 11:8*

David was so relieved he sent a gift along—"a mess of meat."[29] Sorta like sending the guy home with the best leftovers wrapped up in aluminum foil and shaped like a swan.

No doubt the meat was enjoyed...the wife, however, was not.

> But Uriah slept at the entrance to the palace with all his
> master's servants and did not go down to his house.
> *2 Samuel 11:9*

Was Uriah avoiding his wife because he suspected something fishy was going on? Not at all. He was honoring his service to the king, adding further fuel to David's burning sense of shame and no doubt Bathsheba's as well.

It seems Plan A—have Uriah sleep with Bathsheba so he'd think the baby was his—failed miserably.

> When David was told, "Uriah did not go home," he asked
> him, "Haven't you just come from a distance? Why didn't you
> go home?" *2 Samuel 11:10*

What he *really* wanted to ask him, of course, was "Why didn't you save us both a lot of grief, buster, and sleep with your wife?"

> Uriah said to David, "The ark and Israel and Judah are
> staying in tents, and my master Joab and my lord's men
> are camped in the open fields." *2 Samuel 11:11*

How patiently this soldier reminded his king of the hardships of military service, which offered nothing but tents and fields for beds.

> "How could I go to my house to eat and drink and lie with
> my wife?" *2 Samuel 11:11*

Bet that "lie with my wife" line hurt, huh, Dave?

And what an honorable man Uriah was! He hadn't gone home because he knew what was expected of him. Men headed for battle were supposed to steer clear of female companionship, as David himself once assured a priest: "Indeed women have been kept from us, as usual whenever I set out."[30]

Then Uriah further honored the king who had dishonored him by making an oath.

> "As surely as you live, I will not do such a thing!"
> *2 Samuel 11:11*

Uriah's loyalty only served to heighten David's disgrace.

No doubt with a growing sense of panic, the king bought himself some time.

> Then David said to him, "Stay here one more day, and tomorrow I will send you back." So Uriah remained in Jerusalem that day and the next. *2 Samuel 11:12*

It was time for Plan B.

Uriah was called back into the palace.

> At David's invitation, he ate and drank with him, and David made him drunk. *2 Samuel 11:13*

David, have you *no* shame? As one of the minor prophets moaned, "Woe to him who gives drink to his neighbors, pouring it from the wineskin till they are drunk."[31] It appears David made Uriah drunk but didn't join him in the debauchery. There's something even more contemptible about that.

So calculated. So cruel.

And so ineffective.

> But in the evening Uriah went out to sleep on his mat among his master's servants; he did not go home. *2 Samuel 11:13*

Plan B down the drain!

Even *drunk* the man behaved himself better than his sober king, who'd been intoxicated with lust only weeks earlier.

Desperate, David moved to Plan C.

> In the morning David wrote a letter to Joab and sent
> it with Uriah. In it he wrote, "Put Uriah in the front
> line where the fighting is fiercest. Then withdraw from
> him so he will be struck down and die." *2 Samuel
> 11:14–15*

The *nerve* of this king, making Uriah carry his own death warrant to the battlefront! Somebody embroider a pillow for David's office with this cheery verse: "Cursed is the man who kills his neighbor secretly."[32]

Honestly, David. *Disgusting* isn't the word for it.

What must Joab have thought when he got this letter? Did he imagine that Uriah was guilty of some crime and David was passing sentence? Or did he add things up—next-door neighbor, wife home alone—and wisely not ask questions?

Joab did what any good military leader would do under orders from the commander in chief. He followed the king's instructions to the letter and produced the desired results.

> Uriah the Hittite was dead. *2 Samuel 11:17*

Unfortunately, Plan C worked.

Joab sent a messenger to David with the whole story, cleverly inserting the important detail about Uriah falling in a heap amidst his other battle news. Like a Trojan horse, Joab's message was harmless on the outside yet harbored deceit and sin on the inside.

David's response to the messenger was equally circumspect.

> "Say this to Joab: 'Don't let this upset you; the sword devours
> one as well as another.'" *2 Samuel 11:25*

Good grief, now he's sending his commander motivational messages! Why not put it on a coffee cup for him, Dave? "The sword kills one as well as another!" (NLT).

This time, the sword killed Uriah.

What must Bathsheba have thought of the sad news? Did she know about Plans A, B, and C? Whether she resisted David's advances that moonlit night or welcomed them, we can be fairly certain the whole thing was *not* her idea. Killing her husband must have been *less* so.

Oh, Bathsheba…don't you wish you'd said no on that fateful night?

> When Uriah's wife heard that her husband was dead, she
> mourned for him. *2 Samuel 11:26*

Mourning was a ritual act—not necessarily an emotional one—involving a whole set of duties and required lamentations.

Was she relieved, then, or truly grieved? Heartened or heartbroken? Like so much of Bathsheba's inner workings in this sordid tale, her thoughts are hidden from view.

> After the time of mourning was over, David had her brought
> to his house, and she became his wife and bore him a son.
> *2 Samuel 11:27*

From David's standpoint, his problems were solved.

The beautiful Bathsheba was his. He would no longer be an adulterer but would be a husband to her. Their child would be born with a proper name in his proper home—the palace. All was well.

How many of us often think the same way? As long as everything turns out well, we're willing to overlook the crooked path it took to get there. This particular path included breaking three of the Ten Commandments—coveting his neighbor's wife, committing adultery, and committing murder. Despite the "happy" ending, no way had David acted heroically. If he'd managed to get Uriah into Bathsheba's bed back at Plan A, you know David would have never claimed the child or the woman who bore him.

The success of Plan C required he claim both of them, beginning with his new bride. Literally he "sent for and collected her." Whether Bathsheba even *wanted* David for her husband was a moot point in those days.

Smile for the wedding pictures, darling. You might want to adjust your gown, see if you can cover…ah, that's better.

Look, anybody with basic math skills must have figured this thing out: a conveniently dead husband, a hasty wedding, a child born suspiciously soon after the nuptials.

One thing is clear: Nothing got past God.

> But the thing David had done displeased the LORD.
> *2 Samuel 11:27*

Which "thing," I wonder? David did so many things wrong. Was it the stolen wife? The illegitimate babe? The one-man drinking party? The murdered husband?

Note that it does not say, "The thing *Bathsheba* had done displeased the LORD." Ah. That may be our biggest clue that she had little choice in all the sinful proceedings.

> The LORD sent Nathan to David. *2 Samuel 12:1*

Nate was a prophet, a good guy—though David may not have thought so once he heard what the man had to say.

> When [Nathan] came to [David], he said, "There were two men
> in a certain town, one rich and the other poor." *2 Samuel 12:1*

Jesus was not the first to teach with parables. Nathan is telling David a story to convey a lesson. Considering how closely drawn the parallels are— King David was rich, Uriah was poor—it's amazing Dave didn't pick up on the moral of the story sooner.

> "The rich man had a very large number of sheep and
> cattle…" *2 Samuel 12:2*

I'm cringing at the comparison Nathan used here, equating David's wives and concubines to livestock. Boo. Make that *moo*.

> "...but the poor man had nothing except one little ewe lamb
> he had bought." *2 Samuel 12:3*

And that one little lamb would be, of course, Baaa-thsheba.

> "He raised it, and it grew up with him and his children.
> It shared his food, drank from his cup and even slept
> in his arms. It was like a daughter to him." *2 Samuel 12:3*

Nate is quite the storyteller. Remember how Uriah would not eat or drink or sleep with his wife? David should have made the easy connection here. Not only that, but the prophet said the poor man treated his little ewe "like a daughter." The Hebrew word for daughter is *bath*...hint, hint, Dave!

> "Now a traveler came to the rich man, but the rich man
> refrained from taking one of his own sheep or cattle to pre-
> pare a meal for the traveler who had come to him. Instead, he
> took the ewe lamb that belonged to the poor man and pre-
> pared it for the one who had come to him." *2 Samuel 12:4*

The traveler—representing that unwelcome adversary, Satan—came to visit the rich man—David—whetting the man's appetite until it consumed him, demanding his attention like a stranger knocking at his door on a moonlit night.

At mealtime the rich man didn't reach for one of his own wives—uh, sheep—but instead stole the one little ewe that belonged to the poor man and served it for dinner to the traveling serpent.

Horrors...lamb chops!

This story offers the strongest grounds for proving Bathsheba had no more choice about sliding into David's bed than the poor little ewe had about sliding into that hot oven. Speaking of hot...

David burned with anger against the man and said to
Nathan, "As surely as the LORD lives, the man who did this
deserves to die!" *2 Samuel 12:5*

Uh…David? You just pronounced your own death sentence.

Then Nathan said to David, "You are the man!" *2 Samuel 12:7*

That's right, King D. *You.*

Imagine the look on David's face: shock at first, then disbelief, then
guilt, and finally fear. Nathan proceeded to dress down the stunned king,
relating the words of the Lord directly as he reminded him of all God's
blessings on him.

"Why did you despise the word of the LORD by doing what is
evil in his eyes?" *2 Samuel 12:9*

Nate didn't even give him time to answer, just hammered away at Big
Dave's sins, in particular Uriah's death. Then Nathan pronounced a troubling, prophetic promise on behalf of the Lord:

"Before your very eyes I will take your wives and give them to
one who is close to you, and he will lie with your wives in
broad daylight." *2 Samuel 12:11*

And it happened just that way when Absalom later slept with all of
David's concubines on a rooftop.³³ Not too subtle there, Lord.

"You did it in secret, but I will do this thing in broad daylight
before all Israel." *2 Samuel 12:12*

God never makes a promise he doesn't keep. Of all people, David
surely knew that.

Did he toss Nathan out on his ear, denial ringing down the corridors
of the palace like a discordant gong? Or did he—should *we*—confess and
repent?

Then David said to Nathan, "I have sinned against the
LORD." *2 Samuel 12:13*

Bravo, Dave! In a single sentence he admitted his guilt and correctly
identified the One whom he wronged the most.

Nathan replied, "The LORD has taken away your sin. You are
not going to die." *2 Samuel 12:13*

Whew! Now *that's* what I call a happy ending.
Hope. A future. And undeserved salvation!

"But because by doing this you have made the enemies of the
LORD show utter contempt, the son born to you will die."
2 Samuel 12:14

Wait, Lord. What kind of happy ending is *that*? To take the life of a
helpless baby? To let the guilty go free and the innocent son die? To force
a mother to watch her child suffer unto death at your bidding, just to pay
for the sins of...
Oh my.
We know this story well.
Jesus, son of David, the innocent One whose death was foreshadowed
in the death of this newborn babe...this was also his story.

After Nathan had gone home, the LORD struck the child that
Uriah's wife had borne to David, and he became ill.
2 Samuel 12:15

The child was not born sick. *The child was struck by God.* I know this
is almost impossible to comprehend. It brings to mind a similarly difficult
passage. When Christ went to the cross, the Scripture says, "Yet it was the
LORD's will to crush him and cause him to suffer."[34]
And it crushes *me* to read that. To think of almighty God *pressing* his

own Son against the cross, holding him there until all the life went out of his body, because he loves us so much.

Sisters, don't turn away! See him hanging there—for David and Bathsheba, for you, for me, for all who have sinned and fallen short of the glory and goodness of God.

The psalms described a Redeemer who would be sent by God to save his people. That same God offered forgiveness—then and there—to David, but not without the shedding of his Son's blood.

The penitent David stretched himself across the ground and prayed, hoping that the Lord might yet be gracious and let the child live.[35]

> The elders of his household stood beside him to get him up
> from the ground, but he refused, and he would not eat any
> food with them. *2 Samuel 12:17*

I know David's actions all through Uriahgate have been less than honorable, but the days he fasted and begged God to have mercy on his baby boy were extraordinary. Monarchs seldom grieved like that over one sick infant—not with so many wives and concubines giving birth all over the place. After several months together, David's feelings for Bathsheba had obviously grown, extending to this infant son of their union.

His prayers were heard. Though the answer was different than David had hoped, it was exactly what David expected.

> On the seventh day the child died. *2 Samuel 12:18*

Just as Nathan had prophesied. A tragic disappointment but not a surprise. Notice how it happened on the seventh day, the number of completion or perfection. And one day before the baby's circumcision would have taken place.

During those seven days on his face, praying with all his heart, a song came to David. Perhaps the most beautiful psalm he ever wrote. Written for public performance and confession, these song lyrics were prefaced by a description of when it was written and why: "When the prophet Nathan came to him after David had committed adultery with Bathsheba."[36]

Wow. Talk about your true confessions!

Suppose after you committed some big, messy, disgraceful sin, you not only poured your heart out to God, but you set it to music and had Michael W. Smith sing it for the whole *world* to hear.

That's in essence what David did.

Listen as he sings to us.

> Have mercy on me, O God,
>> because of your unfailing love.
> Because of your great compassion,
>> blot out the stain of my sins. *Psalm 51:1* (NLT)

The Lord loves a man with a humble heart. No wonder he loved David. Though the king had seduced a forbidden woman fresh from her bath, he now realized it was his own soul that needed washing.

> Wash away all my iniquity
>> and cleanse me from my sin. *Psalm 51:2*

It's a refrain that runs all through David's psalm: "Wash me, cleanse me, make me new." It's hard to begrudge a guy who was *that* sorry and expressed it so eloquently.

> Cleanse me with hyssop, and I will be clean;
>> wash me, and I will be whiter than snow. *Psalm 51:7*

How many hours a day do we devote to washing our bodies when it is our hearts and souls that desperately need a bath?

> Create in me a pure heart, O God,
>> and renew a steadfast spirit within me. *Psalm 51:10*

Eugene Peterson's take on this verse in *The Message* knocks my socks off: "God, make a fresh start in me, shape a Genesis week from the chaos of my life." Amen to that! It was only when David's heart was pure again, cleansed by time alone with God, that the repentant king (who had to be filthy after seven days on the floor!) even bothered washing his external self.

> Then David got up from the ground. After he had washed,
> put on lotions and changed his clothes, he went into the
> house of the LORD and worshiped. *2 Samuel 12:20*

David understood repentance. Do you, beloved?

When we turn back to embrace the One who loves and forgives us, we are made new. The old sin is washed away and gone for good, like that sudsy water from your shower that disappears down the drain, never to be seen again.

Some of us put in a drain stopper, though, and insist on bathing in that same polluted water every day, beating ourselves up for last week's dirt still swirling around us rather than letting God wash it off us for good.

This isn't about *deserving* forgiveness. It's about *accepting* it.

When your skin is covered with sweat, dust, and grime, you take a bath, yes? You don't say, "I'm too filthy to get in this tub. I'll just have to stay grungy." No way. *You get in and get clean.*

How Satan blinds us to this truth! We think we have to be "good" to deserve God's grace. That's like saying you have to be clean to take a bath! Dear one, the more grimy our lives are, the more we need Jesus. The dirtier your body, the better that bath feels.

The sensation you have in the physical realm when you step out of that cleansing hot shower—"Ahh!"—is exactly what happens in the spiritual realm when you bathe in the living water of God's grace. And the Lord's forgiveness is every bit as available as that shower in your bathroom, sister. *Reach for the faucet!*

God forgave David for killing a man after stealing his wife. *Think* about that!

Whatever sins you need to confess, it's clear God can handle them.

Furthermore, because of his sovereignty—and not their goodness—the Lord blessed their union.

> Then David comforted his wife Bathsheba, and he went to
> her and lay with her. *2 Samuel 12:24*

Again David shows us his tender heart. He "comforted" her, not just with sex, though the shortness of the verse makes it sound that way. She's called *his* wife here, not Uriah's wife—good sign—and she found consolation from her grief in the arms of the man who'd saved her from shame.

Just as David sought forgiveness, so must have Bathsheba.

As David's desire to please God grew afresh, so did his love for Bathsheba, which means she must have sought after God as well or David would not have found her so desirable. I'm thinking of hardhearted Michal, David's first wife, who turned her back on her husband's worship. David did *not* comfort her nor fill her womb with children. Michal died childless.

Bathsheba, on the other hand, gave birth to five sons, of whom four lived and one became king of Israel.

> She gave birth to a son, and they named him Solomon.
> *2 Samuel 12:24*

Solomon, meaning "peace or completeness."

Sigh. I love happy endings, especially when they don't come easily, yet come eventually.

> The LORD loved him;... *2 Samuel 12:24*

Solomon isn't the only one! We, too, are showered with God's favor. "This is love: not that we loved God, but that he loved us."[37]

> ...and because the LORD loved him, he sent word
> through Nathan the prophet to name him Jedidiah.
> *2 Samuel 12:25*

Jedidiah means "beloved of the Lord." And Solomon was.

Bathsheba loved her son Solomon as well and years later made sure that David fulfilled his promise to name Solomon as his successor.

Tradition tells us Bathsheba was the one who composed that famous passage in Proverbs 31—"A wife of noble character who can find?"[38]—as "an admonition to Solomon on his marriage to Pharaoh's daughter."[39]

Nifty, huh? To know that a relationship that began on shaky ground became rock solid before all was said and done. Their marriage was blessed, their home was blessed, and through the centuries the son of Bathsheba and David would be honored, right into the New Testament listing of the lineage of Christ: "David was the father of Solomon, whose mother had been Uriah's wife."[40]

Uh-oh. Typo there—right, Lord? Otherwise why at the start of his gospel account did Matthew bring up Uriahgate a thousand years after the fact?

It's there to point out that God uses broken people. Sinful people. Less-than-perfect people. Even Uriah's adulterous wife, Bathsheba. To the end, she honored her second husband who had once dishonored her, yet who was also washed clean and made new by God's grace.

> Then Bathsheba bowed low with her face to the ground and, kneeling before the king, said, "May my lord King David live forever!" *1 Kings 1:31*

David himself no longer lives…but his anointed offspring does. May our Lord King Jesus live in our hearts forever!

What Lessons Can We Learn from Bathsheba?

Just say no.
Bathsheba needed a "Just Say No" button on her bathrobe. She could have said no to the messengers, asking them to bring a written request in the morning, then slipping out to stay safely with a friend. Once at the palace she might have said no to the king, offering any number of valid reasons

for not joining him in his bedchambers. When she discovered she was pregnant, she could have said no to involving David further and thrown herself at the mercy of her husband, asking him to forgive them both and claim the child. Seemingly irresistible temptations and almost impossible situations plague us all. Put on your own buttons, girls, and just say it with me: "N-O!"

> Resist [the devil], standing firm in the faith. *1 Peter 5:9*

Plans A, B, and C weren't prompted by God.
I can make lists and write out plans with the best of them—ask my family! But unless my plans line up with God's will, certain failure awaits me. I'm not talking about the little stuff—where should we go for dinner tonight?—but the big, life-altering, course-changing stuff. God's will was nowhere to be found in David's plans for Uriah. Deception, drunkenness, and murder are man's way of solving problems, not God's. David learned the hard way and lost his son in the process. David and Bathsheba no longer get to plan their lives over…but we do. Plan ahead, and put God at the top of your list!

> But the plans of the LORD stand firm forever,
>> the purposes of his heart through all generations.
>> *Psalm 33:11*

Know whose toes you're stepping on.
When Nathan challenged David with "You are the man!" David didn't hesitate for a second to name the one he'd offended most: God. Not even the wrongs he did to Uriah, Bathsheba, and Nathan compared to the shame he brought upon the Lord. When we sin, it is God's forgiveness that matters most. Asking the forgiveness of others comes next. Frankly, that job is much easier when God has washed all our guilt away and given us a clean heart to work with!

> Against you, you only, have I sinned
>> and done what is evil in your sight. *Psalm 51:4*

Bathsheba cleaned up her act...we can too.

A story that starts with a bath should end with a splash. Bathsheba's certainly did. In spite of David's sinful invitation and her own sin of omission—foolishly omitting the word *no* from her vocabulary—Bathsheba managed to stand next to David as a faithful, godly wife to the end of his life. When she visited the aging, infirm David, he was glad to see her and happy to grant her request. Her youthful beauty was gone. Her girlish charms were packed in mothballs. But she served her king, honored his King, *and* gave birth to a king in the lineage of the King. Not bad for a girl who couldn't say no!

> Charm is deceptive, and beauty is fleeting;
>> but a woman who fears the LORD is to be praised.
> *Proverbs 31:30*

Just Desserts

Sweet is revenge—
especially to women.
LORD BYRON

The pew cushions at Wilderness Community Church needed replacing, Rhoda decided, shifting restlessly in her seat. New carpet would be a welcome improvement as well. *Too spiritually minded to be any earthly good, this bunch.* She stifled a noisy sigh as a burst of late October sunlight streamed through the narrow stained-glass windows, spreading a blanket of transparent color across half-empty pews and silvery heads.

Rhoda watched Pastor John approach the pulpit and felt her spine stiffen. His messages were getting more bothersome by the week. "Turn to the fifth chapter of Matthew, if you will," the thirty-something preacher announced, holding up his Bible to get their attention. "Verses twenty-seven through thirty-two. We'll begin reading following the anthem."

Pastor John was marching his way through Matthew's gospel, never failing to raise his voice when he hit a word like *repent* and extolling the virtues of baptism until Rhoda was certain her ears were waterlogged. *Puh-leeze!* On previous Sundays she'd suffered through the Beatitudes—all that meekness and weakness nonsense—but last week's sermon on anger had made her so mad she'd barely enjoyed Sunday dinner at Sperry's.

As the choir rose to their feet, awash in royal blue robes, Rhoda yanked her bulky coat out from underneath her, still trying to get comfortable. Not that she had the slightest chance of feeling at home in this place ever again. *Not since I divorced Philip.*

She nodded in time to the organ's spirited staccato and fought a mischievous smile, thinking of the old hens who had spent last week's Tuesday Morning Circle brooding over her affairs—or so the rumor went.

Her leaving Philip wasn't what set their beaks clucking. Rhoda was hardly the first divorcée at Wilderness Community. It was her marriage to her ex's younger brother, Henry, at a private ceremony in Judge Harman's chambers at the courthouse the very hour her divorce was final—*that's* what made feathers fly.

As if on cue, Henry glanced down at her and winked, squeezing her hand affectionately. The man was good-looking, she had to admit. And an enthusiastic lover, much more so than his brother. *What a wuss!* In bed and out, old Philip hadn't measured up to her expectations. She should have married Henry in the first place, but who knew?

Unlike his indecisive brother, Henry lived by the Nike philosophy of Just Do It—in fact, had framed the slogan and hung it in his corner office at Osbourne & Smith, the biggest law firm in town. Rhoda's wry smile broadened. Marrying Henry was the smartest thing she'd done to date. He had more money, more clout around Nashville, and more chutzpa than Philip ever dreamed of having.

"Mom, look!" A girlish whisper at her shoulder snapped Rhoda back to the present. The choir had long finished their anthem, and Pastor John was reading aloud his text for the morning.

Rhoda glanced sideways at her daughter's oval face with its ear-to-ear scowl. "What is it, Sally?"

The ten-year-old rolled her eyes. "Can't you see? People are staring at us."

Rhoda watched as one salt-and-pepper head turned and shot a withering glance their way. Then another senior member swiveled around to arch a haughty eyebrow at the couple.

The nerve of these people!

Hoping her lowered head would cover the telltale heat that had rushed to her cheeks, Rhoda cursed the pale skin that gave her away. She looked down at the pew Bible in her lap and pretended to follow along as Pastor John ranted and raved about a nation steeped in moral decay.

"The Word says, 'Anyone who looks at a woman lustfully has already committed adultery with her in his heart,'" John proclaimed, conviction ringing in his voice.

Well! Her head shot up as the heat in her face rose a few degrees higher. The pastor's piercing gaze momentarily fell on hers. What was he trying to say with that troubled expression of his? That *she* was guilty of adultery? *Nice try, John.* She'd divorced one man and married another. So what? In quick succession, yes, but it was perfectly legal. When Philip had threatened to contest the divorce, Henry had handled it. Swiftly. Privately.

"Just do it, Henry," she'd said, and he did.

Money wielded a power all its own.

Pastor John's attention was drawn elsewhere now, though his words still seemed aimed at her. "It is better for you to lose one part of your body," he intoned, "than for your whole body to go into hell."

Rhoda resisted the urge to snort. *Watch it, pastor, or you'll lose one part of your body you'll sorely miss: your head.* Who did he think he was, trotting out passages like this as if such straight-laced foolishness still applied today? *Get with the program, John. It's a new world with new rules.*

The man was hopelessly out of touch. His camel-colored suit, for example, should have been retired on Labor Day, yet there he stood, wearing beige—in the pulpit of all places!—well into October.

Her cheeks cooled with the comforting realization that her second husband held the opinionated preacher's fate in his hands. As head of the church's board of elders, Henry had the final say on whether John remained at Wilderness Community. Or not.

They were the fifth congregation in as many years to call John as pastor. He was already on shaky ground with their denomination. "Too conservative!" said one church. "Too liberal!" another argued. "Too different!" insisted a third. One more demand for his resignation, and John Boy would not only lose this pulpit, he'd be stripped of his ordination and tossed out on his ear.

Relieved, Rhoda patted the open book in her lap with a sigh of satisfaction. *Another sermon like this one, fella, and you're dead.*

Clearing his throat, John continued in an authoritative tone, "Let's see what the next verse has to teach us. 'But I tell you that anyone who divorces his wife, except for marital unfaithfulness, causes her to become an adulteress—'"

That does it. Rhoda closed her Bible with a vehement slap. *How dare he!* More heads were turning her direction. As her sainted grandmother was fond of saying, John had "quit preachin' and moved to meddlin'." She felt Henry's shoulders stiffen next to her. At least she wasn't alone in this. Ignoring the faint murmur around them, Henry and Rhoda both looked straight ahead as John finished reading.

"And anyone who marries the divorced woman commits adultery."

Says you. Rhoda ground her teeth and suffered through another thirty minutes of pointed stares and even sharper words from the pulpit. John would not get away with this. Not if she could help it—which she most certainly could. Henry wouldn't like what she had in mind. But Henry would do it.

Rhoda checked her watch. *Six thirty.*

Dozens of men already packed the Belle Meade's ornate ballroom, slapping each other on the back and shouting good-natured insults at Henry, the birthday boy, while Rhoda and Sally warmed the furniture in the hallway outside.

The appeal of growing older was beyond her, but Henry's well-connected family celebrated birthdays in a big way. She felt certain Philip would be the only no-show among them. Before the evening ended, the room would be overflowing with the younger members of Nashville's social elite and everyone that mattered from Osbourne & Smith.

Everyone male, that is. Henry's birthday bashes over the years had evolved into a guys-only event. She'd never minded when old Philip went without her. A bunch of out-of-shape jocks discussing the merits of Vanderbilt's starting lineup was boredom incarnate. Now that it was her own husband's party from which she was none-too-gently excluded, it stung a bit.

No matter. Rhoda had a special guest appearance planned that would put her mark on this day —permanently.

A small hand touched hers. "Should I go in now, Mom?"

Rhoda shook her head, a finger to her lips. "We'll wait right here, Sally," she whispered. "I'll tell you when it's time."

Henry hadn't hit his four-beer limit yet, an indulgence he allowed himself once a year—October 24. The point was to get loose, not drunk, he explained. She wanted him as close to the edge as possible. For her plan to work, he needed to reach the stage of inebriation where judgment was impaired and emotions ran high.

Another agitated glance at her watch. *Almost seven.* They had at least an hour to kill. Perched next to her daughter on a stiff love seat outside the ballroom doors, Rhoda smiled as more guests disappeared into the semi-darkness of the banquet hall. Dinner was being served at the moment. It was standard male fare—crisp fried chicken, barbecued ribs, inch-thick onion rings, and more Miller draft. No doubt the kitchen staff cringed at the menu, but if that's what Henry wanted, that's what he got.

Sally sat quietly with a backpack full of homework balanced across her lap and a thin raincoat loosely tied over her costume. Only the girl's size-five boots in polished white leather hinted at the night's entertainment to come.

The hour crawled by. Finally, when the dinner plates were cleared away and only dessert remained to be served, Rhoda watched as the huge, tiered birthday cake was rolled toward the doors by a white-jacketed waiter.

"Psst!" She motioned him over. "Let my daughter wheel that in, won't you?" Rhoda offered her most engaging smile, though it was hardly necessary. She was the one paying the bill. "Sally, think you can manage?"

The girl closed her geography book with obvious relief and jumped to her feet, shedding her flimsy coat to reveal a dazzling sequined vest and short flared skirt the likes of which even the Grand Ole Opry had never seen. Knowing Henry would hit the ceiling if he caught a glimpse of the price tag, Rhoda had snipped the evidence into little pieces in the club's bathroom.

The effect was more than worth the expense.

If Sally had been three years older, she might have looked cheap, like a too-young prostitute. The partygoers would have been turned off by her little routine, or—even more risky—turned *on*. If she had been three years younger, she would have looked overdressed, a second grader wearing her big sister's dance outfit, forced to perform against her will.

Instead, with her sequins and long, coltish legs, Sally struck the perfect note of youthful charm and sparkling innocence. Her Thursday afternoon dance lessons were about to pay off, big time.

"Is the music ready, Mother?" She looked a bit nervous now. Despite her bright satin skirt shimmering in the light of thirty-eight tiny candles and the cake's bold proclamation in matching red icing—*Have a Good One, Henry!*—Sally seemed less than sure of herself.

"I have the D.J. waiting for my cue at the door, sweetheart." Rhoda patted the girl's arm, hoping to buoy her confidence. "As soon as the doors open, the man will point a spotlight at you and start the music. Just wheel the cake over to the head table, park it in front of your stepfather, then start dancing. See how easy it will be?"

Sally nodded slowly, clearly not convinced, yet determined to do her part.

"When you finish," Rhoda added, standing, "give the men plenty of time to whoop and holler. Then, if Henry asks you what he can do for you in return, or if you'd like to be paid for your efforts—anything like that— you come find me right away." She patted the envelope in her pocket, adrenaline pumping through her veins. "Understand?"

Her daughter swallowed and grabbed the metal cart, pointing it toward the ballroom doors.

Oh, brother. Whose idea was this?

Sally noticed her hands shaking and gripped the handles harder.

She was a good dancer, wasn't she? One of Mr. Granger's best students—or so he'd insisted. There was nothing to this two-step business, though it was more fun with a whole line of people.

Lifting her chin, she moved toward the doors as they swung open for her. All at once a blinding spotlight hit her square in the face, and a huge roar of approval swelled through the ballroom. The opening notes of a honky-tonk tune poured out of the speakers, and the party guests—her audience—clapped in time to the upbeat rhythm.

Here we go.

Taking a deep breath, she plunged into the room, the sea of grinning faces around her a blur except for one—her stepfather's. His smile seemed wider than anyone's, though his eyes were glazed and bloodshot, as if he hadn't slept in a week. *So much for your four-beer limit, Uncle Henry.* The empty shot glasses scattered around him explained a lot.

"Wellll, look whoosh here!" he called out above the music, slurring his words something awful. "'S my new daughter, Sally. Ish'n she a beauty?"

Her real father never drank. Uncle Henry scared her, this big man with his reddish eyes and sideways grin. Still, her mother expected her to do this. Sally had learned years ago it didn't pay to argue; her mother always won.

Once the cake was safely stationed in front of her uncle—well, her stepfather—she stepped back, swallowed hard, and kicked up her heels. Stepping, dipping, spinning, bobbing, she worked the small dance floor area like a trouper and never missed a move, even when the men cheered and hollered, almost drowning out the music.

In spite of the noise and confusion, Sally liked the way her skirt bounced along with her, the satin ruffles doing a dance of their own. Her

boot heels pounded out the incessant beat until the last guitar chord re-
verberated through the room. The applause was thunderous. Henry rose
to his feet, swaying a bit as he lifted his nearly empty glass in a wobbly toast.

"Thas mah fav'rite present raht there, fellas. Yuh lookin' at her. Mah
girl, Sally. Ten goin' on twenty." Henry dropped back into his seat with a
less than graceful thump while the next tune started at a much lower volume. "Tha' was wunnerful, honey. I'm s'proud of you."

Proud? Is that all?

Her mother was wrong, then. Henry wasn't offering her a thing except
his slobbery praise!

"So…Daddy." Even saying it made her feel queasy. "Don't I get a present from *you?*"

The still-attentive crowd grunted in agreement.

"Yeah, Henry! Give the little princess a pony, why don'tcha?"

"C'mon, birthday boy. Pay the young lady for her trouble!"

Henry nodded, dipping his head up and down half a dozen times,
obviously mulling it over. "Okay, okay." His bleary gaze met hers. "What'll
I give ya, honey? You don't really wanna pony, do ya?"

She shook her head.

"Good," he said, punctuating it with an exaggerated nod. "Long's it's
not a pony, you can have anything your li'l heart desires."

"Anything?" She looked at him one last time, making certain he meant
it. "Anything I want?" Elated, she skipped out into the hallway, where her
mother pressed an envelope into her hand with a knowing wink.

"Give this to your father, dear. He'll know what to do."

Sally stared at the plain envelope, puzzled. Maybe it was a whole list of
things she could ask her new father for. *Like Christmas.* New clothes, a full-
size bike, some Nintendo games. *Yeah!*

Seconds later she hurried back into the room and thrust the envelope
into Henry's meaty hands with a shake of her auburn curls. "Here's what I
want."

A chorus of voices hollered, "Give her what she wants, Henry!"

"I will, fellas, I promise." He offered a lopsided grin, then tore the envelope open, almost ripping the single sheet of paper inside. Smoothing it out, he stared down at it, his features graying with a suddenness that frightened her.

Uncle Henry...um, Dad?

Sally stole a sideways glance at the mostly blank sheet. *Oh, drat.* It wasn't a list at all. It was a head shot of Pastor John cut out of last week's church newsletter with a clipping from a Nike ad pasted below it: "Just Do It."

Her forehead crinkled in confusion. Had her mother lost her mind? What was *this* all about?

Her stepfather's face showed he knew exactly what it meant. And didn't like it one bit. Looking more sober by the second, he patted the paper. "Uh...well...I'll give it some thought, darlin'... "

At that, her mother flung open the double doors and made a grand entrance, her hands clasped behind her, a wicked grin stretched across her face. "Hen-ry," she sang out. "You offered your daughter anything she asked for, remember?"

"Right." He lowered his voice, though in the heavy silence it still carried. "But we're talkin' about a man's career here. His livelihood, Rhoda. His life."

Sally watched her mother draw closer, commanding every eye in the room as she sashayed forward.

"A man's life? So we are." With that, her mother produced a long, silver cake knife, its sharp edge gleaming in the candlelight. "But it's *your* future I'm thinking about now, dear husband. Before all these witnesses, Henry, you made a promise to your daughter that I'm sure you plan to keep. Yes?"

"Ah...yes...well..." He looked as if he'd been poleaxed with a two-by-four. "Whatever you say, Rhoda."

"Good." She held the knife high, then plunged it down into the cake with a lethal slice and a smile to match it. "Happy Birthday, Henry..."

Some Mother-Daughter Banquet *That* Was: Herodias and Salome

Herodias. A name perfectly suited to her odious self.

When it came to evil, this woman took the cake—and every other dessert one might serve in first-century Rome.

Her family tree was an arborist's worst nightmare. Branches intertwined at whim, were pruned in the wrong season—for the wrong reason—and bore singularly rotten fruit.

From the trunk of that diseased tree grew Herod the Great, infamous for having all the toddler boys in Bethlehem slaughtered after the Magi announced Christ's birth.[1] Horrid, that Herod. No wonder Mary and Joseph fled for Egypt and stayed there until the brutal ruler died.

Herod wielded his power close to home as well, executing two of his sons and his favorite wife, the lovely Mariamne, merely because he heard a faint rumor they were plotting his demise.

If only they'd succeeded…

Herod-the-Not-So-Great had at least two surviving sons: Herod Philip and Herod Antipas. His grandniece Herodias came along and married Herod Philip—that's right, her uncle—and they remained husband and wife long enough for her to give birth to a daughter (more about Salome later). Our biblical story begins when Mrs. H dumped Herod Phil and married his brother Herod Antipas—that's right, also her uncle.

Meet Herod. And his other brother Herod.

Except this isn't a comedy routine; it's a dysfunctional family with a capital *D*, who intermarried because—get this—they didn't think any other family was good enough for them![2]

If that wasn't trashy enough, Herodias not only abandoned a living husband to marry another (big no-no), she convinced her new hubby, Herod Antipas, to toss aside *his* wife as well. That meant by the law of

Herod's Hebrew subjects, Herodias committed *incest* by marrying her two uncles and *bigamy* by remarrying while her first husband still lived.

Incest *and* bigamy—simultaneously?

It beats any soap-opera plot I've ever seen.

No wonder the Herod clan was called "the most despicable family that ever lived on the face of the earth," a nest of vipers that "left their slime on everything they touched."[3]

Eeww.

Serpentine or not, Herodias must have been an eyeful in her royal robes (or out of them) to seduce Uncle Number Two into breaking Hebrew law and order—outrageously offending the people he ruled over. It's reputed that her grandmother, the doomed Mariamne, possessed a beauty rivaling that of her contemporary, Cleopatra. It seems Herodias inherited the same genes but *not* the same victim status. Nobody would find Mrs. H dispensable—not if she could help it.

Herodias's bed-hopping routine started when Herod Antipas came to Rome on political business. She decided he was the more powerful of the two brothers, and so her plot to move up the political ladder was hatched.

No question in my mind, Mrs. H started the affair.

After all, she had more to gain. He had more to lose.

But, oh, the possibilities, the court intrigue, the risky nature of it all! Clearly, "sin and scandal meant nothing to her."[4] Freud identified the two basic drives behind human behavior as "pleasure and power."[5] Herodias got a two-for-one deal, since "power was her favorite aphrodisiac"[6] and Herod Antipas had a more powerful position to offer than his brother.

It was a sleazy business, her manipulation of the two brothers. She no doubt played them against each other—feeding the ego of Antipas while emotionally starving her soon-to-be ex-husband. We can easily imagine the sort of lies she told Antipas, rubbing her hands across his torso, batting her kohl-lined eyes at him, stretching her berry-stained lips into a lazy smile.

"You're more handsome than your brother…but you know that, don't

you?" A flick of her veils, a broad wink. "I've always regretted not marrying you when I had the chance." The sultry voice trained midway between
whisper and purr. "We can remedy those wedding vows, of course. Philip
will barely notice I'm gone…"

There's no other word for Herodias but *hussy*.

Trust me, I know one when I see one. Two dozen years ago, two-timing
Herodias was the face I saw in my own mirror.

They were roommates—two hunky guys who'd been good friends
since high school—until I came along. When my relationship with Beau
Number One fizzled, I took charge of the situation by marching across the
hall and knocking on future Beau Number Two's bedroom door, humiliating Beau Number One and driving a stake through their friendship. It was
risky—what if he rejected me?—but I thrived on risk and loved flying in
the face of convention.

Even spiritually bankrupt and immature as I was, I should have known
better.

The older and craftier Herodias *did* know better.

But a woman determined to win—in finance, romance, or politics—
thinks only of her own gain. Of Mrs. H's many sins, it's her unbridled selfishness I understand—and grieve over—most of all.

Mr. and Mrs. H both left their spouses behind and went on to Tiberias,
where they were greeted (if not welcomed) by their new constituents, who
clearly found their marriage arrangement illegal and distasteful. Did they
interfere? Make a fuss? They did not. Herod was their new tetrarch, and
Herodias, this "grasping and self-centered woman,"[7] was obviously *not* the
sort one crossed without peril.

The smart citizens of Tiberias kept their mouths shut.

John the Baptist, however, did not.

> John rebuked Herod the tetrarch because of Herodias, his
> brother's wife, and all the other evil things he had done.
> *Luke 3:19*

Nervy, huh?

You gotta love this fella John. Called sin *sin*. Even when he knew it might cost him his freedom, if not his life.

"Atta boy, John!" we say with pride. "Let 'em have it with both barrels!" After all, we never get upset when someone *else's* sins are pointed out.

But let a radio preacher step on *my* toes, and I bristle in a hurry. "Humph! Who are you calling a glutton, buddy?"

The closer to the true nature of our sin someone gets, the more agitated we become. As an astute writer put it three hundred years ago, "Herod respected him, till he touched him in his Herodias."[8]

> For Herod himself had given orders to have John arrested,
> and he had him bound and put in prison. *Mark 6:17*

'Twas a dangerous time to be a prophet, as Jesus would soon find out for himself. Truth was no more welcome in the streets of ancient Rome than it is in modern Gotham City.

John the Baptizer, called by God to preach repentance, cared about Herod's very soul.

Herod cared only about Herodias's sharp tongue.

Jail it was for John, then.

> [Herod] did this because of Herodias, his brother Philip's
> wife, whom he had married. *Mark 6:17*

"Because" doesn't quite cut it. "In order to please Herodias" (CEV) is closer to the mark. The bridges that once linked Herod to his brother and to his first wife were in ashes. Joined now in sin to Herodias, Herod must have decided pleasing her was prudent, even if it included breaking the social code of the land *and* throwing a man in jail who he knew full well was innocent.

Interesting how Herodias is still called "Philip's wife" in the verse above, as well as the one below.

> For John had been saying to Herod, "It is not lawful for you
> to have your brother's wife." *Mark 6:18*

It was right there in black and white (make that ink on parchment) in the Mosaic Law: "Do not have sexual relations with your brother's wife; that would dishonor your brother."[9] Of course, if the husband was dead, not only was it honorable, it was *required* at one point in Jewish history, as you'll soon learn in Tamar's story.

The problem here was that Herod the First Hubby was very much alive.

That's why John B was in the tetrarch's face, which made Hubby Number Two nervous…and Herodias angry.

> So Herodias nursed a grudge against John…

Good wording. She *nursed* her anger, feeding and tending that volatile emotion to keep it alive, reminding herself of how much she deserved Antipas, the more powerful uncle, as her husband. While John languished in prison, she concocted a grand scheme to put the holy man down for good.

Hmm. An evil queen killing a good prophet. Sounds like that Bad Girl of Old Testament fame, Jezebel. Jez wanted Elijah snuffed out, precisely the way Herodias longed for John the Baptist to disappear. Why? Two reasons: (1) Nefarious women have little use for righteous prophets who dampen the fun they find in flagrant sin. And (2) in both cases, the prophets were urging their husbands to turn away from sin and back toward God.

That's the message John B was known for: "Repent, for the kingdom of heaven is near."[10] Scary stuff for a Jezebelian wife like Herodias. The last thing she wanted was to see her man softening his heart toward God. Maybe her greatest sin wasn't selfishness after all. Nor bigamy, nor incest. It was rejecting the truth of the gospel.

Imagine if Herod *had* confessed his marital sins, repented, and sent Herodias back to her first husband. My, wouldn't Philip have been thrilled to see his adulterous wife?! Or worse yet, Herod might have expected her to stay, repent, and change her ways.

Huh-uh. Herodias couldn't take that chance.

Something had to be done to stop this outspoken prophet with his strange camel's-hair clothes and his locust-and-honey diet.[11]

Something permanent.

> ...and [she] wanted to kill him. But she was not able to.
> *Mark 6:19*

Mark's gospel, written around A.D. 50—the earliest of the four—makes it clear that Herodias wanted John dead. But according to Matthew's gospel, written ten to twenty years later, she wasn't the only one who dreamed of wringing John's neck.

> Herod wanted to kill John, but he was afraid of the people,
> because they considered him a prophet. *Matthew 14:5*

So Herod didn't like what the man had to say either, eh? Then again, maybe Herod's guilty conscience was talking.

No matter the reason, neither Mr. nor Mrs. H could risk killing the popular prophet, though hubby seemed a bit more sympathetic than his wife was toward John's plight.

> Herod feared John and protected him, knowing him to be a
> righteous and holy man. *Mark 6:20*

Does that beat all? Herod knew the man was innocent, sent from God, and yet he imprisoned him as a form of protection, to keep him alive and "preserve him from the machinations of Herodias."[12] We'll see in a minute that even those cell walls couldn't protect John from his female nemesis.

Herod, meanwhile, realizing that John was holy and righteous, engaged him in conversations about topics he didn't quite grasp but found fascinating.

> When Herod heard John, he was greatly puzzled; yet he liked
> to listen to him. *Mark 6:20*

Over the years I've had friends who weren't professing Christians but loved to debate the merits of organized religion or a particular Bible passage. When I shared my faith, their curiosity was piqued, and though our ideas weren't always in sync, they enjoyed the discussions. That was Herod. Confused yet curious. "He was miserable with guilt—and yet he couldn't stay away. Something in John kept pulling him back."[13]

That pull wasn't hard enough, or soon enough, to save John...*or* Herod. Herodias was counting the hours until she could put her evil plans into action. Revenge beat a deadly rhythm in her dark heart.

> Finally the opportune time came. *Mark 6:21*

No question who we're talking about here: "Herodias found her opportunity" (NEB). Premeditated murder, the courts would call it today. And what a "strategic day" (NASB) she chose.

> On his birthday Herod gave a banquet for his high officials
> and military commanders and the leading men of Galilee.
> *Mark 6:21*

Birthdays were a big deal in those days. Party time. Drinks all around. Notice "all the brass and bluebloods" (MSG) were there but not the women. Good Girls didn't go to these parties, no matter how well they knew the birthday boy. Not even Herodias would have attended.

The only women found at such gatherings "were 'evil' women, ones who danced or entertained the men after the meal."[14] You know—*babes*. The kind that climb out of a giant cake.

If you've ever read the story of that queen among Good Girls, Esther, you know how she ended up on the throne. Her predecessor, Queen Vashti, was invited by King Xerxes to make an appearance at his all-male shindig. Not to dance, mind you, just to show up (and show off). To her credit, Queen Vashti refused.[15]

Two points for Queen V.

Queen Herodias, however, scores a minus ten for sending her young daughter alone into this stag party, knowing full well what it would do to the girl's reputation. All Herodias cared about was making a scene and getting what she wanted, even if it did bring shame on her offspring. Add *terrible mother* to Herodias's growing list of beastly attributes.

When the daughter of Herodias came in…

We know the girl as Salome, though she's never called that in Scripture. The Salome you *do* find named in the Gospels is another woman altogether, a Galilean follower of Jesus. It was Josephus, a first-century Jewish historian, who recorded the name of Herod's stepdaughter as Salome.

…and [she] danced…

Honey, she's been dancing ever since. Bring on the veils! Heat up some music! Paint those toes a shocking red! Spray the room with a heady perfume!

Could someone turn on the air conditioner?

Over the last two millennia, Salome has been painted—literally and figuratively—as a temptress and a vamp. The justification goes something like this:

1. Dancing was verboten, especially in public.

Good Girls back then did *not* do the two-step. Period. "Salome…did a shameful thing. Dancing by women was only ever done before family and kin."[16] That she was a princess of the royal house made her fancy footwork even more scandalous.

2. Salome's dance was bound to be erotic.

Why else would she be dancing, if not to incite their collective lust? If indeed "the rhythmic dances of the East are voluptuous in the extreme,"[17] then hers must have been off the chart—"wild, exotic, indecent and unbecoming,"[18] the "most sensuous dance ever performed."[19] *Whoa!*

3. What about those seven veils, peeled off one by one?

We can easily picture Herod's wine-besotted guests checking out Salome's nubile young body, "seen through the flowing flimsy garment."[20] Our imaginations drape her in diaphanous veils with peekaboo slits, her bare feet exposed or wrapped in the slightest of sandals, her eyes painted Jezebel-style, a jingling sistrum in her hands.

4. Hateful Herodias, Herod, and Salome were in cahoots.

Scholars insist the woman "used her own daughter to inflame Herod's passions,"[21] depicting him as "a dirty old man"[22] and Salome's moves as an "astonishing act of abasement that appealed to his perverted mind."[23] Three rotten eggs in Tiberias.

5. Everyone knows dancing leads to death. Or sex. Or both.

In a commentary from 1890, fully *ten* of the eighteen pages about Herodias were devoted to the dangers of dancing, which "injures the health, dwarfs the intellectual powers, and destroys spirituality."[24] Using Salome's slender story as his only textual proof, a writer in the 1960s insisted the outcome of her dance was "sufficient to condemn dancing as we know it."[25]

Stop right there, ladies and gents.

None of these assumptions—*not one word*—comes from the Bible!

For starters, there's no such thing as a "dance of the seven veils." That theatrical addition came eighteen centuries later on the stage of Richard Strauss's 1905 opera *Salome*.[26] His opera was based, not on Scripture, but on Oscar Wilde's play from 1894, in which Salome's dialogue was crammed with the most…um, *evocative* lines from Song of Solomon.[27]

You know the ones.

The movie versions that followed in the twentieth century were drawn from those two dramatic sources, as well as from many famous paintings from the Middles Ages on, depicting Salome as a tart of the first order.

All of which left the scriptural version of Salome in the dust.

Girls, it's our job to unveil the truth.

Using solely the New Testament accounts, we'll need to eliminate the heavy cosmetics, the skimpy costume, the seven disposable veils, the sultry music, and the suggestive undertones. We definitely gotta do away with the unsubstantiated notion of that health-injuring, intellect-dwarfing, spirituality-destroying exercise known as dancing.

All the Bible says is that the daughter of Herodias *danced*.

You know—danced? As in "you put your right foot in, you put your right foot out…" As in, "a time to mourn and a time to dance."[28] And since she was a child, dancing by herself, the potential for hanky-panky (let alone hokey-pokey) was reduced to almost nil.

Despite what some commentators insist, "to dance" is not synonymous with "to sin." Not today in our contemporary churches filled with praise dancing, and not three thousand years ago when King David "danced before the LORD with all his might."[29] The psalmist charged us to "praise him with tambourine and dancing,"[30] which is precisely what Miriam, the sister of Moses, did, "and all the women followed her, with tambourines and dancing."[31]

Ah, but Liz! Salome wasn't dancing "before the Lord;" she was dancing before her stepfather Herod.

Good point.

So *how* was she dancing? Innocently? Or provocatively?

The Greek word used by Mark—*orcheomai*—means simply "to dance." The same word was used in Aesop's fables referring to "children at play."[32] *That* sounds innocent enough.

And the Greek word describing the daughter is *korasion,* meaning "little girl or maiden," the same word Mark used for Jairus's twelve-year-old daughter.[33] Thankfully, twelve isn't the age of your average striptease artist.

In other words (drum roll, please), I'm asking you to *toss out* all your preconceived notions about Salome and her dirty dancing routine and picture a young girl, perhaps nine or ten years of age, doing an impromptu recital for her stepfather. Though her straight-as-a-stick legs were starting to lengthen

and her baby fat slowly disappearing, the child was hardly a woman. No cur-
vaceous hips, no full breasts. A winsome young girl, not a wanton seductress.

My precious (and precocious!) daughter, Lillian, performed a dance
for me soon after she turned ten. Her eleven-year-old brother was in
charge of lighting and sound, since this was a sophisticated show with
much flicking of the light switch and computerized music from our tinny
desktop speakers.

On the first note, Lillian commenced her dance with a dramatic leap.
She swirled. She hopped. She spun on one foot without falling (very
impressive). She also tried one brief, hip-wiggling move borrowed from a
more mature dancer's repertoire that made me stuff my knuckles between
my teeth to keep from laughing.

The child was adorable. Utterly charming. And totally innocent.

When her father took in her encore performance an hour later, he was
equally delighted—though I assure you, not in the least bit enticed—by his
daughter's dancing.

And how was Salome received?

> …she pleased Herod and his dinner guests. *Mark 6:22*

Pleased. Loaded word, that. Sunsets give me pleasure—but so does
my husband. This word *pleased* in the Greek is *eresen,* translated as "ac-
commodating someone, or doing something that someone will approve."[34]
The term decidedly does *not* refer to sexual pleasure of any sort.

Simply put, she made her stepdad happy. In fact, Salome "so delighted
Herod and his guests" (NEB), that he wanted to reward her.

> The king said to the girl, "Ask me for anything you want, and
> I'll give it to you." *Mark 6:22*

"Anything" she wanted? Clearly the tetrarch got "carried away" (MSG)
seeing Salome dance for him. Granted, her movements *could* have been a
sexy romp in see-through veils. We have no evidence one way or the other.
However, if a young, half-dressed woman gyrated her way into a roomful

of drinking men, I fear the outcome wouldn't have been "What can I give you?" but rather "Hey, baby, what can you give *us*?"

That's why I vote for the more innocent approach. It isn't hard to imagine a young girl (we don't know her exact age) abruptly taken from her real father, Herod Philip, and brought into a new household in a strange, foreign town. Her great uncle was now her stepfather. Stress city.

Maybe the adjustment wasn't a smooth one, and this whole dancing business was her mother's idea: "C'mon, honey, it's your stepdad's birthday. Do something to please him for a change."

Whatever the emotional state of their relationship and whatever Salome's dance steps, Herod was "drunk on the wine of his own self-importance"[35] and made the girl a rash offer.

> And he promised her with an oath, "Whatever you ask I will give you, up to half my kingdom." *Mark 6:23*

You'll notice he repeated his generous proposal and made it more specific, echoing the words spoken by King Xerxes to Queen Esther, "What is your request? Even up to half the kingdom, it will be given you."[36] I'll say this for Herod: The man was not a tightwad.

> She went out and said to her mother, "What shall I ask for?" *Mark 6:24*

Here's another hint that she was quite young. Rather than answering Herod herself, the girl went and found her mother. No way would a teenager do such a thing! "Hey, Pop, how 'bout my own sport-and-utility chariot?" Salome's need for adult guidance is our surest sign she was too young to tango.

"Went out" suggests she left the banquet hall—remember, no women allowed—and found her mother lurking outside the entranceway. I suspect this was prearranged. The scheming Herodias had no doubt counseled her, "After you dance for your stepdaddy, if he offers to give you something, track me down pronto."

"Prompted by her mother..." wrote Matthew.[37] Poor Salome. Could she possibly have guessed the ghastly gift her mother would ask for?

"The head of John the Baptist," she answered. *Mark 6:24*

No hesitation there, honey. Herodias was ready. She didn't merely want John executed; she wanted him disgraced and humbled in such a vile manner that word would spread far and wide: Herodias was right and John the prophet was dead wrong.

One woman commentator confessed, "I have moments when I wonder why all men's heads can't be cut off and served up on platters."[38] Yeah, we get that. Any woman who's ever been dumped on by a man—and who hasn't at least once in her lifetime?—might indulge in a momentary fantasy involving a thick neck and a sharp blade.

But the fact is, this man John was right about her sins, no matter how much Herodias protested otherwise. There was only one way to silence him. She "usurped God's position of judge and put a man to death."[39]

Young Salome must have died inside a bit herself. A beheading? How horrible! *She* would have asked for pretty gowns or pricey jewels. Or the first-century version of a Web site. Who wants a bloody old head?

But her mother was not one to be kept waiting.

At once the girl hurried in to the king with the request:...

"At once" is right. One couldn't waste time at a moment like this. A few extra seconds and Herod's enthusiasm might have cooled along with his offer.

...."I want you to give me right now the head of John the
Baptist on a platter." *Mark 6:25*

Interesting. Salome added to her mother's request and left the woman's name out of it besides. Not "Mom wants," but "I want." And "right now," not after there's been a fair trial, or Herod has had time to change his mind, or the audience of witnesses has stumbled home in a wine-besotted stupor.

Nope. Right now.

And "on a platter." There's a grisly touch. To make a show of the thing? So she could serve her mother on a silver platter this "food of death instead of the bread of life"?[40]

Yuck. Sometimes it pays to leave the banquet before the entertainment starts.

I'm stumped on Salome's motivation though. Is she an innocent pleasing her mother or a guilty co-conspirator thrilled to see this purveyor of lies put to death? If you're uncertain too, join the club, because in the same breath one commentator calls her "an obedient daughter" who was also "selfish, immoral, heartless."[41]

Of this much we can be certain: Her stepfather was anything but overjoyed with her request.

> The king was greatly distressed…

To be more accurate, he was "deeply pained *and* grieved *and* exceedingly sorry" (AMP). Nothing about his reaction suggests he was in on the dastardly deal, though he's in up to his ears now. John's ears, actually.

> …but because of his oaths and his dinner guests, he did not want to refuse her. *Mark 6:26*

Herodias knew her husband's pride and his need for public approval would win out over doing what was right. She'd orchestrated the scene with deadly precision. All the key players of Galilee were on hand. Her daughter gazed up at Herod expectantly. Herodias waited behind the scenes, holding her breath. After his foolhardy offer, Herod would dishonor the whole family if he didn't deliver, and like any parent caught in a trap of his own making, "he did not want to slight her [by breaking faith with her]" (AMP).

So he immediately sent an executioner with orders to bring
John's head. *Mark 6:27*

Herod was defying Jewish law—again—which "prohibited both execution without trial and decapitation as a form of execution."[42] So defiantly—
and repeatedly—did Herod and Herodias break the law, they barely noticed
two more strikes against them.

The executioner, meanwhile, struck the most painful blow of all.

The man went, beheaded John in the prison, and brought
back his head on a platter. *Mark 6:27–28*

Herod had offered his stepdaughter up to half his kingdom and instead
gave her something worth infinitely more: a man's life. John the Baptist,
the last of the Hebrew prophets—he who came to prepare the way for the
Lord Jesus—lost his head to a manipulative woman who used her daughter's innocence and her husband's pride to buy her freedom from hearing
the voice of her detractor ever again.

Instead, John the Baptist was the one eternally set free by his martyr-
dom, while Herod and Herodias were imprisoned in their sin, doomed to
hear the voice of the accuser forever.

Back in the banquet hall, it was time to serve a truly "gruesome
dessert."[43]

He presented it to the girl, and she gave it to her mother.
Mark 6:28

Ick. I'm not looking. Are you looking?

"The death glare is still in the eyes; the locks are all dabbled with gore;
the features are still distressed with the last agony."[44] *Ugh.*

Legend says that when Herodias saw John's severed head she "bent
forward and thrust a bodkin through the tongue that had dared to challenge her."[45] Once again, that bit of high drama with a sharp instrument

isn't in Scripture. But it doesn't take much imagination to fathom what the sight of a bloody, severed head did to young, impressionable Salome. Scarred for life, poor thing.

Although it was her mother's idea, it was *she* who requested it. Salome's guilt in years to follow would be a great deal heavier than that platter. Herodias's daughter, on the world stage for one brief dance, disappeared into the history books, never to be heard from again.

The partygoers probably scattered too. Who'd want to hang around after seeing a severed head dished up as the final course? Some happy-birthday finale. Herod's joy was ruined for certain, thanks to selfish, sadistic Herodias.

We're never told what this Really Bad Girl did with her repulsive prize. As for the rest of John the Baptist, he was claimed by those who loved him.

> John's disciples came and took his body and buried it. Then
> they went and told Jesus. *Matthew 14:12*

Jesus and John had been colaborers in repentance. How it must have grieved Jesus' heart to lose his relative and friend! Surely he must have seen it as a foreshadowing of his own death, in part by Herod's own hand.[46]

Later, when Jesus was ministering in the neighborhood, performing miracles like those of the prophets of old, some said he was John the Baptist back from the grave, which must have given old Herod a migraine.

> But when Herod heard this, he said, "John, the man I
> beheaded, has been raised from the dead!" *Mark 6:16*

Though he did it for the sake of his wife and daughter, Herod took full credit for the holy man's death.

In the years that followed, Herodias continued to make a pill of herself, pushing her husband to seek higher office until eventually the couple were banished from the land in A.D. 39 and sent to Gaul, a frontier territory not unlike Siberia.[47]

Gaul! Is that all? What a letdown!

I want this dreadful woman to *pay* for her crimes, don't you? At least with Jezebel we got a sense of justice when she was shoved out the window by two guys who worked for her. Messy but a well-deserved sort of closure for a Very Bad Girl.

As for Herodias, her head stayed firmly on her shoulders. We're not told if she relented. Nor if she repented. Two thousand years later Herodias is remembered as "one of the most vile and vicious"[48] women who ever walked through the pages of human history.

The baddest of the Really Bad Girls? Perhaps.

Hell must have welcomed her with open arms.

Yet for a woman like Herodias—seething with anger, hatred, cruelty, vengeance, bitterness, and evil—she lived every day in a hell of her own making.

What Lessons Can We Learn from Herodias?

If someone gently points out your sin, don't chop her head off.
I'm the first to admit I don't take correction particularly well. My natural reaction when someone catches me in an act of obvious disobedience is to look for something wrong with *that* person or, failing that, to slice him or her to shreds with my words. Ouch! But it's a mark of maturity to admit when we're wrong and to welcome the kind of loving, gentle correction our heavenly Father gives us. Next time such reproof comes from the Lord or one of his most trusted servants, let's pray for humility, wisdom, and a teachable, "non-Herodias" spirit.

> Blessed is the man whom God corrects;
> so do not despise the discipline of the Almighty. *Job 5:17*

Pointing out someone else's sin may get *your* head chopped off!

When the opportunity arises to draw attention to another person's disobedience, think carefully. Not many (any?!) of us are as holy or righteous as John the Baptist. He was called by God to a specific work of preaching repentance. We are called—over and over—to love one another and bear one another's burdens. As parents, we're charged with the task of correcting our children when they sin. But as brothers and sisters in Christ, we are to resist judging and to put our own lives in order first.

> "First take the plank out of your own eye, and then you will
> see clearly to remove the speck from your brother's eye."
> *Matthew 7:5*

Pleasing others can get you in trouble.

Because his daughter pleased him, Herod made a reckless promise to please *her,* an offer that cost a man's life...and ultimately perhaps his own. Those of us who are "people pleasers" have a difficult task ahead of us: letting go of the need for approval. Pleasing people is exhausting at best, dangerous at worst. Let's go for a new goal: pleasing God.

> If I were still trying to please men, I would not be a servant
> of Christ. *Galatians 1:10*

Anger and revenge are bad for your digestion.

Herodias was a woman who ignored the consequences of her actions. She fed her lustful desires until they destroyed her first marriage. She fed her anger until it consumed her and resulted in an unholy beheading of an innocent man. Yet she was always hungry, manipulating those around her to feed her need for more power, more worldly goods, more control. Wise is the woman who studies carefully everything Herodias did...and does the exact opposite!

> A fool gives full vent to his anger,
> but a wise man keeps himself under control. *Proverbs 29:11*

Veiled Threat

*When women go wrong,
men go right after them.*
MAE WEST

Beneath the wide brim of her elegant black hat, Tammy's gaze followed the mahogany casket as it disappeared into the parched Nevada desert. Though Boulder City coaxed its lawns and gardens to life with constant irrigation, six feet down the soil was dry and sterile as a bone.

Just like me. Tammy blinked away a faint threat of tears.

"Ashes to ashes, dust to dust."

She merely nodded at the words spoken by the stranger in a dark suit. Her father-in-law's choice, no doubt. Judd Tucker knew everyone in Eldorado Valley and half of Las Vegas besides. *The better half.*

Judd dropped a shovelful of dirt on the lid of the coffin while Tammy watched in silence. His expression was stoic, daring anyone to suggest he couldn't handle himself like a man, even if he was burying his beloved Oliver, the second of his sons to die mysteriously in as many years. He blamed Tammy for both of their deaths, of course.

"It's all your fault, you murderess!" That's what he'd shouted at her this morning over breakfast. It wasn't rashly spoken in a fit of anger. Judd meant every word.

First, there'd been Edward, Judd's oldest son and Tammy's first husband.

They were married less than a year. No children. But then, how could there have been?

When the coroner declared Edward dead of natural causes two Novembers ago, not a soul in the Tucker family believed the man. There were too many unanswered questions. Ed was healthy one minute, stretched out cold on the plush carpet of his father's foyer the next.

And now Oliver. Younger than Ed, but every bit as dead.

Oliver was Judd's second son. And Tammy's second husband. No offspring there either, of course.

The August sun hovered high above them now, bleaching the scene with a blinding brightness. Huge floral arrangements stood about like a wilted color guard, their silent presence a grim reminder that death was the business at hand that morning.

Tammy noticed a host of impatient stares aimed in her direction and stumbled forward with a guilty start. Judd's clod of sandy soil was to be followed by her single-stemmed rose. She'd been through this ceremony before. How could she have forgotten her duties so quickly?

Placing one black patent high heel in front of the other, Tammy approached the yawning grave, fearing if she got too close, Oliver's cruel hands would reach up and pull her down with him. She tossed the limp rose onto the casket with a nervous flick of her wrist and made a hasty retreat, murmuring "dust to dust," if only to keep herself from saying what she wanted to say: *Good riddance!*

Despite the heat, her body felt chilled. *It's the numbness, Tammy. Stay there. Don't let them watch you sweat.* Exhaling a deep breath, she lifted her head to face the solemn gathering. Not a friendly eye met hers. Tammy saw suspicion, curiosity, anger, even fear. *As if this was my doing!* She kept her chin steady and squeezed the purse tucked under her left arm, grateful for the dark sunglasses that hid her too-obvious relief at Ollie's demise.

She'd survived seven long months as Mrs. Oliver Tucker. Funerals and false accusations were a cinch after a nightmare like that.

Moments later the formalities were blessedly over. Judd clamped a sun-tanned hand on his wife's elbow and steered the impeccably dressed Sharyn Tucker toward the black Seville waiting for them at the curb. Tammy followed a safe distance behind, watching as Judd deposited Sharyn into the backseat, then turned on his heel, piercing Tammy with a steel-edged squint.

"This changes nothing, you know." His words hissed like water on a hot skillet. "My will stands as is. Without children, you don't get a dime, Tammy. Got that? Not one thin dime."

She shrugged. *Old news, Judd.* "I didn't marry Ed or Oliver because of your money, Mr. Tucker." She never could call him *Judd* to his face—let alone *Dad.* "I married Ed because you told him that siring children with a woman like me was his best insurance for inheriting your millions."

His grin held no hint of amusement. "So I did."

A fine mist filled the air as the sprinkler system along the cemetery's entranceway kicked on. Her black linen dress drank up the moisture like a sponge as she forced a smile to her lips. "And I married Oliver because he asked me to."

"Uh-huh." Judd stepped closer. "But you didn't give me grandkids by either of them, like *I* asked you to." He bent his still-youthful body over hers. All the Tuckers married young. Died young too, some of them.

"I wanted a pauper with good bones," he reminded her with a scowl. "Someone who couldn't afford to leave when the going got tough. What's the matter with you, Tammy? Not woman enough yet for the task?"

She bristled. "You chose me, Mr. Tucker. I was perfectly happy at that Hardee's restaurant near the Strip until you walked in and talked me into coming to Boulder City to meet Ed."

He laughed at that. "You were what—eighteen?—and poor as a church mouse. Living in that ramshackle excuse for a house with your whole miserable family." Judd brushed a bit of unseen lint off his suit jacket. "I did you a favor, girl. Too bad you didn't return it."

Some favor. He'd ruined her life with their little business arrangement. Spun out magical promises of the good life in beautifully green Boulder

City and the fortune that awaited her as the mother of his grandchildren. When Edward balked at the idea, Judd demanded Edward marry her or risk being written out of the will.

That blasted will! He held it over them all like a lighted torch. Threatened to disown them. Cut them off without a cent. The usual control-freak jargon.

She wouldn't tell him—couldn't tell him—why there had been no children. Even thinking about it now brought a fresh wave of heat to her cheeks. Judd would never believe her, nor did she have proof. Besides, they were his sons and they were dead. What was the point of telling their father now that both his sons were—

"So." He cut off her thoughts, abruptly snapping open his flat leather wallet and pulling out a perforated paper. "This should take care of things."

He handed over the paper with a flourish as though it were a hefty check. It was a CAT Pass. A one-way bus ticket to Las Vegas.

"Go home to your family." His derisive laugh hit her hard, like a blow to her stomach. "If they'll take you back, that is."

She stared at the inexpensive ticket, stunned. Was the Tucker family done with her then? They'd groomed her, trained her, filled her closets with the right sort of clothes, and now…nothing?

"But…but my family *won't* take me back. When I left…" Tammy swallowed hard, all at once feeling lightheaded in the harsh sun. "When I left with you that day, they accused me of thinking I was too good for them. They said they never wanted to see me again. Unless…"

He wrapped a hand around her bare upper arm and yanked her against him, whispering in her ear. "Unless you came home with some of my money. Is that it?"

Judd read her like the front page of the *Sun*. All she could do was nod, her face hot with embarrassment.

He released her with a slight shove. "You signed the prenuptial, Tammy. You knew how this worked. No money for you, ever, unless you provided me with grandchildren."

Moistening her sun-parched lips, she made herself speak the truth. "Yes, I signed it. But I never dreamed I'd be a young widow. Twice. I never dreamed that…well, that I wouldn't get…pregnant." She dropped her head until only her black patent shoes were in view. Murmuring more to herself than to Judd, she added, "I thought I could win your trust, prove to you I wasn't a gold digger." Her voice faded to a faint whisper. "I hoped I could change your mind about me."

A masculine hand reached under her hat and tipped her head up. His grip on her chin was warm, and for one brief moment their gazes locked. A flicker of compassion crossed his features, then quickly disappeared.

His eyes narrowed. "Nothing has changed, Tammy, except that I've lost two sons. I intend to keep my youngest under lock and key, where you can't cozy up to him like you did Oliver."

Son Number Three. *Steffan*. A young man of eighteen, two years her junior. The vicious glint in the boy's gaze had told her all she needed to know. No, she would not seek comfort in Steffan's arms. In fact, she would drown herself in Boulder Basin before she'd even consider it.

"Steffan is safe from me," she assured her father-in-law, shifting her chin out of his grasp. "I'll find my own way to the bus station, thank you." Close to fainting at Judd's heartless dismissal of her, Tammy propelled herself along the sidewalk with all the grace she could muster. She'd never been to the Citizens Area Transit station in Boulder City. Had no idea which direction to begin walking.

She reminded herself that she'd lived through worse days than this. *Oh, much worse.* All the money in the world couldn't change some men into gentlemen. She would find her bus, get on it, and never look back.

Judd's voice followed her down the street. "Don't think you can turn up pregnant in a month and have me accept that child in this family!" The man was shouting, not caring who heard him. "Do you hear? I'll do DNA testing if I have to." He was bellowing now. "Don't even try it. Don't even *think* it, witch!"

I am not a witch! She refused to acknowledge Judd's rantings and kept marching toward City Hall, vaguely remembering having seen a CAT bus parked out front.

Her pointed shoes pinched her toes with each step, a painful reminder of the comfortable life she was leaving behind. What would she tell people back in Vegas if they asked why both her young husbands dropped dead? "Because they deserved it" didn't seem a reasonable answer, though Tammy thought it might just be the truth.

Judd's constant harping about wanting "a full quiver of grandchildren"—his favorite phrase—made his own sons angry and resentful. Made them meanspirited and hateful. Made them break her heart every night without fail.

Disinterested in how their father earned his millions, they'd focused instead on cruelty as an art form. Edward, the older brother, forced her to pleasure him any way she could except the one way that would produce children. He never touched her, never kissed her, never held her. He laughed at her tears and mocked her when she pleaded with him to love her as a husband should.

"What, and watch my inheritance disappear into a child's greedy pockets when I could keep it all myself? You really are a fool, Tammy."

When Edward died—*oh, happy day!*—Oliver was there to comfort her, putting his arm around her shoulders, something Edward had never done. She melted at Oliver's gentle touch. Weeks later, when he kissed her, she nearly swooned. When he proposed, she leaped into his arms with joy.

How could she know that once they'd married, Judd's demand for offspring would bring out a side of Oliver she'd never imagined? He, too, had no wish for children and even less desire to bed his older brother's wife merely to accommodate his old man. Instead, Oliver spent his evenings surfing the Internet, stopping at every disgusting pornographic site he could find.

When he did remember his husbandly duties, he did so with little concern for her feelings, spending only enough time with her to satisfy his own desire, spilling his seed into a hand towel, leaving her frustrated and ashamed.

And childless.

She couldn't even pretend she was sorry both men were dead.

But she was very sorry she hadn't been blessed with children.

Squinting up at the sun to measure the hour, Tammy felt the hot sting of tears at last. No man—not Edward, not Oliver, and certainly not Judd Tucker—was going to steal her dream of motherhood in a mansion. "No way!" She ground the words out, her confidence building with every determined step. "Not for one Las Vegas minute!"

Ten minutes after nine.

Time really didn't matter on the Strip. The casinos didn't bother with clocks, so Tammy wore a watch. If Judd followed his usual pattern on these business trips—something she knew even three long years wouldn't alter— he'd be walking through the doors of the Arabian Nights Resort right about nine.

Whatever the time, Tammy was ready.

He'd never recognize her. Not after three years, and not in this outfit. She adjusted the flimsy veils, making sure they revealed more than they concealed, and tucked a tendril of her much longer, much blonder hair behind her ear.

Judd liked blondes, she remembered.

Tammy hoped he'd like this one enough to buy her for an hour.

It was the only way—the *only* way—she could get what she wanted. Edward and Oliver were dead, and Steffan had been packed off to college in Utah. Judd was her final option, however distasteful the prospect. His will had clearly promised his fortune to his children—and *her* children.

Was it her fault his sons hadn't cooperated? *No.* A share of the Tucker fortune was rightfully hers—morally if not legally. A child would make it legal. And binding.

Besides, Tammy didn't want just anybody's baby—she wanted a *Tucker* baby. Maybe Judd's obsession had become her own. Who knew? She simply had to try, if only to prove him wrong and put her sense of failure to rest. *It's what he wants too,* she reminded herself. *Children.* A legacy and a future.

When she read the article in the *Sun* that mentioned an upcoming meeting of the Colorado River Commission, Tammy knew it was time to make her move. Naturally, Judd's name was listed among the CRC attendees. He'd always arrived the night before for these meetings, always stayed in this hotel, and—since Boulder City was the only town in Nevada with a no-gambling law—he'd always lost a little money at the gaming tables.

But he'd never flirted with the beautiful women that made Las Vegas famous. It was a source of pride for him. "After all," he'd insisted, patting Sharyn's arm, "I'm a happily married man."

Not anymore. Sharyn had died two months ago in a boating accident on Lake Mead. It was the lead story on the ten o'clock news. "Prominent businessman Judd Tucker suffered a tragic loss today…"

Tammy had stared at the television in disbelief. Sharyn dead?

That was when she began to formulate her plan.

Risky? That wasn't the half of it. Prostitution was legal enough in Vegas, but with a power player like Judd, a woman had to be careful. Judd knew too many people, could pull too many strings.

Her only trump card was her carefully chosen disguise and the changes the past three years had made in her appearance. If he recognized her, it was all over. But if he didn't…

She sneaked a glance at her watch, hidden underneath a sequined cuff, and took a deep breath to calm her nerves. *Nine fifteen.* She'd parked herself in a comfortable chair at a strategic spot in the lobby where two hallways converged. She'd be sure to see him. And he'd be sure to see her.

The lighting was softer there as well. The last time he'd laid eyes on her was at Oliver's funeral. *A lifetime ago.* She'd spent the months since then finding a decent clerical job, an apartment of her own, a dependable car.

But not one boyfriend. Who went out with a woman with two dead husbands to her credit? *No one.* She'd kept her married name, like the widows of her grandmother's generation: "Mrs. Oliver Tucker." It gave her a feeling of belonging to *someone,* even if he was only a memory and not a pleasant one at that.

Anyway, it wasn't a husband she longed for. It was children. She would be a good mother. No, a *wonderful* mother. She *would!* With her big heart and Judd's big wallet, a child would have everything he or she needed—past, present, and future.

The huge iron gates of the Arabian Nights Resort swung open, and a familiar man swaggered in. *Judd!* She held her breath as he checked in at registration, one small bag and his hand-carved German walking stick by his side—a trademark accessory, purely for effect.

Seconds dragged into minutes. Tammy fiddled with her borrowed outfit, one that matched the gold and purple hues of the hotel's Arabian theme. She hoped the layers of chiffon and sparkling coins struck the right note of availability without seeming—*heaven forbid!*—cheap. The idea was to look and sound like a high-class call girl, not a low-class whore.

At last Judd finished at the front desk. Waving away the bellman, he grabbed his overnight bag, then turned and headed for the hallway to her right, his walking stick in hand, his gaze taking in the noisy confusion around him before landing on her and settling there. A slow-growing grin softened his lean features as their eyes met.

Her heart leaped into her throat. Was it her imagination, or was he slowing his steps?

No turning back now, Tammy. She offered him a frank gaze of approval in return and rose to greet him, pitching her voice lower than usual. "Sir, may I assist you in finding your room?"

He looked down at her, still smiling, though nothing in his eyes indicated recognition. Only admiration. And unmistakable interest. "Young lady, I can think of nothing I'd like more than your…assistance."

Summoning all her courage, she slipped a hand into the crook of his elbow and steered him toward the elevator. "We're in agreement then." Ten steps later she pressed the button and looked up at him with the most businesslike expression she could manage. "Rather than spoil things later, suppose we discuss the financial details now."

He nodded as the elevator doors opened, shutting just as silently behind them in seconds, enclosing them in privacy. *Thank goodness!* There was no point in delaying any longer. "So," she began as the elevator headed upward, "what will you give me for an hour of pleasure?"

His laugh bounced off the mirrored walls. "Wait a minute. Aren't you supposed to quote *me* a price?"

"You look like a man of good taste and some means." She lifted one perfectly arched brow. "I rather hoped you might be more generous than the...average man."

The doors slid open with a *whoosh.* "And so I will be. Say...a thousand dollars?"

The man was daft! She shrugged, checking the room number scribbled on his key folder. "I suppose that will have to do. Cash, is it?"

Now it was his turn to shrug. "Sure, unless you take American Express." He winked and shoved the key in the door. "I hadn't counted on company tonight."

Tammy had counted every day until she could be certain it wasn't hormones or nerves or a case of the flu.

Clearly it was none of those things. She was pregnant. *Pregnant!*

Granted, the time of the month had been ideal, and his efforts in their darkened room at the Arabian Nights Resort most thorough. But anything could have happened. Or nothing.

Instead it was the precise something she'd hoped for. In a few months she would hold her child—their child—in her arms. She'd kept the secret to herself those first weeks, then shared her news with a few trusted friends at work.

How to tell Judd though? A phone call? A letter? A telegram? Simply show up on his doorstep and let him see the results himself?

Judd solved that dilemma for her.

With a warrant for her arrest.

The knock on her door came on a Friday afternoon. "What am I being charged with?" she demanded, throwing open her apartment door so hard it dented the wall.

One cop consulted his paperwork while the other cuffed her with a mumbled apology. "Mrs. Tucker, you are wanted in connection with the murder of Edward Tucker of Boulder City."

"Nonsense!" Tammy suddenly felt faint, and her stomach tightened. "Look, you'll have to forgive me. I'm...pregnant." *And innocent.* Neither was obvious yet. Her voice was audibly shaking as she stalled for time and fought a sense of nausea. "Who signed this warrant?"

Tammy recognized the name: one of Judd's friends on the bench.

The arresting officers were patient but firm. "You'll need to come downtown now, ma'am."

Sniffling, she gathered a few necessary items, including a certain walking stick she pretended to need. Judd's AmEx card slipped easily into her jeans pocket. Surely he'd missed it within hours of that night and cancelled it, dismissing both his liability and his embarrassment at being taken for a fool.

It wasn't the credit line that had interested her though. It was the name boldly imprinted across the bottom: *Judd Randolph Tucker*. When he'd nodded off for a moment that night, she'd slipped out the door with his card and his cane, knowing they'd be needed someday.

Someday had come.

Having read Tammy her Miranda rights, the two cops guided her down the steps and into the backseat of the cruiser. No lights, no sirens. But the destination was awful just the same.

She'd never been to the police station, never seen the seamier side of humanity draped across chairs, propped against walls, waiting to stand before a judge who barely knew their names. Catching a glimpse of herself in a mirror—her hair shorter and brown once again, the circles under her eyes dark with strain—she sank into a folding chair and waited her turn, fearing the worst.

Hours seemed to pass before her name was called. "Tucker!" the sergeant behind the desk hollered out. She was already standing when she heard a familiar male voice behind her answer, "Right here."

She didn't need to turn around to know who'd walked through the station doors. *Judd.*

He was next to her in an instant, his expression triumphant. "I had to watch this little drama in person." He stole a glimpse at her abdomen. "Not showing yet, I see."

Her mouth dried to dust. "H-how did you know?"

"I know everything about you, Tammy, including your due date." His smirk was an ugly scar across his face. "A date that will find you in prison. Death row, if I have anything to say about it." Judd's eyes narrowed to slits. "My lawyers finally have the evidence they need to convict you. I always knew you'd murdered Edward, and now I think we can prove it. We're still working on Oliver's case, but I'm not buying natural causes there either."

"Why?" She bit her lower lip to keep it from trembling. "Why are you doing this to me?"

"Because it's the truth." He closed in on her, his voice low and menacing. "And because that baby in your belly is an affront to me. You couldn't manage to give me grandchildren when you were my daughter-in-law, but now you've let some no-good swine father a child that—"

Her laugh was so loud it startled even her. The activity around her ground to a halt as the noisy room quieted to an uncanny silence.

Tammy lifted her chin and smiled, her own sense of victory growing. "It seems you don't know everything after all, Judd. The doctor tells me I'm carrying not one child, but two. Twins. Boys."

Judd's forehead knotted in a frown.

Surprise, Dad.

She turned to the young policeman on her right. "Officer, show Mr. Tucker the item I asked you to carry for me."

Confused, the man held out the elegant walking stick. "You mean this?"

Tammy watched the color drain from Judd's face. Watched his Adam's apple dip up and down. His voice was hoarse as he struggled to speak. "Where...where did you get..."

"I'm pregnant by the man who owns it." She slipped the American Express card out of the front pocket of her jeans and held it toward him. "And this. Recognize it, Judd?" She laughed, more softly this time. "Maybe you should have left home without it..."

What's So Bad About Wanting to Be a Mother?: Tamar

Hol-ly-WOOD!

Girls, this Bad Girl is ready for the big screen. Her story has it *all*: mysterious deaths, deceptive relatives, mistaken identities, hidden babies, even a woman sentenced to burn at the stake!

Come to think of it...why *hasn't* a nail-biting drama about Tamar been flashed across a Technicolor screen by now? Delilah got her own epic (though she had to share billing with Samson). Bathsheba nabbed her share of reel time. So did Jezebel and Salome.

Why not Tamar?

I'll tell you why, and it isn't because Tamar's name makes her sound like a boy. Or a camel. Any way you tell this story you eventually come to a scene that, even in our anything-goes society, doesn't sit well on the psyche: A young woman poses as a prostitute so she can sleep with her father-in-law. On purpose.

I can hear Cecil B. DeMille now: *"Cut!"*

You won't find much enthusiasm for sermon skits about Tamar and Judah at church. Not many weekly women's meetings are called "The Tamar Circle." And yet Tamar gets an honorable mention in the book of Ruth. Before her own story ends, Tamar is declared more righteous than Judah, who was one of God's chosen. And here's the big *ta-da!* In the first chapter of Matthew, Tamar is listed in the genealogy of the Messiah.

Tamar, the temporary tramp, in the lineage of Christ?

Unbelievable. Unimaginable. And so like the Lord.

Tamar means "palm tree." Perhaps she grew into a tall young woman, a willowy but tenacious presence amidst the strong desert winds, bending but never breaking. We don't know if she was beautiful or homely, but her quick mind made an appearance soon enough.

Some might even say she was devious. Victorian feminist Elizabeth Cady Stanton refused to include the texts on Tamar in her studies, finding them "unworthy a place in the 'Woman's Bible.'"[1]

Picky, picky, picky.

Other women commentators insist Tamar is "not a wicked woman at all"[2] and in truth offers a "ray of hope."[3]

So...Good Girl or Bad Girl?

Honey, she was just like us, only more so. Her good deeds were exemplary, the stuff of role models. Her one truly bad deed was off-the-chart bad. But it ended well and was handled in keeping with the customs of her time and place. See, that's the key with this story: understanding what kind of rules and regs the woman was up against.

We'll find Tamar's tawdry tale in Genesis, which right off the bat tells you it's o-l-d. Pre-Moses stuff. No Ten Commandments hanging on the walls of their tents, no praise choruses of "Let My People Go" sung around a Sabbath meal. "The law had not yet been given, and the prophets had yet to prophesy."[4] Nor had the judges judged or the kings kinged. We're talking *ancient* history.

Tamar and Judah's sidebar story sits smack-dab in the middle of Joseph's saga. At the end of Genesis 37, Joseph has just been sold into slavery by his brothers. *Oh no!* Then Joe's future is left dangling while we toddle after one of his brothers for thirty verses.

> At that time, Judah left his brothers and went down
> to stay with a man of Adullam named Hirah. *Genesis 38:1*

Judah, a son of Jacob the patriarch, left his family in "an act of willful indiscretion"[5] and started hanging out with an Adullamite guy called Hirah. Judah was a pup, barely old enough to shave, yet plenty old enough to choose a wife.

The rabbis considered the marriageable age for young men to be "thirteen years and a day."[6] Judah, like any hormone-happy adolescent, wasted no time.

> There Judah met the daughter of a Canaanite man
> named Shua. He married her and lay with her;...
> *Genesis 38:2*

Uh-oh. This was literally and figuratively a step down for young Judah. The Canaanites lived almost exclusively in the plains[7] *and* were the bad guys in God's eyes. Judah yoked himself to Bathshua (NEB)—"daughter of Shua"—and to her people, emotionally, physically, and soon parentally.

> ...she became pregnant and gave birth to a son,
> who was named Er. *Genesis 38:3*

Er? What kind of name is that? Must be short for *Error.*

Two more sons followed: Onan was born when Judah was about fifteen, then Shelah joined the nursery a year later.[8] Talk about babies having babies!

Judah waited the appropriate baker's dozen years until it was his turn to play matchmaker for his young sons.

> Judah got a wife for Er, his firstborn, and her name
> was Tamar. *Genesis 38:6*

We know zip about Tamar's background or where Judah found her. For our purposes she simply showed up in her wedding veil. Young, no doubt, though well established in her menses. In the sixteenth century B.C.—give or take—fertility was a woman's primary claim to fame.

> But Er, Judah's firstborn, was wicked in the LORD's
> sight;...

Wicked in what way? Did he thumb his nose at God? Dishonor his father and mother? Misuse his bride? Most likely it was all three. Rabbinical tradition points to "unnatural intercourse" (no specifics, thank goodness) as the nature of Er's wickedness, with the "intent being to prevent the woman from conceiving."[9]

Shame on you, Er. Don't you know it isn't nice to fool Father Nature?

> ...so the LORD put him to death. *Genesis 38:7*

Yes, God is patient. But God is also just. Knowing the spiritual state of Er's heart, God decided Er was wicked through and through. So Er was...uh, through.

Next.

> Then Judah said to Onan, "Lie with your brother's wife
> and fulfill your duty to her as a brother-in-law to produce
> offspring for your brother." *Genesis 38:8*

Welcome to Levirate Marriage 101.

Later, when customs and decrees became the Law, it would be described like this:

> If brothers are living together and one of them dies without
> a son, his widow must not marry outside the family.
> *Deuteronomy 25:5*

Good heavens! In those days you not only had to check out the groom but all his brotherly ushers, too, just in case. (The one on the end isn't bad...)

> Her husband's brother shall take her and marry her and fulfill
> the duty of a brother-in-law to her. *Deuteronomy 25:5*

"Fulfilling his duty" meant making sure she gave birth to a son who would carry on her dead husband's name and inherit his land. One writer explained that it wasn't a true marriage at all but more of a "stud service" for the widowed woman.[10] Lovely.

The good news was, it rescued her from destitution.[11] Widowhood was a reproach, a dishonor. Without children, a widow had no financial provision and was forced to beg or worse. The law of levirate marriage prevented that hardship.

The bad news was, she had to sleep with her brother-in-law, and he with her, until a healthy son was produced. Only the most considerate of men would make such an awkward situation bearable. Onan, brother of the deceased, was many things. "Considerate" was not one of them.

> But Onan knew that the offspring would not be his;...

No dummy, that Onan. What benefit would he enjoy from impregnating his sister-in-law, other than...well, other than the act itself? Better for him that Tamar never had children. Then the land would be split only two ways—between himself and his younger brother—instead of three. It didn't take a mathematical genius to figure out the solution to *that* problem.

> ...so whenever [Onan] lay with his brother's wife, he spilled
> his semen on the ground to keep from producing offspring
> for his brother. *Genesis 38:9*

Your health teacher called it *coitus interruptus,* one of the oldest forms of birth control.

In Tamar's case it was doubly cruel, because his swift departure from her body not only prevented pregnancy—the thing she longed for most— but it also robbed her of any possible pleasure in the process.

Onan used Tamar shamelessly, treating her like a whore instead of a wife.

His Bad-Boy behavior even earned him a place in the dictionary. Look up *onanism,* and you'll see among its meanings "self-gratification."[12] That was Onan, all right—selfish to the extreme.

Once again, God was not amused.

> What he did was wicked in the LORD's sight; so he put him to death also. *Genesis 38:10*

I'm biting my lip to keep from cheering, "Go, Lord!"
Judah, naturally, was *not* thrilled with this second funeral.

> Judah then said to his daughter-in-law Tamar, "Live as a widow in your father's house until my son Shelah grows up."
> *Genesis 38:11*

Though Papa Judah's deceit wasn't as flagrant as the chicanery his two sons pulled, he, too, behaved badly. Only a true widow could be properly welcomed back into her father's household. Tamar was still "married" to this family as long as a living son remained for her to wed...and bed.

That was a situation Judah couldn't bear to sanction.

> For he thought, "He may die too, just like his brothers."
> *Genesis 38:11*

I'll bet the neighborhood gossips—if not Judah himself—pegged Tamar as a mistress of the black arts, casting a spell on her two husbands, with a deadly potion ready to pour down the throat of unsuspecting Son Number Three.

By withholding his son, Judah dishonored Tamar, then added to his sin by sending her back home penniless, childless, and disgraced.

> So Tamar went to live in her father's house. *Genesis 38:11*

Can't you hear her sisters now, greeting her at the front gate?

"Who invited *you* back? Humph. No way you're sharing *my* room!"

And imagine what they called her when they thought she wasn't listening: *Jinx. She-devil. Murderess.*

The woman was an outcast, with three strikes against her: She was young but not marriageable, barren (or so it appeared), *and* a widow—twice. She wasn't homeless, but she *was* rootless, with no provision made for her future. The parties involved probably wished Tamar would quietly die and spare them all further embarrassment.

Tamar didn't die. But Bethshua did.

> After a long time Judah's wife, the daughter of Shua, died.
> *Genesis 38:12*

"After a long time" is very telling. It meant years of loneliness for Tamar. Those of us who've struggled with depression and feelings of worthlessness or abandonment find a familiar resting place in Tamar's weary soul.

Abused, deceived, forgotten.

Over at Judah's house, there was plenty of pain to go around as well. No grandchildren. No daughters or sons, save one whom he couldn't rightfully betroth to anyone but the dreaded Tamar.

And now no wife.

> When Judah had recovered from his grief,…

Judah's grieving was genuine, but when it ended, he tossed aside his mourning clothes and jumped back into life with both feet pointed toward the biggest excuse to party in the plains: sheep-shearing season. Like a carnival with its revelry and relaxed rules, it drew a crowd that threw away loose change on loose women, among other attractions.

> …he went up to Timnah, to the men who were shearing his
> sheep, and his friend Hirah the Adullamite went with him.
> *Genesis 38:12*

The Bible is full of irony, few passages more so than this one: Judah went off to shear his sheep, but *he* was the one about to get fleeced!

> When Tamar was told, "Your father-in-law is on his way to
> Timnah to shear his sheep,"... *Genesis 38:13*

A casual conversation. A bit of overheard gossip. Judah was the head of his clan, so people surely talked about his comings and goings. The forgotten Tamar saw his impending trip as an opportunity to remedy a terrible injustice rendered against her by her father-in-law.
Judah deceived her first.
Now it was her turn.

> ...she took off her widow's clothes,...

The *New English Bible* calls them "widow's weeds." Gives you a vivid picture of the alluring nature of *those* dreary threads, eh?
Off with the gray/brown/black. On with the red/purple/blue.
Something sheer, please. *Oh, good.* One size fits all.

> ...covered herself with a veil to disguise herself,...

Considering what Tamar had in mind, concealing her identity was of paramount importance.

> ...and then sat down at the entrance to Enaim, which is on
> the road to Timnah. *Genesis 38:14*

A woman sitting alone by the side of the road? Sounds like an invitation to disaster. Or maybe it was just an invitation.
Not only is there no modern location for Enaim, but an eleventh-century French rabbi admitted, "We have searched through the whole of Scripture and found no place called 'Petach Enaim.'"[13]
The translation "where the road forks in two directions" (NEB) is closer to the mark. It was a place where one was obligated to make a decision.

Tamar felt she had no choice but this one because of the poor choice Judah had made.

> For she saw that, though Shelah had now grown
> up, she had not been given to him as his wife.
> *Genesis 38:14*

Realizing Judah would never honor the levirate law, Tamar took matters into her own hands. This is the one thing that labels her a Bad Girl, if only for a night. Perhaps a Good Girl would have accepted her childless status as God's choice on her behalf and lived out her days in a state of quasi widowhood, shunned by society, poor but righteous.

Tamar, however, was more concerned with being a mother than with being good, and so she devised a plan. It was Bad-Girl stuff and waaay beyond risky, but she obviously felt Judah left her no other recourse.

One commentator thought that by not giving her his third son, Judah exposed Tamar to fleshly temptation. *Nah.* This wasn't about needing sex. This was about carrying on the family name.

From Tamar's point of view, she was about to do Judah a favor, and not just a sexual one. It wasn't marriage she was after, or honor, or revenge—it was children and the future they represented, both for Judah's lineage and her own financial security.

Today a woman might visit her local sperm bank, plunk down a sizable sum, and choose some designer genes. Tamar, though, had only one option, and he was walking in her direction.

> When Judah saw her, he thought she was a prostitute,...

Was it the veil? Something in her eyes? A come-hither tilt to her head? Her pungent perfume? The Hebrew word in this verse is the one used for a "common prostitute"—*zonah*. In any millennium, the body language is the same: "Then out came a woman to meet him, dressed like a prostitute and with crafty intent."[14]

Tamar wasn't crafty so much as she was desperate. This man had something she needed, and whatever attire, attitude, or action it took, she was going to get it.

Ah, how well we understand.

Those of us who have spent more than one Saturday night sitting on a barstool, dressed like a prostitute, hoping some man would give us an identity—girlfriend, fiancée, wife, mother to his children, something, anything—lived with a deep-down fear that we would get only what we'd advertised for: sex.

We understand fully the power of a veil.

> ...for she had covered her face. *Genesis 38:15*

Though by Assyrian law common prostitutes were to remain un-veiled,[15] Canaanite cult prostitutes were heavily veiled. And not just veiled while waiting between customers but during the act of intercourse as well, giving their partners the illusion that they were "actually engaging in the sexual act with the goddess herself."[16] That way, the men could convince themselves it wasn't sex...it was worship.

Well, now.

No wonder the Israelites had such a tough time tossing out the Canaanite religious practices! And no wonder the Word of God speaks so strongly against this "abominable form of idolatry."[17]

Whether Judah thought of it as venerating the goddess of fertility or venting his pent-up passions, his "sin began in the eye"[18] when he gazed upon the veiled vamp by the side of the road.

> Not realizing that she was his daughter-in-law,...

I know, I know...how could he not recognize his own daughter-in-law?! Remember that Judah hadn't seen her in ages. People change. I find the mental image I carry of people is based on the *first* time I saw them, not the last. I've walked right past an old friend at the mall, realizing several steps later, "Hey! Wasn't that so-and-so? Boy, does she look older!" (*Uh-huh*. Like I don't!)

Maybe that's what happened at the fork in the road to Timnah. Years had passed since Judah last saw Tamar. She was older. Fine lines creased the fragile skin around her dark eyes. Instead of widow's weeds, she was wearing the latest in harlot haute couture.

Toss in the fact that the man was a widower with certain unmet needs, and it's easy to grasp why he didn't see Tamar, per se—he saw an available woman, period.

> …he went over to her by the roadside and said, "Come now, let me sleep with you." *Genesis 38:16*

A real sweet talker, that Judah. Like many men, he preferred to cut to the chase.

Tamar was probably relieved. No games, no false flirting required. She went straight to the bottom line as well.

> "And what will you give me to sleep with you?" she asked. *Genesis 38:16*

With her keen bartering skills, Tamar is one of several women in the Bible known as a "sexual trickster,"[19] cleverly trading feminine favors to advance her cause. Notice she didn't state her price as a professional prostitute normally would. She asked Judah what he was willing to *pay*.

> "I'll send you a young goat from my flock," he said. *Genesis 38:17*

Now look who's desperate! A *goat*? Ladies of the evening were often paid as little as a loaf of bread for a roll in the wheat. But a *goat*? Maybe Judah was new to the ways of fallen women. Or maybe Tamar in that veil was a sight to behold. Could have been the man was feeling generous. Or frisky.

Whatever the case, it's a good thing he forgot his wallet, because the story would have had a very different ending if he'd paid cash on the spot. Instead he promised to *send* her his payment.

Oh sure, Judah. The goat is in the mail.

> "Will you give me something as a pledge until you send it?"
> she asked. *Genesis 38:17*

Clever woman. Despite what she was up to here, it's hard not to root for Tamar. In what had to be the most difficult circumstance for this Former Good Girl about to go Bad for a Good Reason, she kept a cool head and focused her eyes on the prize: children in her womb, in her arms, in her life, in her lineage. And money in her bank account.

Judah didn't balk at her request.

> He said, "What pledge should I give you?" *Genesis 38:18*

Psst! Shoot high, Tamar, shoot high!

> "Your seal and its cord, and the staff in your hand," she
> answered. *Genesis 38:18*

That's like asking for his driver's license, his wallet, a stack of business cards, *and* his photo ID. Judah should have laughed and walked away. But the veiled Tamar, knowing him well, banked on her outrageous request appealing to his sizable ego.

The seal, or "signet" (NKJV), was a small hollow cylinder engraved with Judah's identifying markings, which he pressed into soft clay on documents, like a signature. It hung around his neck on a cord where he could keep it safe and handy when needed, which surely was often on a business trip like this one.

His staff, or "walking stick" (CEV), might have been fancy or plain, a simple shepherd's crook or the symbol of clan leadership. In any case it was a useful item, not a decorative one.

However valuable those things might have been, Judah presented them to her with one hand while he happily untied his tunic with the other.

> So he gave them to her and slept with her,...

Thank you, Lord, for leaving out the details. We all know how this works.

> ...and she became pregnant by him. *Genesis 38:18*

Well, well. Tamar got her wish.

At the moment of conception, not even Tamar knew that. It would be months before Judah would hear the news. The two of them didn't perch on a couch before a TV camera, early-pregnancy test in hand, tears streaming down their faces. "Look, everybody! We're pregnant!"

Only *the Lord* knew, because he alone bestowed the blessing. "Sons are a heritage from the LORD, children a reward from him."[20]

God was in that child's life from the beginning.

Just as he was in yours. Just as he was in mine.

No matter what the circumstances of our conception—whether done in love or in lust, within the sanctity of marriage or the certainty of sin—God is sovereign.

To say he had a grand plan for the fruit of her womb is an understatement.

> After she left, she took off her veil and put on her widow's
> clothes again. *Genesis 38:19*

Her sin was deliberate, it was purposeful, and it was over. Once and done.

That reality does not make her actions "good," but it does make her motivation clear. Sex with her father-in-law was a necessary evil to produce a necessary good.

(It goes without saying, the rules have changed. Don't try this at home. Ever.)

> Meanwhile Judah sent the young goat by his friend the Adul-
> lamite in order to get his pledge back from the woman,...

I can hear Judah now. "C'mon. *You* go, Hirah! You know the place better than I do. Be a pal and find her for me, will ya?"

...but he did not find her. *Genesis 38:20*

Surprise, surprise.

> [Hirah] asked the men who lived there, "Where is the
> shrine prostitute who was beside the road at Enaim?"
> *Genesis 38:21*

Now, instead of being labeled a *zonah*—a common prostitute—she's
become a *qedeshah*, a temple prostitute. You don't suppose old Judah cleaned
up his story in order to make himself look more religious to his Canaanite
friend? Or had he convinced himself that because her veil stayed in place
she was a shriner, so to speak?

> "There hasn't been any shrine prostitute here," they said.
> *Genesis 38:21*

Those shrine prostitutes, by the way, were devotees of the mother-
goddess Ishtar. (*Silly me.* All this time I've thought *Ishtar* referred to the
worst movie ever made!)

> So [Hirah] went back to Judah and said, "I didn't find her.
> Besides, the men who lived there said, 'There hasn't been any
> shrine prostitute here.'" *Genesis 38:22*

Mr. J, you've been had.

> Then Judah said, "Let her keep what she has, or we will
> become a laughingstock." *Genesis 38:23*

As the leader of his clan, he couldn't afford to get a "bad name" (NEB),
so Judah reasoned, "We'd better forget about the goat, or else we'll look like
fools" (CEV).

You already look like a fool, you old goat.

> "After all, I did send her this young goat, but you didn't find
> her." *Genesis 38:23*

Why, you sneaky blame shifter! "I did *my* part, Hirah. My conscience is clear. Too bad you didn't handle *your* half of the deal."

Give me a break!

Since he couldn't walk through the front door without them in hand, Judah probably had his staff and seal replaced by artisans sometime between the sheep-shearing extravaganza and arriving home. You can imagine how he explained that away. "Musta lost it somewhere last night at a party. See, there were these dancing girls…"

You just *know* the man was ready with a story if anybody asked what happened to his original seal and staff, though no one had reason to suspect Judah of anything untoward. Yet.

> About three months later Judah was told, "Your daughter-in-law Tamar is guilty of prostitution, and as a result she is now pregnant." *Genesis 38:24*

We're back to the word for a common whore—*zonah*—even though she didn't entertain multiple paying partners every night. Interesting how in our own culture some people find nothing wrong with a woman sleeping with a man she just met at a bar or living with a man who isn't her husband. But let her charge a fee for one hour of illicit sex, and suddenly she's trash. Somebody call the vice squad.

So it was with Tamar. As a widow, she was not permitted to have sex with anyone. Pregnant? A prostitute, then. There were laws about such things.

> Judah said, "Bring her out and have her burned to death!"
> *Genesis 38:24*

Mercy! *Burned* to death? The usual punishment was stoning. Burning was only employed when the woman was a daughter of a priest.[21] Why was Judah outraged enough to suggest such a beyond-the-pale death sentence?

Maybe he blamed this woman for everything that had gone wrong in his life and wanted finally to even the score.

Maybe he was angry because she had never conceived a child by either of his sons and yet here she was, pregnant by a stranger.

Maybe he really did think she was a witch, worthy of death by burning.

Or maybe—just maybe—he'd realized after the fact why the woman had seemed so familiar that day on the road. Burning Tamar to death would quickly destroy any telltale evidence of his own involvement in the crime.

The truth? We will never know.

The facts on hand? Tamar had shamed him with two dead sons.

Judah intended to see that she would not shame him again with a live son. The execution order stood.

As she was being brought out,...

Wait. Stop!

My heart is in my throat—isn't yours? I can see that waiting stake surrounded by a bundle of sticks, imagine the ominous snap and crackle of the flames mere minutes away, feel the scorch of Judah's red-hot anger burning her to ashes.

Speak up, Tamar. Do *something*!

...she sent a message to her father-in-law. "I am pregnant by the man who owns these," she said. *Genesis 38:25*

Of course! The seal and staff. Tamar, you brilliant woman.

But why did she wait until the last minute? Wasn't that taking too great a risk? No. Catching Judah off guard like that would make it harder for him to stall or try to turn things around in his favor.

Besides, Tamar had nothing to lose at that point. She had already taken her greatest risk back at the fork in the road.

This scene was all about timing and control.

And she added, "See if you recognize whose seal and cord and staff these are." *Genesis 38:25*

Note, she didn't accuse him via her messenger or do her own version of Nathan's charge to adulterous David: "You are the man!"[22] This Canaanite woman must have realized that favor had been bestowed on her and was growing in her womb. That gift gave her the generosity of spirit to stretch out the seal, cord, and staff to her father-in-law and allow him to claim them—and their child—and confess his disobedience before God and his witnesses in his own words, in his own way.

Judah was at a crossroads again.

He could have charged her with stealing his valuables. He could have described how she deceived him by the side of the road and so perhaps whipped up sympathy for his foolishness. He could have painted himself as a victim and her as an incestuous whore. Whatever Judah's accusations, all would have believed him, and Tamar would have died, taking her babe with her.

Instead, Judah did the right thing.

Judah recognized them...

Or better translated, he "acknowledged them" (AMP). We can imagine him nodding, not in defeat, but in acceptance.

...and said, "She is more righteous than I,..."

The crowd gasps. The music swells. Tamar is saved!

Judah has chosen life over death—for her, for the child in her womb who would bear his name, and for himself, since only with a clear conscience could Judah truly live out his days in peace.

One minor point: Though Judah admitted, "she is more in the right than I am" (NEB), by no means does that justify her actions or make her righteous in the eyes of the Lord. "More" right isn't the same as "all" right.

If she'd slipped into Judah's house and seduced his son—her rightful third husband—she would have been truly righteous. Wonder why she *didn't* try that? My feeling is, she would have feared being (1) caught by Judah, (2) rejected by Shelah, or (3) guilty of sending Son Number Three to an early grave.

Besides, her father-in-law had proven to be a virile man with healthy seed. Tamar—a woman who would not be "manipulated or intimidated or ignored"[23]—instead took a calculated risk that paid off.

Judah took the blame (about time!) for his negligence that had forced her to do so.

> "…since I wouldn't give her to my son Shelah." *Genesis 38:26*

Judah knew his actions at the crossroads had been "motivated by physical desire, while her motives had been noble."[24] Again, her *method* wasn't noble, but her *motives* were. In God's economy that counts for something, simply because *none* of us gets either the actions *or* the motivations right much of the time. We're assured by Paul, "There is no one righteous, not even one,"[25] and by Isaiah that "all our righteous acts are like filthy rags."[26]

Here's the good news: He loves us anyway. He died for us anyway. He blesses us anyway, though we clearly don't deserve it.

That unmerited grace makes me *want* to do the right thing, out of sheer love and gratitude—and because the Holy Spirit won't let me rest if I do otherwise.

A properly chastised Judah made sure he did right by Tamar.

> And he did not sleep with her again. *Genesis 38:26*

That was both the honorable—and legal—thing to do, as the Law would later record: "Do not have sexual relations with your daughter-in-law."[27]

Nor did he marry her, nor give her to Shelah. But undeniably the sons in her womb were his. That's right—*sons.*

> When the time came for her to give birth, there were twin boys in her womb. *Genesis 38:27*

How like God. A double blessing. Twins to replace the two dead sons of Judah. As any mother of twins will tell you, the birth process can be…er, tricky.

Three hundred years ago a commentator declared Tamar's delivery "was hard to the mother, by which she was corrected for her sin."[28] Oh, for Pete's sake! Thanks to Eve (and bigheaded babies), *all* births are hard, twins especially.

We're with you, Tamar. Breathe, honey. You can do it.

> As she was giving birth, one of them put out his hand; so the midwife took a scarlet thread and tied it on his wrist and said, "This one came out first." *Genesis 38:28*

Make a note to read Rahab's story in Joshua, chapters 2 and 6. That "scarlet thread" will take on new meaning. Here the red thread was meant to mark the firstborn, an important distinction when you're talking about a future inheritance.

> But when he drew back his hand, his brother came out, and she said, "So this is how you have broken out!" And he was named Perez. *Genesis 38:29*

Perez meant "breakthrough" (ouch), or as another translation phrases the midwife's words, "This breach be upon you!" (NKJV). A breach refers to (1) a violation of a law and/or (2) a broken, ruptured, or torn condition or area.[29] We've got both definitions at work here.

The Lizzie Revised Version says: "That was some entrance, kid!"

> Then his brother, who had the scarlet thread on his wrist, came out and he was given the name Zerah. *Genesis 38:30*

Good name, since Zerah meant "redness."

Her travail wasn't easy, but Tamar got what she wanted. Despite Judah's near miss with the burning stake incident on the edge of town, the patriarch got what he wanted too.

What matters is this: God's will prevailed.

As Eugenia Price wisely observed, these Old Testament stories are not "little 'morality plays.' We are not to try to be like them or not to be like them. *We are to look for what God did in all they did.*"[30]

My sense is, this Canaanite woman probably did not see God's hand at work in her life, just as we often don't. Who knows? Maybe she came to appreciate that truth later.

Here's proof of God's sovereignty in this story, from top to bottom, sordid as some of it was: When you follow the lineage of Judah's son, Perez, you find a few generations later a certain King David. Keep moving down the genealogy until you reach the final verse and you discover "the father of Joseph, the husband of Mary, of whom was born Jesus, who is called Christ."[31]

Tears spring to my eyes at the very thought!

Tamar, who posed as a harlot by the side of the road, was used by God for his holiest of purposes.

Yet if we allow the fact that she is in the lineage of Christ to excuse her "badness" in the situation, we lose the ability to learn a lesson from her story. Tamar is not to be praised—*God is.*

The Lord used her *in spite of* her sin. That's the hook we hang our hope on, sisters. Not in "getting it right," but in knowing that although we get it wrong—over and over, consistently, even blatantly—God's power to accomplish his will is not limited to our meager efforts.

Whew. What a relief!

We are made for one purpose: to worship and glorify God. Our challenge is to stop trying to make things work out for *our* good and let God work things out for *his* good and perfect will through us.

What Lessons Can We Learn from Tamar?

Men can be such jerks. So can women.
It's tempting to blame Tamar's behavior on Judah and his sons, especially with sins so gender-specific as theirs were. But Tamar sinned too and in a

frankly female manner. Men and women are equally lost without God. And equally forgiven at the cross. When we find ourselves fuming about "those *men*" in our lives, we might want to pull back and see how "we *women*" are contributing to the problem.

> There is neither Jew nor Greek, slave nor free, male nor
> female, for you are all one in Christ Jesus. *Galatians 3:28*

Sex is meant for procreation and recreation...not manipulation.

Our God-given sexuality is not a force to be trifled with. Even within the bonds of marriage, it can be misused. More than one wife among us has faked a headache—or an orgasm—in order to wield some sort of power over her husband. We know that God was displeased with how Er and Onan performed in Tamar's bedroom. Are we willing to examine our own bedside manners and see if they genuinely honor the man we married and the Lord we love?

> The wife's body does not belong to her alone but also to her
> husband. In the same way, the husband's body does not
> belong to him alone but also to his wife. *1 Corinthians 7:4*

Prostitution is not the unpardonable sin.

Don't misunderstand—the Lord *hates* the sin of prostitution. He also died that prostitutes might be forgiven. The only "unpardonable sin" is reject-ing the grace of God. No matter what your sexual past—or present—your future can be one of walking in newness of life. I am haunted by the face of a young mother, tiny tots in tow, who came to one of my book signings, leaned forward to look at me with pain-stricken eyes, and whispered, "Is there any hope for a prostitute?" There is more than hope, beloved. There is life everlasting in Jesus.

> Jesus said to them, "I tell you the truth, the tax collectors and
> the prostitutes are entering the kingdom of God ahead of
> you." *Matthew 21:31*

In all things, our God reigns.

The genealogy that opens the book of Matthew, from Abraham to Jesus of Nazareth, is full of sinners. Some obviously so—Rahab the harlot, David the adulterer, Tamar the trickster—and some whose sins aren't recorded in Scripture but whose transgressions are fully known by God. Every person in that lineage was put there by God for his purposes. Not because they were righteous or deserved to be there, but because God created them for one purpose: to glorify him.

> "You are worthy, our Lord and God,
>   to receive glory and honor and power,
> for you created all things,
>   and by your will they were created
>   and have their being." *Revelation 4:11*

Tears of a Clown

We are healed of a suffering
only by experiencing it to the full.
Marcel Proust

Veronica leaned toward the dingy mirror and exhaled in anticipation. The harsh lighting in the Greyhound bus station rest room was hardly flattering, but it would have to do. It was time for "Vera" to make her appearance.

Veronica lightly skimmed a finger across the jar of Mehron Clown White perched on the grimy porcelain sink and then rubbed her hands together, warming the grease paint to her body temperature. It went on her face smoothly, covering every inch of her small, plain features until no trace of the real Veronica showed through. She lightly patted her skin to even out the base, then surveyed her reflection.

Good start, Vera.

Clowns came in several varieties, but the one called "neat whiteface" was the perfect choice for a woman with no hair. "Look how her white skullcap disappears!" the other clowns would marvel, while Veronica merely smiled at the irony of it all.

She hadn't needed a skullcap for twelve years. Not since she lost all her hair—all over her body.

Alopecia areata universalis the doctors called it.

Veronica called it *ugly*.

When small clumps of hair began rubbing off on Veronica's pillow at age nine, her mother had done her best to shine a positive light on things. "Count your blessings, child. Be glad it isn't fatal or contagious."

Both were true—but neither was comforting.

"No pain either," her mother had reminded her.

On that count, Veronica knew better.

Outside the rest-room door, the organized chaos of the Great Circus Parade was gearing up. Less than two hours from now an agile prankster dressed as the Statue of Liberty on stilts would start the grand procession. Hundreds of horses would follow, along with exotic animals and antique circus wagons, winding their way through downtown Milwaukee.

Vera the Clown would be among them.

Reaching for a cotton swab, she pictured the colorful gathering of a hundred or more clowns, including mimes like her who preferred using their whole body to communicate rather than their voice. She carefully removed grease paint from the spots that would soon come alive with black and red creme liners. A narrow line for the eyebrows she no longer had, room for a small comical nose, and a dramatically drawn rosebud of a mouth.

Soon she would add pigment and look almost normal. Whatever that was. Could she even remember having hair?

A sense of desperate hope overwhelmed her.

Please, let this be the man who can heal me!

She would see him within the hour, the man they called a miracle worker. *Maybe, maybe, maybe…*

Veronica pressed the corner of her eye with a tissue, catching a tear before it ruined her makeup. *Easy does it. You're Vera the Clown today, remember?* Vera, who hadn't a care in the world except making other people laugh. The only tears she'd permit herself today would be painted ones.

"Who are *you*?" A child toddled up, pointing at her in-progress costume and half-finished makeup. "Are you in the parade?"

Veronica nodded and pantomimed adding a big hat and oversize shoes.

"But where is your hair?" the child asked, curiosity squeezing her tiny features together. She reached a small hand toward Veronica's head before her mother snatched the child's fingers in her own.

"Now, honey, you know better. We don't talk to strangers."

Veronica forced a smile to her lips. "I'm not a stranger. I'm Vera the Clown." Blinking to hold her tears at bay, she added. "I'm very safe indeed."

The child beamed at her. The mother, staring at her shiny scalp, seemed less convinced.

Veronica turned back to the mirror, determined to get in full costume and lose herself in the crowd as quickly as possible. Deftly holding an art brush, she dipped it into baby oil, then pigment, and drew a cherry red nose and mouth.

Voilà! She had a face again.

Vera was her alter ego, a playful excuse to look different on purpose. During all her trips to the hospital, she'd met others in much greater pain than she was. It had humbled her and prodded her into action. Now she poured her energy into making others smile. Though her own was painted on, the real smiles of others made her feel a tiny bit useful, a tiny bit needed. Birthday parties and schools, children's homes and hospitals—wherever someone longed for a reason to smile again, Vera the Clown appeared, turning balloons into giraffes and tears into laughter.

Today Vera was her ticket to the parade, her only hope of getting close enough to the Grand Marshal—closer than the crowds on the curb, past the scrutiny of his handlers—so she could present her case and plead for his assistance.

She'd traveled seven hundred miles on the strength of one Web site headline: *Healer to Lead Milwaukee Parade—Record Crowds Expected.*

Two months back she'd scanned the article on her computer screen that described miraculous healings. It was unbelievable. Crazy. The man was apparently proficient at curing all sorts of ailments. His satisfied patients—and their numbers increased daily—insisted that his healing efforts took no time at all. They also appeared to be subsidized by some unnamed source because *the man didn't charge a dime*!

It was too good to be true, of course.

But what if it *was* true?

What if he could help her? What if he could *cure* her?

She didn't let a little thing like common sense get in her way, not after twelve years. It cost her the bulk of her savings and a very long, uncomfortable ride in a crowded bus to land in this Wisconsin city she'd never visited before and knew next to nothing about.

But she had to try. She *had* to!

After all, the medical world had offered few answers, and they'd all sounded like *no*.

No, they weren't certain what caused alopecia areata.

No, it wasn't her fault.

No, there wasn't a cure at the present. It might spontaneously grow back all by itself, or it might not.

Not, it seemed. Not even a little.

Quickly cleaning the grease paint off her hands with a towel, Veronica wagged a finger at her image in the mirror. "If you don't quit sniffling, the parade will start without you." Unthinkable after all she'd gone through to get there.

Baby powder came last. It set the makeup and kept it from melting off in a puddle. Milwaukee in July wasn't as steamy as her screened-in porch back in Dalton, Georgia, but it was still plenty hot. Tipping her head back, she held a cotton sock over her face and shook it, sending a fine mist of powder over her white makeup. She dressed with care, guiding her black-and-white jumpsuit and stiff ruff around her carefully applied features, then reached for the finishing touch: her tall, black-and-white polka-dot hat.

The moment of truth had come.

And with it, another prayer.

Please, let this be the man who can heal me!

Veronica was outside moving among the throng within minutes. All along Lincoln Memorial Drive, floats and marching bands lined up, ready to move at the strike of two. She spotted a troupe of colorful clowns and slipped in among them, nodding and flashing her painted-on smile.

Craning her neck to see how far down the line the Grand Marshal's entourage was, she jumped when a trumpet blast from the lead marching band suddenly launched the Great Circus Parade into motion as a thunderous cheer rose from the crowd.

Here we go!

Vera the Clown would live up to her calling today, she decided, waving at the children and their parents packed ten deep along the curbs. Popcorn, cotton candy, and balloons were everywhere. The deafening sound suited her mime routines well as she worked her way forward, dancing along the periphery of the main attractions. Registered clowns were free to move back and forth near the parade watchers, highly visible yet invisible at the same time.

As the parade rolled down Wisconsin Avenue, she passed the century-old float of "The Old Woman Who Lived in a Shoe" and did an impromptu skit for a child perched atop a six-foot ladder. The elephants had just made the turn north onto Water Street when she found herself mere feet away from the motorcade bearing the guest of honor himself.

The Grand Marshal.

She stopped, rooted to the pavement. He looked so ordinary—yet so extraordinary. His eyes exuded warmth, his hands stretched out to clasp all who came near. The crowd along the sidelines surged toward the car, pushing past the Keystone Cops who were doing their best to protect him.

The Grand Marshal didn't seem the least bit rattled. He wasn't dressed like a clown, but he sure did *laugh* like one. *Look at him, throwing his head back like that!*

Surely she could trust this man. He was joy itself.

Veronica elbowed her way toward the convertible where he sat on top of the backseat—waving, smiling, reaching out, shaking hands.

Touch him.

The impulse seemed to come from outside herself, strong and very insistent. Could touching him really do any good? Wouldn't healing require medicines and tests and office visits and—

Touch him.

Well, it wouldn't hurt to try, she reasoned. He was wearing a white linen sports jacket. Maybe she could just touch *that*. He would hardly notice or care if she—

Touch him.

Veronica was almost on top of the car before she sidestepped the bumper, sparing herself yet another bruise. She slid along the side of the Cadillac convertible, her heart pounding in her throat. His white jacket was in reach now. Eyeing the crisp hem, she stretched out her right hand—it was shaking, but at least it was moving—as the voice in her head grew louder by the second.

Touch him!

She did it. One quick touch, enough to feel the smooth texture of the linen. No one saw her. No one cared. No one—

Ohh!

Something was wrong.

No!

Something was right. Very right.

Her scalp was…was…tingling! A shiver ran up and down her arms.

Underneath her oversize hat, she felt an odd sensation, a strange heaviness on the crown of her head. She couldn't bring herself to slip a hand underneath her hat, but she knew *something* was happening, no doubt about that.

"Oh!" She said it out loud this time. Not very loud, but loud enough. She shrank back, hoping he wouldn't notice her.

But he did. "Driver, stop the car please." The motorcade came to a sudden stop as he straightened taller still. "Who touched me?" His voice was like the ocean, vast and deep, almost frightening.

Two of the closest Keystone Cops leaned toward him. "What, are you kiddin'? This big a crowd, and you wanna know who touched you?"

Up and down the street, gigantic floats and gaily decorated caravans slowly ground to a halt, realizing there was some delay. Elephants trumpeted impatiently, swinging their trunks around. Caged lions roared as their trainers gazed down the parade line, wondering what the holdup might be. Clowns and parade goers alike drew closer, trying to see what had happened, staring right at her as she stood trembling a few feet behind the Grand Marshal.

He waited in silence for an answer.

Though it surely was her imagination, the whole of Milwaukee seemed to wait as well.

Veronica finally stepped forward, her face hotter than the July sun. "I...I d-did it. I touched you."

He turned to her with eyes full of compassion. "Did it help?"

She nodded her head, afraid if she said the words it would no longer be true.

The crowd grew quieter still, straining to hear him. Even the birds that swooped down for a closer look withheld their cries.

"If you are well," he asked at last, "then why aren't you smiling?"

So she smiled. Just a little, hardly much.

How good it felt! How right. Her smile broadened until it almost hurt her cheeks. She felt the heavy grease paint and powder creasing beneath the unfamiliar pull of her facial muscles.

His smile grew wider too as he leaned forward and grabbed the brim of her hat.

"Stop!" Instinctively her hands flew to her head in protection, remembering all the times meanspirited kids had yanked off her wig. Surely he wouldn't...

Surely he did.

He swept off her hat with a flourish.

"Nooo...ohh, my!"

As if released from prison, a headful of glorious brunette hair escaped from the hat and cascaded over her shoulders.

Hair. It was...*hair. Her own hair!*

The curly brown locks she hadn't seen in a dozen years bounced along her shoulders like an old friend.

A furtive glance at her outstretched arms confirmed what she suspected. Both forearms were covered with a fine, dark glisten. She lifted a shaky hand and felt an eyebrow—a real one, not drawn on—hiding beneath her makeup, with thick eyelashes framing the fresh tears that were surely ruining her clown face for good.

"So." His grin was very contagious indeed. "How do you feel?"

"I feel…" She gulped. "I feel…*whole!*"

All at once she made a sound. A funny sound, the sound joy might make if joy had a voice. Light and airy, like wispy clouds without a hint of darkness behind them.

"Ha!" There it was again, that joyful sound.

She looked up, as though in a trance, and realized that everyone within earshot was waiting, eyes wide, mouths agape, no doubt wanting to know what this miracle man had accomplished.

Of course!

They didn't know, but she did.

Tell them!

"I have…" She faltered, then gulped and blurted out, "*Had*, that is…no hair."

Several clowns drew closer, nodding, offering their support as she described her struggles. Her gaze inched higher, meeting the Grand Marshal's eyes, then dipped down again in embarrassment, remembering all those years of feeling different. She admitted softly, "People can't bear to look at me, let alone…touch me."

"Ah." The Grand Marshal spoke again. "Did you think touching my jacket would make you well?"

"Yes," she whispered. "And…it did."

"It wasn't the jacket, child." He patted her hand then turned to wave at the crowds again. "Your faith has healed you. Go and join the others now."

As if cued by an unseen hand, up and down the parade route marching bands struck up a cheerful cacophony of sound. The elephants lumbered forward, and the antique caravans turned their wheels once more.

Veronica watched as all around her clowns did jigs and handsprings, tossing their many-colored hats into the summer air and leaping with joyful abandon. Within seconds they were calling her by name, pulling her into the dance, embracing her as one of their own.

When the Grand Marshal's motorcade rolled out of sight, Veronica waved, shouting her thanks, drowned out by the celebration that swirled around her.

It was a sight to see, a parade that no one in Milwaukee ever forgot. The clowns with sad painted faces were laughing, and the ones with happy faces were crying, and one clown with curly brown hair couldn't stop singing, "I love a parade!"

○

Miracle on Main Street: The Bleeding Woman

Ah, dear Jesus.

You always hung out with the ill and infirm, didn't you?

Called on the sick, the hospitalized, the bedridden—every day, not just, say, Tuesday mornings. Never worried about catching some incurable disease. Offered your hands to strangers, willing to touch anyone who was ready to be healed.

Luke, himself a doctor,[1] must have loved writing down your words for his gospel account: "It is not the healthy who need a doctor, but the sick."[2]

Luke healed with medicines.

You heal with miracles.

Once upon a time you were on your way to Jairus's house to spare a young girl from an untimely death, when a miracle seeker furtively reached for the hem of your garment and stopped you in your tracks.

Walk us through the story, Lord. It's one of our favorites because it infuses us with endless hope and unspeakable joy.

We are, every one of us, sick.

Please make us well.

> Then one of the synagogue rulers, named Jairus,
> came there. Seeing Jesus, he fell at his feet and pleaded
> earnestly with him, "My little daughter is dying."
> *Mark 5:22–23*

What does this little girl have to do with our hurting woman?

Patience, beloved. She's right around the corner.

In his version of the biblical story, Dr. Luke tells us that the little girl was about twelve.[3] Her papa was a major player, a ruler in the church. Yet illness, that great human leveler, brought Jairus to Jesus as a humble beggar—not a haughty big shot—pleading for the life of his dying daughter.

> "Please come and put your hands on her so that she will
> be healed and live." *Mark 5:23*

That was all Jesus needed to hear. This grief-stricken father believed Jesus' touch could make a difference, so Jesus agreed to help. Period. He didn't run a multitude of medical tests or ascertain Jairus's ability to pay. After all, Jesus didn't take money for his miracles.

Let me say that again: *Jesus didn't take money for his miracles.*

When someone promises you a miracle then quotes you a fee, that someone is not Jesus.

> So Jesus went with him. *Mark 5:24*

Just like that, no questions asked.

The promise is unmistakable: Jesus, who often commanded other people, "Follow me," is also willing to follow us, to meet us where we are, to go where he's most needed.

When you're that kind of leader—a servant leader—people will follow you without even being asked.

> A large crowd followed and pressed around him.
> *Mark 5:24*

Honey, they pressed him flat as a pair of dress pants! In fact, they "thronged behind" (NLT) and "almost crushed him."[4] It makes the hairs on the back of my neck stand up just to picture it. I'm fairly claustrophobic anyway, especially when people are jammed all around me—say, at a large speaking engagement—and everybody is trying to catch my eye at the same time. Even as I'm smiling and shaking hands, genuinely grateful, inside I feel dizzy, and my stomach rolls over and begs for mercy, and I pray I won't faint.

If only I could be more like Jesus. He was accustomed to people pressing against him, tugging at his sleeve, tapping his shoulder, snagging his elbow, doing all the things we do to capture someone's attention.

Everywhere he went, exciting things happened, so of course, no one wanted to miss the parade. Some came seeking help for loved ones too sick to rise from their beds. Others came asking for healing for themselves, which is invariably tougher and more humiliating.

Not "Will you help my daughter?" but "Will you help...um, me?"

When my children are sick, calling their pediatrician for an appointment is as natural as breathing. I know his phone number and the Higgs chart location by heart. But when some infernal bug takes up residence in my own body, I hem and haw and find a dozen excuses for not visiting the doctor:

"I'm too busy."

"I'll feel better tomorrow."

"All they'll say is I'm sick. I *know* I'm sick."

"It's too expensive."

"There's nothing they can do for this anyhow."

Ring any bells, sis? It's hard for do-it-all women to admit we're hurting and need help.

This woman we're about to meet was smarter than that. She knew she needed help.

> And a woman was there who had been subject to bleeding
> for twelve years. *Mark 5:25*

Just "a woman," no name. Just "there," part of the scenery. I think of her as the Woman at the (Un)Well. This poor, anonymous sister had a serious medical condition that went on and on and on for a dozen years.

That's right—twelve years, the same number of years that Jairus's daughter had been alive. That's how long this unidentified woman had been bleeding without ceasing.

Five days each *month* does me in.

Think about 4,380 days in a row…

She had a nonstop "hemorrhage" (NLT) or "flow of blood" (NKJV), what we would delicately call a "female problem." Even in our no-holds-barred twenty-first century, if you tell folks you have "female problems," they ask *no* further questions.

Except those of us who are naturally curious. What *was* this woman's medical dilemma, do you suppose? Her constant bleeding could have been "fibroid tumors, or an endocrine gland disturbance…or a tear in the cervix, or it could have been a polyp."[5]

Ugh to all of 'em.

Today's surgical procedures might have made her right as rain in no time. Two thousand years ago, though, a woman suffered in silence—and shame—since the list of restrictions for a bleeding woman was lengthy and tedious, quickly turning her into a social outcast.

In ancient times there was "nothing casual or optional in the demand for cleanness."[6] I'll say! They considered it life-or-death important, and Mosaic Law brooked no argument on this one.

"When a woman has a discharge of blood for many days at a time other than her monthly period…she will be unclean as long as she has the discharge." *Leviticus 15:25*

A dozen years of being unclean.

A dozen years of no houseguests, no public events, no potlucks.

A dozen years of no husband, no children, no visits from family.

A dozen years of never being touched by anyone. Ever.

To be considered "unclean" was to be unwelcome and unwanted. Not only was her body unclean, but so was the bed she slept in and the chairs she sat on.[7] And it wasn't just inanimate objects she threatened with her low hygiene rating. If other people touched those things, they, too, were "unclean" and had to wash their clothes and bathe with water and wouldn't be considered clean again until past sundown, the start of the next day.[8]

My heavens.

What a good way to lose friends. What a horrid way to live.

People back then really *did* believe cleanliness was next to godliness. Since this woman never *got* clean and sullied everything in sight, it's pretty obvious where that left her: right at Satan's doorstep. Demons, after all, were called "unclean spirits,"[9] so you can imagine what people whispered behind her back.

"A spawn of the devil, that one!"

"Cursed, I'd say."

"People won't go near her place."

"Whatever she's got, it's catching."

"I knew it! Must be Beelzebub's daughter."

Though no evidence suggests she was a Bad Girl, morally speaking, the fact is, her community would have seen her as very bad. Dangerous to be around. A terrible role model for young girls. And deserving of her ailment because of her supposedly sinful life.

On another occasion Jesus was preparing to heal a blind man when his disciples asked, "Rabbi, who sinned, this man or his parents, that he was born blind?"[10] To their first-century way of thinking, sin and disease walked hand in hand. Blindness had a cause—not a physical one, a moral one. He was blind because of sin.

This woman's bleeding, then, would have been blamed on her parents or viewed as punishment for her own moral failures. Determined to get well—and prove her detractors wrong—she turned to the medicine men of her day.

Wrong turn, I'm afraid.

> She had suffered a great deal under the care of many
> doctors...

Quacks might be more accurate, and I don't mean the kind with feathers and webbed feet.

The Talmud described myriad remedies for her constant issue of blood, with off-the-wall ingredients like garden crocuses dissolved in wine, sawdust from a lotus tree mixed with the curdled milk of a hare, and ashes from an ostrich egg worn around the neck in a linen bag.[11]

Not exactly FDA-approved, this stuff.

In fact, most of these so-called prescriptions boiled down to a simple astringent or pure hocus-pocus.

Anemic, frustrated, and depressed, our unnamed, unloved woman knocked on one healer's door after another. Arriving full of hope that this time she'd be cured, she soon departed with her heart in tatters, knowing "they had not done anything except cause her a lot of pain" (CEV).

And cost her a lot of money.

> ...and [she] had spent all she had,...

Whether she had a little or a lot to begin with, eventually it ran out, as money always does.

> ...yet instead of getting better she grew worse.
> *Mark 5:26*

Groan.

Emotionally bled dry, she surely despaired when her body refused to follow suit but instead kept right on bleeding. With her resources gone and her health deteriorating, the woman's frail grip on hope was slipping fast. Dr. Luke himself admitted, "No one could heal her."[12]

She couldn't even ask *God* to help her because, by law, she couldn't go into the temple.

So God solved that problem.

He came out of the temple and into the streets where she could approach him one-on-one.

When she heard about Jesus,...

Ooh, what did she hear, I wonder? That he healed the blind, the sick, the lame? That he loved those who were outcasts? That he didn't condemn them? Another translation says, "She had heard the reports" (AMP). I'll just bet she did! Good news travels fast.

In her heart a tiny flame of hope leaped into a consuming fire.

If Eusebius's history is right, the woman traveled nearly thirty miles *on foot*—from Caesarea Philippi to Capernaum—just to seek out Jesus.[13] A tough trek if you're healthy and wearing new Reeboks. But for a woman to walk thirty miles, apparently alone and critically ill...what faith!

And what a desperate cry for help.

Did she sing the old psalm as she trudged along? "I wait for the LORD, my soul waits, and in his word I put my hope." [14]

Something must have kept her weary feet moving forward. Her journey toward freedom required two days of walking, minimum. Sleeping by the side of the road—if one could call it sleep, if she dared close her eyes. Her money was gone, remember. No denarii for so much as a flea-bitten bed or floor space in a leaky-roofed inn.

And the bleeding, the endless bleeding. Secretly changing and washing the bloodstained cloths, praying she wouldn't be identified as "that woman," the one with the issue, the one who was cursed because of her sin.

Along the route her feet may have been bleeding as well, cut and bruised by the tiny, sharp stones that slipped between sandals and flesh. Thirsty, exhausted, drained in every sense of the word, she found her way to the streets of Capernaum, where throngs of people were pushing and shoving around a central figure.

The man in the middle had his back to her. Could it be... Was it...

Yes!

The time had come for a miracle.

But first she had to be exceedingly brave. Like young Arthur with his small hands wrapped around the pommel of the sword and praying for courage as he faced the blade in the stone, she risked public failure and disappointment by touching that which was sacred and powerful.

Not that anybody was really watching her. In that place? Huh-uh. It was nuts. People everywhere. Voices shouting, "Rabbi! Master, over here!" She had no intention of calling out or drawing attention to herself. A touch, that was all she needed. *One touch.*

This silent, valiant woman, her face covered with the dirt of thirty miles and the tears of a dozen years, reached out one unclean hand. She dared not touch his skin and contaminate him. Even touching his clothes broke the sacred Jewish laws of cleanliness.

Did the voices in her head scream their accusation?

Bad girl! Don't touch!

Bad or good, she'd come all that way in search of a miracle. No turning back now. Her feet carried her forward.

> ...she came up behind him in the crowd and touched his
> cloak,... *Mark 5:27*

Not at the shoulder, not on the sleeve—the bottom. The very "fringe of his robe" (NLT).

The hope-filled humility of it astounds me.

She who had been unclean so long that it felt normal still believed she would be made whole and well if she could reach out to this Jesus, who wasn't even looking her direction. Though she's often called "the woman with the issue of blood," I love this label: "the woman who touched Jesus."[15] It captures her scandalous behavior in a heartbeat!

No one had touched her or allowed her to touch them in twelve years. Yet she dared touch the Messiah.

There's a big difference between brushing against someone and touching them. One is accidental, the other is intentional. One is in passing, the other is on purpose. One might be rough, the other is almost certainly tender.

With a humble spirit and a bent body, she touched him with the only thing she had left: her faith. "Being sure of what we hope for and certain of what we do not see"[16]—*that* kind of faith. Serious faith, not in herself but in him.

Her faith in him to heal her.

Without a word, without a look, without a touch of his hand.

With only a *thread.*

> …because she thought, "If I just touch his clothes, I will be healed." *Mark 5:28*

Shhh! Did you hear that? Something happened.

> Immediately her bleeding stopped…

Listen. You think God doesn't see your hurts, your needs, your sorrow?

Stretch out your hand. When you are ready for God, *God is more than ready for you.*

This woman was *ready.*

After four thousand days "the fountain of her blood" (NKJV) literally "dried up at the source" (AMP).

Somebody shout, "Hallelujah!"

...and she felt in her body that she was freed from her suffering. *Mark 5:29*

Freed! Sisters, "if the Son sets you free, you will be free indeed."[17] Amen and amen!

Here *freedom* is another word for *healing*—"she was healed of her affliction" (NASB). She knew the blood stopped because she *felt* it in her body. She didn't simply *think* her suffering was over; it was *gone*.

Ever been nearby when a fountain was turned off? The water abruptly stops, followed by an eerie stillness as you realize how much racket that fountain made.

Her disease was like that—noisy, demanding, draining.

Until it stopped. *Ahhh.* Relief.

It was a Jesus kind of healing, all right. When we're treated by physicians and their medications, the healing is gradual, over days, weeks, even months. Shakespeare wrote, "What wound did ever heal but by degrees?"[18]

Well, sir...here's one.

Physical wounds that heal quickly are surprising, but spiritual wounds that heal on the spot are just plain suspect. When people are forgiven of their sins—those big, ugly, in-your-face kind of sins—we seem to want their recovery to take awhile. Face it: We want them to *pay.* We want them to *suffer* a little; we want them to *appreciate* that grace.

Maybe that's what *we* want.

But what Jesus wants to do is heal us and set us free *right now.*

What he does in the physical, he does in the spiritual and in the emotional as well: He makes us whole.

At once Jesus realized that power had gone out from him. *Mark 5:30*

"At once," huh? As I said, the Lord does not waste time.

Eugene Peterson's spin on this verse makes my scalp tingle like a lightning storm filling the air with static electricity: "Jesus felt energy discharging from him" (MSG).

Zap!

The word *energy* here—in Greek, *dunamis*—can be variously translated "power," "strength," *and* "miracle." He not only sensed power flowing out of him; it was miraculous, life-changing power at that!

When I studied the *King James Version,* which states that "virtue had gone out of him," I got concerned. *Virtue?* You mean his *goodness* leaked out? No, silly Liz. Tap into those four years of high-school Latin. The word *virtus* means "strength and manliness."

Jesus flat-out *empowered* the woman.

> He turned around in the crowd and asked, "Who touched
> my clothes?" *Mark 5:30*

Her heart must have thudded to a halt!

Did he know who she was? Had he seen her? Would she be punished? Would she—please no!—start bleeding again?

Oh my, oh my.

She hadn't touched his skin, only the hem of his garment—how could Jesus have discerned it? Such is the mystery of a miracle. He hadn't felt her presence with his body; he felt it with his spirit, for "a touch of faith could not be hidden from Him."[19]

It was, as usual, hidden from the disciples.

> "You see the people crowding against you," his disciples
> answered, "and yet you can ask, 'Who touched me?'"
> *Mark 5:31*

These guys miss so much I sometimes think of them as the *duh*-sciples. You can almost hear the sarcasm dripping from their words. What they were really saying, of course, was "Get serious, boss. Look at the size of this crowd!"

But Jesus kept looking around to see who had done it.
Mark 5:32

He knew the power had gone out of him and that the woman was already healed. Why do you suppose he was still looking for her? I think he wanted to touch her back in some way, to acknowledge her value and celebrate her victory. Isn't it glorious that he stopped following Jairus—an important man with a name and a valued position—to minister to an insignificant, unnamed woman?

He had time for her, dear one.

He has time for you.

For Jesus, "interruptions were opportunities."[20] Having healed her, now he could help her reclaim her identity in the community and glorify God in the process.

It was time for her to raise her hand and say, "I'm here, Lord."

Once again she had to be brave.

Then the woman, knowing what had happened to her,...

She knew. He knew. It was time to go public and let everyone know.

...came and fell at his feet...

Despite the fact that she was "alarmed and frightened" (AMP), an overwhelming desire to abandon herself in a posture of worship swept over her. She didn't come forward for healing. *She was already healed.* She came forward to say "thank you," gratitude being one of the steady beats of a heart turned toward worship.

...and, trembling with fear, told him the whole truth.
Mark 5:33

As in "the whole truth and nothing but the truth."

Notice, Jesus did not ask her to do anything more than present herself.

That alone was a big step for her. But when a woman is set free as she was—as I was, as many of us have been—she will tell anyone who'll listen, "I was broken, but now I'm whole!"

> In the presence of all the people, she told why she had
> touched him and how she had been instantly healed.
> *Luke 8:47*

Perhaps at first only Jesus and the disciples were paying attention, straining to hear this woman's soft voice amidst all the hubbub. Soon, however, people began to hush one another. A thick blanket of quiet anticipation unfurled over the scene.

Faces registered amazement. Mouths began hanging agape.

She had *what*?

And he did *what*?

Not only was the blood gone, her *shame* was gone as well. By confessing her story, by speaking the "whole truth" perhaps for the first time in her life, she was healed and whole in every way. Not a drop of blood remained on her soul.

By listening to her testimony, "the community was healed and made whole too."[21]

And what was Jesus doing while she poured out her private thoughts in this very public venue? Simply looking at her. Listening with his eyes and ears and heart. Augustine wrote, "God loves each of us as if there were only one of us to love!"[22]

At last he spoke. A gentle reminder, girls: Rabbis did not speak to women in public. As usual, Jesus broke a rule that needed breaking.

> He said to her, "Daughter, your faith has healed you."
> *Mark 5:34*

"Daughter." Oh, we like that! So personal and familiar and yet honorable. It is the only gospel account where Jesus addressed a woman as "daughter,"[23] suggesting that she was a younger woman, though in no way young enough to be his own daughter.

She was now, however, in the greatest sense *family*.

On his way to heal Jairus's daughter, he'd paused to minister to this "daughter" with a tender word of encouragement. If there were other women in that crowd, they got the message loud and clear: Jesus thought women were important. Worth stopping for. Worth listening to. Worth talking to. Worth ministering to. Worth healing. "With one blessing, he proclaimed female bodies holy."[24]

And check this out: He didn't take credit for healing her! He credited her faith—not his power. What can that mean? I think it means we participate in our own healing. We can't do it without him, of course. *But he won't do it without us.* Ever the gentleman, he waits for us to reach toward him. Our demonstrated faith—"your trust and confidence in Me, springing from faith in God" (AMP)—against all odds and reason, is what identifies us as daughters of the King.

A word of caution here: Don't put your faith in the garment he was wearing. He healed with water, with mud, with a word, with a touch, not wanting us to make a ritual out of anything. His cloak was a conduit for his power, not the power itself.

Magic cloths and expensive vials of "healing water" are little more than powerless placebos. The word *healed* in this passage is the Greek word *sesoken—saved*.[25] And salvation is found in Christ alone. We are healed in the way that matters most—spiritually—when we are saved by the One who loves us most.

Having been saved, she was now sent.

> "Go in peace and be freed from your suffering."
> *Mark 5:34*

Get out there, new woman! No more hiding in your house. You now have peace with God and you are "free for ever from this trouble" (NEB).

Not from *all* trouble, mind you, but at least *this* bloody one was con-
quered.

Such a happy send-off: "Live well, live blessed!" (MSG).

By the way, if you've been wondering what happened to Jairus's daughter while Jesus lingered to heal this woman, the answer is, she died.

She *what*?

Yup. Dead. No pulse, no breath, no kidding.

Death never stopped Jesus.

> Jesus told the synagogue ruler, "Don't be afraid; just believe."
> *Mark 5:36*

Witnesses laughed at him, but Jesus ignored their scorn and went into
the young girl's room. Taking her by the hand, he commanded her to get up.
Immediately the girl stood up and walked around…

> At this they were completely astonished. *Mark 5:42*

Was he late getting to this little girl? On the contrary. He was right
on time. He healed the Bleeding Woman, knowing the child would die,
thereby giving him an even greater opportunity to reveal the power of God.
He never wastes time. He never ignores our needs. He knocks on our door
at precisely the right moment to create maximum impact for the gospel.

In the scenes that follow this one in Mark's gospel, it's evident that news
of the Bleeding Woman's miraculous recovery traveled ahead of Jesus like a
frontman for the circus.

> And wherever he went—into villages, towns or countryside—
> they placed the sick in the marketplaces. They begged him
> to let them touch even the edge of his cloak, and all who
> touched him were healed. *Mark 6:56*

Aha! They'd heard about that touch-his-cloak move, all right!

Even at story's end we still don't know her name, yet her demonstration of faith has already spanned two millennia, with no sign of losing power. The early church had a name for her though. They called her "Veronica."[26]

A beautiful name, don't you think?

The legends that surround this first-century Veronica are cloaked in mystery. One has it that on Christ's slow, painful journey to Calvary, she followed alongside him and wiped his brow dripping with sweat and blood. Such cloths came to be known as Veronicas,[27] sold for their supposed healing powers. To this day, Catholics celebrate Saint Veronica's Feast Day every July 12.[28]

Another tradition holds that she erected two bronze statues outside her home, one of a woman on bended knee with hands stretched out, the other of the Savior reaching toward her in compassion. In front of them grew a plant that offered a "marvelous antidote to many diseases."[29] Specifically, the plant "Veronica Speedwell" is an ancient remedy used to purify the blood.[30] Well, well. Again an attempt to capture supernatural power in a nothing-but-natural object.

We know the truth. So did the real Veronica.

Our only hope for true healing is Jesus.

Remember our fictional Veronica who introduced this chapter? The characteristics of alopecia areata were first described by Cornelius Celsus in A.D. 30.[31]

That's right, A.D. 30. The time of Christ.

He has been healing our hurts for two thousand years, dear sister. Stretch out your hand and be whole.

> There is balm in Gilead
>> to make the wounded whole.
> There is a balm in Gilead
>> to heal the sin-sick soul.

What Lessons Can We Learn
from the Bleeding Woman?

Hope does not disappoint.

Many of us fear we'd lose hope if an illness dragged on for years as hers did. Clearly she was a woman who allowed her suffering to refine her character into sterling silver. All around us that same miracle is taking place among women battling cancer, diabetes, heart disease, and other life-threatening illnesses. As we support and encourage them, so shall they teach us a new meaning of the word *hope.*

> Suffering produces perseverance; perseverance, character; and character, hope. And hope does not disappoint us, because God has poured out his love into our hearts by the Holy Spirit whom he has given us. *Romans 5:3–5*

Jesus is well-acquainted with bleeding.

Consider this: The Lord stopped her flow of blood even as he prepared to shed his own blood that the whole world might live. As women who understand only too well what it means to bleed, we are grateful that her endless flow ceased. But we're exceedingly more grateful that the blood of Jesus has not stopped flowing for two thousand years. It is in his blood that we find our freedom!

> In him we have redemption through his blood, the forgiveness of sins, in accordance with the riches of God's grace. *Ephesians 1:7*

Know your source of power.

Women love to talk about empowerment. We've been encouraged to take charge of our lives and to stop letting our present circumstances—or the people around us—determine our future. This woman did everything she could to make her life better, yet it was only when she put her faith in Jesus that she found the life-changing power she'd been looking for. True empowerment comes in realizing that our own power is limited—make that laughable—and God's power is limitless. Let go of your do-it-yourself battery pack, and plug into the *real* power generator.

> His divine power has given us everything we need for life and godliness through our knowledge of him who called us by his own glory and goodness. *2 Peter 1:3*

Faith is a gift.

This woman had the faith to stretch out her hand and expect a miracle. Where does faith like that come from? Do we build it up ourselves by reading motivational or inspiring books, by improving our self-talk, by watching other faith-filled people in action? Those activities are not without value—but they're not the source of faith. It comes from God. It is a *gift*. Watch the progression: He *gives* us the desire to seek him. When we act on that desire, he *gives* us the faith to believe in him. When we believe in him, he *gives* us the power to confess his name. When we confess his name, he *gives* us grace and forgiveness of sins. When we receive his grace, he *gives* us eternal life. It isn't us, babe—it's *him*! He starts the process *and* he completes it!

> Let us fix our eyes on Jesus, the author and perfecter of our faith. *Hebrews 12:2*

Rebel's Heart

What would happen if one woman
told the truth about her life?
The world would be split open.

Muriel Rukeyser

I am a rebel, through and through.

I did, however, change my allegiance—from the prince of this world to the Prince of Peace. Because he loves me, he is teaching me daily to stop fighting his leadership and relax under his grace-filled command. I'm not fully relaxed yet...but I am at least sitting down!

Rebellion was born in the Garden of Eden, in the heart of a woman and a man who both sinned against God. Though humankind has never stopped sinning, God has never stopped offering forgiveness, despite the depths to which we sink trying to escape his all-seeing eye.

Listen to Lizzie. No matter what you've done, "God is not shockable."[1] Whatever your particular pit might be, he sees you there, he loves you there, and he stands ready to carry you out.

It has not been my goal to shock you, dear reader, by including my own stories from my sinful past. Be assured, my walk with God today is as solid as a Rock. But if I deny my past before I knew him—and my daily failings now—I miss the opportunity to honor the one who loves me "as is" and to serve him in the ministry to which he has called me.

My intent has never been to glorify sin. Quite the opposite. Seeing my foolish actions on paper takes away any of their glamour, excitement, or mystery. They show themselves to be what they were and still are: sin.

The truth?

I care little what you think of Liz, beloved. I care only what you think of this Jesus who died that you might be set free from the pain, shame, and burdens of your past. Putting mine on paper doesn't bind them to me; it frees me of their power to hurt me any longer.

If we point out the sins of others, it's judgment.

If we point out our own sins, it's confession.

And when we confess our weaknesses, we give others permission to confess their own.

Oh, dear heart, how I long for you to know that kind of freedom! These words, written by the apostle Paul to young Timothy, are the very heartbeat of my life in Christ. I pray you'll embrace them as your own.

> Here is a trustworthy saying that deserves full acceptance:
> Christ Jesus came into the world to save sinners—of whom I
> am the worst. But for that very reason I was shown mercy so
> that in me, the worst of sinners, Christ Jesus might display
> his unlimited patience as an example for those who would
> believe on him and receive eternal life. *1 Timothy 1:15–16*

Amen and amen. Love you, sis.

Spoken Word:
Lord, We're Talking Some Really Bad Girls Here

Athaliah and Herodias were a mean and murderous pair.
Different eras, equal loathing for things honorable or fair.
Mother-daughter skills were lacking,
Bad-Girl traits beyond compare.

Fair Bathsheba and the Medium learned the truth one moonlit night:
When the king's men come a knockin', it can give a girl a fright.
Do his bidding, you're a Bad Girl—
Little chance to do what's right.

Hostess Jael, well-veiled Tamar lured their men into a trap.
Female wiles their sharpened weapons, Good-Girl heart, but Bad-Girl rap.
One man killed, another humbled.
All who heard were quick to clap.

In a crowd appeared two women, one by choice, the other not.
One was bleeding, one was silent; both were hurting, both were caught.
Both set free, washed clean, forgiven,
So a lesson could be taught.

If you call yourself a Bad Girl, sister mine, you have a choice.
Put your faith in One who loves you; hear his tender, mighty voice.
Feel his power, know his freedom,
Shout his glory, girl. Rejoice!

LIZ CURTIS HIGGS

Discussion Questions

If your book club will be exploring *Really Bad Girls of the Bible* in a single session, here are eight questions to spark your conversation. Or use them to enrich your personal takeaway when you've finished reading the book.

1. Regarding the Medium of En Dor, consider this statement: "Though her actions appeared good, her motives and beliefs were wrong."[1] Do you agree or disagree? How did you reach that conclusion? What's your definition of a really bad person? What might God's definition be?

2. In the story of Jael, why do you suppose God allowed Sisera to escape death on the battlefield only to die hours later at the hand of Jael? What lesson might there have been for the Israelites? For the Canaanites? For Jael? And for us today?

3. During his encounter with the adulterous woman, Jesus wrote in the dust of the temple floor. What do you think he might have written, and why? Do you believe it was his spoken words or his written words that drove the Pharisees away that day?

4. How do you suppose evil Athaliah justified to herself her violent actions? And how might she have convinced others to support her for six long years? If you've ever worked for an unethical employer, did you confront that person regarding his or her actions? If so, what was the result?

5. When David abandoned his duties as a soldier, trouble soon followed. And when Bathsheba abandoned her duties as a wife,

things got worse. Describe a time when you tried to avoid some unpleasant duty and then found yourself in hot water. What did you learn from the experience? And what will you do differently next time?

6. Herodias was anything but a good wife and mother. Then and now, manipulation and a deep need for control are often factors that lead a family into dysfunctional behavior. What other factors could there be? Consider some practical ways to stop the generational cycle of dysfunction and to move toward healthier family relationships.

7. When Tamar and Judah had their rendezvous on the road to Timnah, who committed the greater sin—Tamar, the pretend prostitute, or Judah, the paying customer? Do you believe God views sins in categories—bad, really bad, horrific? What makes you say that? And how could you support your answer biblically?

8. What if instead of healing the Bleeding Woman, Jesus had given her sufficient strength to bear the pain for another dozen years? Would that also have been a form of grace? If he answered your prayers for healing by giving you the courage to go on instead of curing you, how would you continue to trust in his goodness and glorify his name?

Study Guide

This in-depth guide is designed especially for Bible study groups. Whether you meet for four sessions, eight sessions, or several months, these chapter-by-chapter questions should enrich your learning experience. You can also use this guide and the other resources mentioned here for your personal growth.

Acquired knowledge is a good thing; applied knowledge is even better. So we'll look at how we can incorporate into our daily lives the truths we're gleaning from these less-than-perfect women. You'll need a place to write your answers—a notebook, a computer, a tablet, whatever works—and a few moments in your busy day to let God's Word sink in.

You'll also find on Vimeo a series of free videos for this study, one for each chapter. Each segment is ten-to-twelve minutes long and can be played through your computer. Go to http://vimeo.com/lizcurtishiggs /videos. Plus, a free Leader's Guide for *Really Bad Girls of the Bible* awaits you at http://tinyurl.com/RBGStudy. And if you or someone in your study prefers to listen rather than read, the *Really Bad Girls of the Bible* audio book is available from ChristianAudio.com.

However you choose to enhance your reading, if you have a heart willing to be changed and a mind willing to be stretched, our God has something amazing planned for you!

Chapter One
Dead Man Talking
Medium of En Dor

Read chapter 1 (pages 11–36).

1. I wrote the opening story about Dora from Peoria on a dark, wind-swept night when my family was out of town and our old farmhouse was empty. Too empty. By the time I finished, every light in the place was blazing! You, too, may want to turn on a few more lights as you consider this ghostly story about a woman who dabbled in the occult at the bidding of a doomed king.

   a. In 1 Samuel 15:23 the words "sin" and "evil" make it clear what God thinks of our Really Bad Girl's activities. Have you ever been drawn—even a little—to horoscopes, fortune-tellers, phone psychics, tarot cards, séances, or Ouija boards? Is the fact that God says in his Word, "Don't do it!" sufficient motivation to keep your distance? What makes these dark activities attractive to certain people?

   b. For some of us, rebelliousness came early in our lives. How might the plea of King David in Psalm 25:7 apply to your life? And what do 1 Samuel 12:15 and Psalm 107:17 teach us about having a rebellious nature?

   c. Addressing the Daughter of Babylon—in truth, an entire nation—the prophet Isaiah railed against the same sins we've seen in the life of the Medium of En Dor, a spiritist who employed magic spells and sorcery. Isaiah 47:10 describes two lies that people who are deceived tell themselves. What are the consequences of believing those lies, according to Isaiah 47:11? Perhaps you've mumbled similar statements under your breath, as I once did. What does David call such people in Psalm 14:1? How has God shown you the futility of that kind of thinking?

2. Many aspects of the scene described in 1 Samuel 28:12–19 challenge our understanding of life after death. All the more reason to examine each verse closely and see what God could be teaching us.

   a. In 1 Samuel 28:12–14 why do you think the Medium of En Dor screamed? How would you explain the medium seeing Samuel yet Saul not seeing him? Was God rewarding the medium's efforts or punishing Saul for seeking her out—or could there have been some other divine purpose?

   b. Continuing with the story in 1 Samuel 28:15–19, how many times in these five verses did Samuel say "the LORD"? Surely a medium, accustomed to consorting with evil spirits, wouldn't risk speaking God's name so boldly, so often? What might that suggest about who was actually doing the talking?

   c. Since God clearly told his people he found such practices detestable, how can we come to grips with this seemingly effective séance? Look at Daniel 2:27–28. What does Daniel say God can do that those trafficking in the dark arts cannot? And according to 1 John 4:2–3, what does the Spirit of God do that the spirit of the Antichrist does not? What assurance do you find in these verses that God was in charge of this eerie scene, start to finish?

3. In truth, the medium had little or nothing to do with Samuel's appearance. Rather, it was a miraculous, utterly God-ordained event created for a specific purpose, delivering a final, humbling blow to Saul.

   a. In 1 Samuel 28:19 what did Samuel explain would happen on the battlefield the next day? Now read Psalm 39:4. David wasn't actually asking God to tell him the day he would die. What *was* David asking?

   b. According to Psalm 139:16b, does the Lord know the exact moment we will die? When was that date and time determined? How could the fact that the Lord knows the number of your days—and you do not—give you a measure of peace? How can you release any need to know what your future holds and simply trust God?

   Read 1 Samuel 28:3–25 once more. What's the most important lesson you learned from the shadowy figure of the Medium of En Dor?

CHAPTER TWO
Lethal Weapon
Jael

Read chapter 2 (pages 37–62).

1. My, isn't this a gruesome tale? It's tempting to skip such stories in Scripture, violent as they are. But if they're included in God's Word, you can be sure there's a positive, life-changing lesson to be learned amid the sharp, pointy objects. Namely, God is in control.

    a. Read Judges 4:1–3. Without a godly leader what happened to the Israelites? How long did the Israelites suffer under Sisera's oppression before they realized they needed help? And to whom did they cry out? What does Isaiah 46:4 tell us about God's ability to rescue his people? Think of an instance in your life when you were aware of God rescuing you. How might you share your story with others to encourage them?

    b. At last a godly leader is introduced in Judges 4:4. What three titles or roles did Deborah have, and what could each one tell us about her? What does 1 Samuel 16:7 reveal about how God chooses leaders— in this case, young David? According to Psalm 47:8, no matter who sits on an earthly throne, who is really sovereign?

    c. Judges 4:4 and 4:17 name the husbands of the two women in our story, Deborah and Jael, both of whom acted independently of their men. Married or single, we

are called to consult the Lord above all human counsel.
Romans 12:2 gives us a succinct method of seeking
God's will on a matter. According to that verse, what is
our responsibility?

2. When the battle lines were drawn, Judge Deborah was on the
scene. Though she did not wield a sword, she nonetheless wielded
great power.

   a. Read Deborah's message to Barak in Judges 4:14. What
was her command? To whom did she give credit—twice?
David's victory song in Psalm 18:39 would suit Deborah
well, as would Psalm 33:16–22. How could she be a role
model for you in serving the Lord on your own daily
fronts?

   b. When Sisera escaped from the battlefield, he ran right
into God's perfect plan. According to Judges 4:18–19,
in what ways did Jael make Sisera welcome? And in
Judges 4:20–21 what did Sisera ask Jael to do? Do
you sense any hesitation or fear in Jael's actions? How
might Psalm 37:28 help you be as calm as Jael was under
pressure?

   c. Now read Judges 4:22–23. Did Jael take credit for killing
Sisera at this time? Who *did* get the credit for the Israelite
victory that day?

3. No one actually saw Jael strike the fatal blow, did they?
Yet Deborah and Barak sing her praises in Judges 5, so Jael
must have confessed what happened and admitted she was
responsible.

a. Read Judges 5:24–27 for Deborah's description of Jael's swift justice. Do you agree that Jael was "most blessed"? Why or why not? Did the end justify the means in this situation? What makes you say that?

b. Many a Sisera—or a Sarsour—gets away with murder today without a brave Jael to stop them. According to Deuteronomy 32:35, how should we expect the Lord to deal with cruel, ungodly people?

c. In the end do you see Jael as a brave heroine or a brutal killer? Would you want her as your neighbor? Your best friend? Your Bible study teacher? What does James 4:12 tell us about judging other believers?

Read Judges 4:4–24 once more. What's the most important lesson you learned from the guts-and-glory story of Deborah and Jael?

CHAPTER THREE
Peculiar Grace
The Adulteress

Read chapter 3 (pages 63–88).

1. The story of a woman trapped in her shame strikes a chord with
   many of us who've had our sins dragged into the light of day.
   Where would we be without Jesus? Just as he rescued this nameless woman from certain stoning, he also saves us from certain
   death.

   a. Read Leviticus 20:10 and then John 8:1–4. Since the
      Pharisees caught this woman in the act, what should
      have been done to the man? Why didn't that happen,
      do you suppose? Would Jesus have extended grace to
      the man as well? How might 2 Peter 3:9 help answer
      that question?

   b. John 8:3 tells us the woman was forced to stand before
      the group. Public exposure and its resulting humiliation
      have a long tradition. Think of some examples from his-
      tory—the stocks, the whipping post, others. What are
      some modern ways of shaming people? As a society, what
      motivates us to put sin on public display?

   c. Though human nature has changed little in two thousand
      years, when the grace of God appears, *everything* changes.
      Read John 8:5–7. How did Jesus extend grace to this
      woman even before he formally released her from con-
      demnation? Keeping in mind that Ephesians 5:1–2 calls

us to follow God's example, how can we apply the
instruction in Galatians 6:1 when someone is caught
in sin?

2. If the teachers of the Law and the Pharisees were supposed to be
the Good Guys, upholding the tenets of the faith, let's find out
where they went wrong.

  a. According to John 8:5, the Pharisees weren't satisfied with
  mere humiliation; they demanded the death sentence.
  The first half of John 8:6 explains their real motive,
  which was what?

  b. What do you learn about the Pharisees in Matthew
  23:27–28 and Luke 12:1? How would you define the
  word *hypocrisy* as it applies to the Pharisees? If you see
  any evidence of hypocrisy in your own life, what steps
  could you take to eradicate it?

  c. According to John 8:9, how did the Pharisees respond to
  Jesus' invitation to throw the first stone? What insights
  do you find in Romans 3:19–20 that could apply to this
  scene in the temple? Who benefited most from the Lord's
  confrontation? Make a case for each one:

    The Adulteress

    The Pharisees

    The onlookers

3. Exodus 20:14 tells us that God expressly forbids adultery. And, as this story demonstrates, in biblical times adultery was so serious a crime that execution was the immediate punishment.

    a. Why do you think adultery isn't taken more seriously—even by Christians—today? If a Christian friend was committing adultery, would you approach her about her sin? What biblical advice would you give her? Jesus offers a cautionary word about considering ourselves righteous because we've avoided adultery. What do you think Jesus is saying in Matthew 5:27–28? Does this mean we are all guilty? If so, what hope do we have?

    b. The only words the Adulteress speaks in this story are recorded in John 8:11. What was her answer to his question "Has no one condemned you?" And how did Jesus respond? Did he qualify his promise, saying something like "I will not condemn you *unless*..." or "I will forgive you *if*..."? Do you sometimes put restrictions on the grace of God when extending it to others? To yourself?

    c. One of the dangers of experiencing victory in any area of our lives is that we turn around and judge others for the very sin we just left behind. What do the following verses teach us: Colossians 3:12–13 and Luke 6:37? And what encouragement do Ephesians 2:3–5 and Isaiah 43:18–19 offer us, no matter how hairy our past?

Read John 8:1–11 once more. What's the most important lesson you learned from this nameless, faceless, yet grace-filled Adulteress?

CHAPTER FOUR
Blood Will Tell
Athaliah

Read chapter 4 (pages 89–115).

1. Women as wicked as Athaliah are rare, but they're out there. Left
    unchecked by the Holy Spirit, some take-charge chicks may bear a
    faint resemblance to this Queen B. Rather than hurrying through
    Athaliah's horrific history, let's lean in for a good, long look—in
    our mirrors.

    a. Both Deborah the judge and Athaliah the queen were
       strong, fearless, and bold, yet they were very different
       women indeed. Note some of the stark differences you see
       between these two female leaders.

       Judge Deborah was...   *Queen Athaliah was...*

    b. Athaliah earned her Really Bad Girl crown because of
       her actions recorded in 2 Chronicles 22:10. How might
       Habakkuk 2:12 address her situation? What does the
       fact that Athaliah executed her own grandchildren reveal
       about her spiritual state?

    c. Corrupt leaders often self-destruct, as described in
       Proverbs 5:22–23. In your professional life or in the
       news, when have you watched a less-than-virtuous leader
       experience a career meltdown? What happened? What
       valuable lessons can you learn from someone's bad
       example?

2. Athaliah's parents were no prize. Few mothers in history have been more deadly than Jezebel, few fathers more evil than Ahab.

   a. Ezekiel 16:44–45, part of God's long diatribe on the nation of Israel, could easily describe Athaliah. In your opinion how much did the negative influence of her parents factor into Athaliah's personality and pursuits? And who bears more responsibility? Jezebel, for raising her daughter to worship Baal? Or Athaliah, for not seeking the one true God on her own? What leads you to that conclusion?

   b. What does Psalm 78:2–7 teach us to do concerning our children's spiritual welfare? And what is the promised result? What significance does the oft-quoted verse Joshua 24:15 have for you and your household? How can we guide our children to rightly choose for themselves whom they will serve? If you don't have children of your own, how might you have a godly influence on the next generation?

   c. One bright spot in this story: Athaliah's grandson Joash survived, as we read in 2 Chronicles 22:11–12. Raised by his aunt and uncle, young Joash would have well understood David's plea in Psalm 64:2. How do you think this godly couple managed to keep Joash's existence a secret for six long years? And how did those quiet years prepare Joash for the throne?

3. When Athaliah's life came to a swift and terrible end, her false god's reputation suffered as well.

a. In 2 Chronicles 23:17 we learn how God's people responded to the queen's detestable worship of Baal. What did they do to the temple, the altars, the idols, and the priest of Baal? God makes it clear in Leviticus 19:4 that idols have no place among his people. What does this suggest about tolerating idols in our midst today?

b. Are there idols in your life—whether physical, emotional, or spiritual—that you need to tear down as thoroughly as Jehoiada and company destroyed the idols of Baal? Write them out and then consider each one. How do they interfere with your worship of our one true God? What will it take to destroy those idols? When and how will you ask God to help you clean house? This is a difficult question, so you may be tempted to skip it. Don't. For your sake—for God's sake—ask him to show you what or whom you idolize and how to put an end to it.

c. Finally, since we don't want to follow in Athaliah's footsteps, what direction do Philippians 2:3 and James 3:13 offer us? Both verses point out the virtues of humility. What does humility look like, sound like, feel like to you? What hope do you find in Luke 1:52 and 1 Peter 5:6?

Read 2 Chronicles 22:10–12 and 2 Chronicles 23:1–21. What's the most important lesson you learned from the violent life of Athaliah, the only woman who ever ruled alone as queen of Israel?

CHAPTER FIVE
Bathing Beauty
Bathsheba

Read chapter 5 (pages 116–152).

1. Your dictionary will tell you that those daytime melodramas we call *soap operas* were so named because their earliest sponsors were soap manufacturers like Ivory and Dove. But the *first* soap opera aired three thousand years ago when a lovely young lady took a springtime bath and made quite a splash before her viewing audience: King David.

   a. Read 2 Samuel 11:2. Do you think David was looking for trouble when he strolled around on his roof? Boredom and routine may find us gazing beyond the safety of home for something to pique our interest, as Proverbs 17:24 describes. Be honest: when have you been tempted to let your eyes wander? And how did you handle the situation? What do James 1:13–14 and 1 John 2:16 tell us about temptation?

   b. As we read in 2 Samuel 11:3, a messenger returned to the palace with important information about David's beautiful neighbor. What two things did he tell David that should have stopped him in his tracks? Sadly, it didn't work. In 2 Samuel 11:4 the facts of their affair are brief and to the point. Excluding the mention of Bathsheba's purification, what four things happened that spring evening as outlined in this verse?

      First, David...

So, Bathsheba...

Then, David...

Finally, Bathsheba...

c. David's sins are obvious. What about Bathsheba's? Was she "Bad to the Bone" or "Had by the Throne," and why? Read Romans 7:18–19 and Galatians 5:17, and consider how they might describe Bathsheba's conflicting desires. If you had been Bathsheba, brought to the king's opulent palace on a warm spring night, could you have said no to David's invitation? What would have made the idea attractive and hard for you to resist? Or repulsive and easy to reject? Even if we have chosen to be bad, God's Word offers incredible hope. What do these verses tell us about our sin and God's grace: Ephesians 1:7; Romans 5:8; and 1 Timothy 1:15?

2. David's story so overshadows Bathsheba's it's easy to miss the lessons she has to teach us, especially without a record of her thoughts or emotions to guide the way.

a. In 2 Samuel 11:5 when Bathsheba finally speaks, what does she say? Why might this have been good news from her viewpoint? She discharged the duty of handling this matter completely to David. What outcome might she have been seeking?

b. To a great extent, this story is about taking responsibility for our actions and facing the consequences. Think back to our story about the woman caught in adultery, John 8:4–5 in particular. What consequences might Bathsheba

have faced as an adulteress? David had other consequences to think about—like her wronged husband, as we
read in 2 Samuel 11:6–7. Is there any indication David
sought God's counsel when devising Plan A, Plan B, Plan
C? What does Proverbs 16:3 reveal about making plans?
Why do you think David ignored such wisdom?

c. If you've ever attempted a simple cover-up scheme only to
find yourself piling lie upon lie, what ultimately happened?
Once we realize we've dug ourselves into a pit of sin and
regret and are ready to get out, 2 Corinthians 7:10–11
shows us the way. Describe the fruit of godly sorrow in our
lives.

3. David's story of rebellion, repentance, and restoration is meaning-
ful for all of us who have fallen short of God's glory (which *is* all of
us, according to Romans 3:23).

a. First, God sent the prophet Nathan to confront David
with his sins. Take note of their remarkable exchange,
recorded in 2 Samuel 12:13.

David said:

Nathan said:

The first was *confession of sin,* the second was *forgive-*
ness of sin. In the New Testament we have the same two-
step process described in 1 John 1:9. How does this bring
comfort whenever you fear, as David must have, that
you've ruined your relationship with the Lord forever?

b. As for Bathsheba, it seems her love for David, and his for her, was genuine, as indicated by 2 Samuel 12:24. And 1 Kings 1:28–31 shows that she remained a favored wife at the close of David's life. What does 1 Kings 2:19 tell us about her relationship with her son Solomon?

c. Matthew 1:1 reminds us that Jesus was called "the son of David," and Matthew 1:6 shows where David falls in the lineage of Christ. How does this passage from the Gospels assure us that not only was Bathsheba forgiven by God but that we can be forgiven as well?

Read 2 Samuel 11:1–27 and 2 Samuel 12:1–25. What's the most important lesson you learned from the soap-opera story of Bathsheba and her king?

CHAPTER SIX

Just Desserts
Herodias

Read chapter 6 (pages 153–179).

1. Her dancing daughter, Salome, may be more famous, but Herodias was the one who whispered, "Off with his head!" Even the worst women still have something worthwhile to teach us.

    a. John the Baptist's calling was clear, as outlined in Matthew 3:1–6. In a word what was his message? And what two things did people do in response to his preaching? Of course, not everyone embraced what he said. According to Mark 6:17–20, who gave the orders to have John the Baptist arrested, and why? What does verse 20 suggest about this accuser?

    b. Herodias, the wife of Herod, is also mentioned in this passage. What do we learn about her? Proverbs 12:4 and Proverbs 27:15–16 suit Herodias well. How might those verses give you pause as you consider your own behavior? Since her motive for marriage was wealth and prestige, one wonders if Herodias had any real affection for her second husband, Herod Antipas. Read Mark 6:17 again and Mark 6:26. What was the apparent motive behind Herod's actions?

    c. From your own observations, what happens when a weak woman marries a strong man? And when a strong woman marries a weak man? What wisdom do Romans 15:1 and Jeremiah 9:23–24 offer for finding balance in our relationships with one another as well as the proper perspective in our relationship with the Lord?

2. According to Luke 3:18–20, John the Baptist didn't get locked up for preaching good news to the people. Rather, he was thrown in prison for preaching bad news to Herod and Herodias.

    a. Has a brother or sister in Christ ever confronted you about an area of sin in your life? If so, were you humbled and grateful? Or (be honest) humiliated and resentful? What does Proverbs 12:1 indicate our response should be? What other response does Proverbs 15:12 describe? Which reaction is more common, and why?

    b. If you reacted to such a confrontation with anger or a critical spirit, how did you convince yourself he or she deserved that treatment? And how did you feel after you cut the person down to size? In contrast, how does 2 Timothy 2:24 tell us we are to respond?

    c. Given a second chance, how would you handle it differently? What guidance do you find in Hebrews 12:11 and Revelation 3:19 for the next time you receive earnest correction from a trustworthy source?

3. Herodias didn't welcome John the Baptist's correction for one second. Unlike King David with his Plan A, B, and C, she had just one plan to solve the problem.

    a. Her revenge unfolds in Mark 6:21–24. Why do you think Herodias used Salome to convey her request instead of simply demanding John's head herself? What can you

deduce about Salome from her actions and words in Mark
6:25? And what does Proverbs 20:11 tell us about measur-
ing a child's character? Was Salome as responsible for this
heartless crime as her mother was? Explain your answer.

b. Herod's daughter—and his own sin—forced his hand.
Read Mark 6:26–28. How does the gospel writer describe
Herod's reaction to Salome's request? Why didn't Herod
simply refuse his daughter? Had you been at the banquet,
what would you have said to Herod to try to convince
him to spare John's life?

c. What a sad day for the followers of John the Baptist!
According to Matthew 14:12–13, what did the disciples
do first? Then second? Why in that order, do you suppose? And how did Jesus respond when he heard about
John's execution?

d. Jude 18–19 well describes a woman like Herodias. What
qualities are listed in those verses that suit her? Hebrews
4:13 assures us that, despite appearances, nobody gets
away with murder, because God misses nothing. How
does that truth help you avoid resentment and focus on
repentance?

Read Mark 6:17–29 once more. What's the most important
lesson you learned from the revenge-driven story of Herodias
and her much-manipulated daughter?

CHAPTER SEVEN
Veiled Threat
Tamar the Widow

Read chapter 7 (pages 180–213).

1. Two dastardly, dead husbands didn't stop Tamar, nor did a disgraceful shunning by her in-laws. Yet when her story was said and done, she had what she wanted, what Judah wanted, *and* what God wanted: a son whose name would be counted among those in the lineage of Christ. Good or bad…what a woman!

    a. We learn in Genesis 28:1 the sort of woman a good Israelite was *not* to select for a bride. Yet, according to Genesis 38:2, what kind of bride did Judah choose for himself? As the son of Jacob, grandson of Isaac, and great-grandson of Abraham, Judah *knew* better than to marry someone of a different faith. Why do you think he did so? In 2 Corinthians 6:14 what cautionary word does Paul offer about marriage? To what extent do you believe Judah's unwise choice was the source of all the sorrow that followed?

    b. Later Judah chose Tamar for his oldest son's bride, but the marriage didn't last long because of Er's despicable conduct. Though his sin is not described, it cost him his life. As required by law, Tamar then married his younger brother Onan. As distasteful as the idea of levirate marriage may be to us, how could the practice have benefited a childless widow like Tamar—*if* Onan had been cooperative? Why were Onan's actions especially cruel?

c. What do Deuteronomy 10:12–13 and Leviticus 18:4–5 tell us about God and his laws? Judah knew God's laws, yet he and his sons demonstrate what happens when God's laws are ignored. In Psalm 119:126 we find the psalmist begging God to intervene when his laws are being broken. When have you seen God's laws being ignored and longed for him to act? In both Genesis 38:7 and 38:10, it is clear that God deemed Judah's sons worthy of death for their wickedness. How do you reconcile a God of judgment with a God of grace? Read Psalm 111:7, and then answer from your heart.

2. Two sons dead and still no grandsons. Judah was *not* happy.

a. Judah brought Tamar into his household, accepted responsibility for her, and then sent her packing. What does 1 Timothy 5:8 tell us about taking care of family members? In Genesis 38:11 we learn what motivated Judah to send Tamar away. According to God's law in Deuteronomy 25:5, was Judah justified in keeping his third son, Shelah, away from Tamar? How do you view Judah's protection of Shelah—was it a sin or parental love in action? What prompts you to say that?

b. However alone and abandoned Tamar must have felt, it's clear that God saw her misery and did not desert her. How might Psalm 68:5 and Job 36:6 fit the widow Tamar in her bereft situation? She may not have had many friends, but somebody kept her informed, as we learn in Genesis 38:13. Because of the swiftness of her response, does her scandalous solution seem spontaneous, or do you think it had been in the planning stages for ages?

c. Some see Tamar as a harlot; others consider her a heroine. Is there anything about Tamar you appreciate? Her
creativity perhaps, or her shrewdness? How might she
have justified her deliberately deceptive actions? From
what we see in the biblical account, Tamar was innocent
of any intentional wrongdoing *except* for her sexual
encounter by the side of the road with Judah, her one
unrighteous act. So do you see her as a Really Bad Girl?
Why or why not? How can Ephesians 5:1–3 help you
answer that question?

d. Do you ever struggle with a biblical story like this one,
where it's difficult to see God's hand at work even though
we know he's in everything? What reassurance do you
find in Hebrews 6:13–18; Colossians 2:2–3; and Romans
8:28?

3. Three months after Tamar's bold and brazen act, things started
heating up.

a. In Genesis 38:24 we learn that Tamar was accused of
prostitution, with her unborn child as proof. Judah's
response smoldered with self-righteous fury. What does
James 1:19–20 teach us about anger, and how is that
truth demonstrated here? What justification do you suppose Judah offered for the harsh sentence of death by
burning rather than stoning? Anytime we are tempted to
justify our sinful actions, how might 1 Corinthians 4:4
keep us honest?

b. When Tamar revealed Judah's seal, cord, and staff, as
recorded in Genesis 38:25, did she openly accuse him of

wrongdoing or allow him to confess on his own? What
wisdom do you find in her way of handling things?
How could you use the same approach in a situation
you are dealing with at work or at home or in some other
relationship?

c. According to Genesis 38:27–30, Tamar gave birth to two
sons—not an accident of nature but a plan of God. What
might those twins signify? What purpose do you believe
God had for including Tamar and Judah in the lineage of
Christ? How could you use this story to help a sister with
a checkered past embrace the hope that God offers?

Read Genesis 38:1–30. What's the most important lesson
you learned from the unsettling, yet ultimately redemptive,
story of Tamar the widow?

CHAPTER EIGHT
Tears of a Clown
The Bleeding Woman

Read chapter 8 (pages 214–239).

1. When I chose "Tears of a Clown" for the title of our afflicted woman's story, I was thinking of the old Motown hit recorded by Smokey Robinson and (drumroll, please) *the Miracles*. You can be sure when this desperate woman reached out to touch the hem of the Lord's garment, a miracle was already in motion.

   a. This chapter opens with a quote from Marcel Proust that captures the paradoxical truth of suffering. Do you agree with Proust? Why or why not? In what circumstances have you personally experienced suffering to the full? What does Romans 5:3–4 tell us about the (often unexpected) benefits of suffering? What have you learned from your pain?

   b. According to Matthew 4:24, what are some of the human conditions Jesus healed? What other infirmities does Matthew 15:30 add to that list? And what was the result of those healings, as stated in Matthew 15:31? Jesus had no qualms about touching those who were unclean, and we are called to follow his example. What do Acts 10:28 and Galatians 6:2 teach us about how we're to treat others?

   c. According to Psalm 77:11–14, God has always been in the miracle business. How would *you* define a miracle? How did Jesus heal the people in the following verses:

Luke 5:12–13; Mark 7:32–35; and John 9:1–3, 6–7?
What differences do you find in these stories? What similarities? Is it the *method* or the *master* that heals?

2. Even a light touch can be a powerful means of communication
between two people. It's both identification and supplication, both
"I see you" and "I need you."

a. Read Mark 5:27–28. Why do you suppose she thought
merely touching him would be sufficient for her healing?
And why touch his garment rather than, say, his bare
hand? Mark 5:29 reveals what happened next. What is
the significance of this dramatic change taking place
immediately?

b. She wasn't the only one who knew that something had
happened. According to Mark 5:30, who else knew, and
how soon did he realize it? The disciples didn't understand the question the Lord asked, but you can be sure
she did! In Mark 5:32 we learn that Jesus kept looking
around for her. Despite her fear she threw herself at his
feet, as we read in Mark 5:33. What do you imagine com-
pelled her to do that?

c. It's clear that Jesus wanted everyone to hear this
woman's testimony. What were the possible benefits for
the woman? For the community? For the disciples?
Romans 1:16 explains *why* we share the whole truth,
and 1 John 5:11–12 explains *what* we tell people about
God. If you've heard someone share a testimony of his
or her faith experience, what effect did it have on your

own spiritual life? No matter how dramatic or common-
place you think your testimony is, write a three-sentence
story of how you came to know Christ—or had a life-
changing experience with him at some point in your
Christian walk. Who might need to hear your story this
week?

3. In her story, in our stories, it all comes down to faith—to what we
believe and how far we are willing to go to demonstrate our faith
in Christ.

   a. How do you reconcile the words of Jesus in Mark
      11:22–24 and miraculous stories like the Bleeding
      Woman's healing with your own day-to-day experience of
      people who pray for healing yet are not healed? Does it
      challenge your faith? If doubts have surfaced, how has
      God answered them and assured you of his love in any
      circumstance? What further encouragement can you draw
      from Hebrews 13:8?

   b. Mark 5:34 records Jesus' final words to this woman once
      her healing was complete and her testimony spoken.
      What endearing term did he call her? And what did Jesus
      credit for her healing? Why do you think he honored her
      faith instead of simply saying, "God has healed you"?

   c. How would you define *faith*? Is it something you feel or
      experience or do? Read Romans 10:10; 10:17; Ephesians
      2:8; and Hebrews 11:1. Then gather your thoughts about
      faith into a single sentence: "Faith is _____
      _____."

d. The benediction Jesus offered this woman in Mark 5:34 is
an apt closing to our study: "Go in peace and be freed
from your suffering." If unanswered questions remain, if
pain or disappointment lingers, if doubts and fears still
threaten to rob you of your joy in Christ, do you believe
you can be freed from your suffering? Where do you need
to go or what do you need to do to be at peace? When
you are ready to take the first step, you can be sure Jesus
will be waiting for you, hand outstretched.

Read Mark 5:24–34 once more. What's the most important
lesson you learned from the miraculous story of the Bleeding
Woman?

Notes

Introduction: Nightfall

1. Alice Ogden Bellis, *Helpmates, Harlots, Heroes* (Louisville, Ky.: Westminster /John Knox Press, 1994), 235.
2. 1 Corinthians 10:12

Chapter 1: The Medium of En Dor

1. Matthew Henry, *Matthew Henry's Commentary on the Whole Bible*, vol. 2 (1706; reprint, Peabody, Mass.: Hendrickson Publishers, 1991), 336.
2. George C. Baldwin, *Representative Women* (New York: Sheldon, Blakeman & Company, 1856), 159.
3. 1 Samuel 15:23
4. Margaret E. Sangster, *The Women of the Bible* (New York: Christian Herald, 1911), 152.
5. Dorothy Kelley Patterson, ed., *The Woman's Study Bible* (Nashville: Nelson, 1995), 491.
6. George Arthur Buttrick, *Interpreter's Dictionary of the Bible*, vol. 2 (New York: Abingdon, 1962), 100.
7. Psalm 83:10, NKJV
8. Edith Deen, *All the Women of the Bible* (New York: Harper & Row, 1955), 106.
9. G. Blakemore Evans, ed., The Riverside Shakespeare (Boston: Houghton Mifflin, 1974), 1307.
10. John 3:19
11. H. V. Morton, *Women of the Bible* (New York: Dodd, Mead & Company, 1941), 102.
12. Baldwin, *Representative Women*, 174.
13. Baldwin, *Representative Women*, 174.
14. Baldwin, *Representative Women*, 168.
15. Baldwin, *Representative Women*, 160.
16. Baldwin, *Representative Women*, 169.

17. Francis Brown, *The New Brown-Driver-Briggs-Gesenius Hebrew and English Lexicon* (Lafayette, Ind.: Association of Publishers and Authors, Inc., 1980), 15.

18. Frank E. Gaebelein, ed., *The Expositor's Bible Commentary*, vol. 3 (Grand Rapids, Mich.: Zondervan, 1992), 781.

19. Henry, *Matthew Henry's Commentary*, vol. 2, 337.

20. Charles Caldwell Ryrie, *The Ryrie Study Bible NASB* (Chicago: Moody, 1978), 455.

21. Gaebelein, *Expositor's Bible Commentary*, vol. 3, 782.

22. Frederick Drimmer, *Daughters of Eve* (Norwalk, Conn.: C. R. Gibson, 1975), 39.

23. Janice Nunnally-Cox, *Foremothers* (New York: Seabury Press, 1981), 66.

24. Morton, *Women of the Bible*, 108.

25. Herbert Lockyer, *All the Women of the Bible* (Grand Rapids, Mich.: Zondervan, 1967), 191.

26. Ann Spangler and Jean E. Syswerda, *Women of the Bible* (Grand Rapids: Zondervan, 1999), 169.

27. Leigh Norval, *Women of the Bible* (Nashville: The Methodist Episcopal Church, South, Sunday School Department, 1889), 126.

28. http://www.nsac.org/

29. Phyllis Curott, *Book of Shadows* (New York: Broadway Books, 1998), 55.

30. Doreen Irvine, *From Witchcraft to Christ* (London, England: Concordia Publishing House, Ltd., 1973), 104–5.

31. Deuteronomy 18:12

32. Curott, *Book of Shadows*, xiv.

Chapter 2: Jael

1. Leonard J. Swidler, *Biblical Affirmations of Women* (Philadelphia: Westminster, 1979), 111.

2. Denise Lardner Carmody, *Biblical Women* (New York: Crossroad, 1988), 28.

3. John Bartlett, *Bartlett's Familiar Quotations*, 16th ed., ed. Justin Kaplan (Boston: Little, Brown, 1992), 756.

4. Exodus 3:11; 4:1,13

5. Janice Nunnally-Cox, *Foremothers* (New York: Seabury Press, 1981), 50.

6. Grace Aguilar, *The Women of Israel,* vol. 1 (New York: D. Appleton & Company, 1851), 221.

7. Judges 9:54

8. Dorothy Kelley Patterson, ed., *The Woman's Study Bible* (Nashville: Nelson, 1995), 390.

9. Laurence J. Peter, *Peter's Quotations* (New York: Bantam Books, 1980), 120.

10. Michael Cardinal Faulhaber, *The Women of the Bible* (Westminster, Md.: The Newman Press, 1955), 81.

11. Ann Spangler and Jean E. Syswerda, *Women of the Bible* (Grand Rapids: Zondervan, 1999), 114.

12. William P. Barker, *Everyone in the Bible* (Old Tappan, N. J.: Revell, 1966), 158.

13. William Shakespeare, *Hamlet,* act 1, scene 5, line 106.

14. Matthew Henry, *Matthew Henry's Commentary on the Whole Bible,* vol. 2 (Peabody, Mass.: Hendrickson Publishers, 1991), 111.

15. George Arthur Buttrick, *Interpreter's Dictionary of the Bible,* vol. 4 (New York: Abingdon, 1962), 573.

16. Frank E. Gaebelein, ed., *The Expositor's Bible Commentary,* vol. 3 (Grand Rapids, Mich.: Zondervan, 1992), 407.

17. F. C. Cook, ed., *Exodus to Ruth,* Barnes' Notes (1879; reprint, Grand Rapids: Baker, 1998), 429.

18. Judges 5:25

19. Morton Bryan Wharton, *Famous Women of the Old Testament* (Chicago: W. P. Blessing, 1889), 129.

20. Herbert Lockyer, *All the Women of the Bible* (Grand Rapids, Mich.: Zondervan, 1967), 71.

21. Rose Sallberg Kam, *Their Stories, Our Stories* (New York: Continuum Publishing, 1995), 96.

22. Lockyer, *All the Women of the Bible,* 71.

23. Jon L. Berquist, *Reclaiming Her Story* (St. Louis: Chalice Press, 1992), 93.

24. Judges 4:9

25. Bartlett, *Bartlett's Familiar Quotations,* 81.

26. Leigh Norval, *Women of the Bible* (Nashville: The Methodist Episcopal Church, South, Sunday School Department, 1889), 86.

27. Berquist, *Reclaiming Her Story*, 105.

28. Nunnally-Cox, *Foremothers*, 49.

29. Luke 1:28, NKJV

30. William Mackintosh Mackay, *Bible Types of Modern Women* (New York: George H. Doran Company, 1922), 92.

31. Elizabeth Cady Stanton, *The Woman's Bible*, vol. 2 (1898; reprint, New York: Arno Press, 1972), 20.

32. Mackay, *Bible Types of Modern Women*, 90–1.

33. George Matheson, *The Representative Women of the Bible* (New York: A. C. Armstrong & Son, 1907), 163.

34. Psalm 18:32,34,38,42

35. Luke 1:37

36. Gaebelein, *Expositor's Bible Commentary*, vol. 3, 415.

37. Deuteronomy 32:35, NASB

38. Bartlett, *Bartlett's Familiar Quotations*, 247.

39. Barbara L. Thaw Ronson, *The Women of the Torah* (Northvale, N. J.: Jason Aronson, Inc., 1999), 256.

40. Swidler, *Biblical Affirmations of Women*, 112.

Chapter 3: The Adulteress

1. John 8:12

2. Herbert Lockyer, *All the Women of the Bible* (Grand Rapids, Mich.: Zondervan, 1967), 240.

3. Deuteronomy 17:6

4. Nathaniel Hawthorne, *The Scarlet Letter* (Pleasantville, N.Y.: The Readers Digest Association Inc., 1984), 15–16.

5. Leviticus 20:10

6. Virginia Stem Owens, *Daughters of Eve* (Colorado Springs, Colo.: NavPress, 1995), 122.

7. Hosea 2:10

8. Lockyer, *All the Women of the Bible*, 240.

9. Deuteronomy 17:5

10. Leonard J. Swidler, *Biblical Affirmations of Women* (Philadelphia: Westminster, 1979), 86.

11. Rose Sallberg Kam, *Their Stories, Our Stories* (New York: Continuum Publishing, 1995), 209.

12. Frank E. Gaebelein, ed., *The Expositor's Bible Commentary*, vol. 9 (Grand Rapids, Mich.: Zondervan, 1981), 90.

13. Julia Staton, *What the Bible Says About Women* (Joplin, Mo.: College Press Publishing Company, 1980), 94.

14. Numbers 5:11–31

15. Matthew Henry, *Matthew Henry's Commentary on the Whole Bible*, vol. 5 (Peabody, Mass.: Hendrickson Publishers, 1991), 792.

16. Deuteronomy 17:7

17. John 3:17

18. 1 John 1:8

19. Matthew 11:15

20. Romans 14:10

21. Albert Barnes, *Notes on the New Testament: The Gospels*, Barnes' Notes, ed. Robert Frew (1884–85; reprint, Grand Rapids: Baker, 1998), 266.

22. *New English Bible* (Oxford, England: Oxford University Press, 1961), note at end of gospel of John.

23. *The Amplified Bible* (Grand Rapids: Zondervan, 1954), note at John 7:53.

24. Revelation 12:10

25. Luke 12:5

26. Owens, *Daughters of Eve*, 126.

27. Romans 8:1–2

28. Kathy Manis Findley, *Voices of Our Sisters* (Macon, Ga.: Peake Road, 1996), 23.

Chapter 4: Athaliah

1. Vicki Leon, *Uppity Women of Ancient Times* (Berkeley, Calif.: Conari Press, 1995), 111.

2. Edith Deen, *The Bible's Legacy for Womanhood* (New York: Doubleday, 1969), 179.

3. Margaret E. Sangster, *The Women of the Bible* (New York: Christian Herald, 1911), 188.

4. 2 Chronicles 21:4

5. 2 Chronicles 21:6

6. 1 Kings 16:25

7. 2 Chronicles 22:3, RSV

8. Athalya Brenner, *The Israelite Woman* (Sheffield, England: Journal for the Study of the Old Testament Press, 1985), 29.

9. 2 Kings 11:1 KJV

10. Leon, *Uppity Women of Ancient Times,* 111.

11. Matthew Henry, *Matthew Henry's Commentary on the Whole Bible,* vol. 2 (1706; reprint, Peabody, Mass.: Hendrickson Publishers, 1991), 595.

12. Herbert Lockyer, *All the Women of the Bible* (Grand Rapids, Mich.: Zondervan, 1967), 33.

13. Frederick Drimmer, *Daughters of Eve* (Norwalk, Conn.: C. R. Gibson, 1975), 38.

14. Psalm 27:5

15. George Arthur Buttrick, *Interpreter's Dictionary of the Bible,* vol. 1 (New York: Abingdon, 1962), 306.

16. 2 Chronicles 23:13, NLT

17. 2 Chronicles 23:15

18. 2 Chronicles 23:19

19. Proverbs 11:10

20. Ann Spangler and Jean E. Syswerda, *Women of the Bible* (Grand Rapids: Zondervan, 1999), 240.

21. Lockyer, *All the Women of the Bible,* 33.

Chapter 5: Bathsheba

1. Jon L. Berquist, *Reclaiming Her Story* (St Louis: Chalice Press, 1992), 112.

2. John Bartlett, *Bartlett's Familiar Quotations,* 16th ed., ed. Justin Kaplan (Boston: Little, Brown, 1992), 455.

3. Frank E. Gaebelein, ed., *The Expositor's Bible Commentary,* vol. 3 (Grand Rapids, Mich.: Zondervan, 1992), 928.

4. Matthew Henry, *Matthew Henry's Commentary on the Whole Bible*, vol. 2 (1706; reprint, Peabody, Mass.: Hendrickson Publishers, 1991), 386.

5. F. C. Cook, ed., *The Bible Commentary: Exodus to Ruth*, Barnes' Notes (1879; reprint, Grand Rapids: Baker, 1998), 93.

6. *International Children's Bible, New Century Version* (Nashville: Word, 1986, 1988), note on 2 Samuel 11:2.

7. Herbert Lockyer, *All the Women of the Bible* (Grand Rapids, Mich.: Zondervan, 1967), 35.

8. J. Cheryl Exum, *Plotted, Shot, and Painted* (Sheffield, England: Sheffield Academic Press, Ltd., 1996), 47.

9. Sue and Larry Richards, *Every Woman in the Bible* (Nashville: Nelson, 1999), 127.

10. Job 31:1

11. Matthew 5:28

12. Elizabeth Cady Stanton, *The Woman's Bible*, vol. 2 (1898; reprint, New York: Arno Press, 1972), 57.

13. Deuteronomy 17:17

14. Deuteronomy 5:18

15. Leviticus 18:20

16. Stanton, *The Woman's Bible*, 57.

17. Psalm 51:3

18. Ross Saunders, *Outrageous Women, Outrageous God* (Alexandria, New South Wales, Australia: E. J. Dwyer, 1996), 83.

19. Beth Moore, *A Heart Like His* (Nashville: Broadman & Holman, 1999), 171.

20. William P. Barker, *Everyone in the Bible* (Old Tappan, N. J.: Revell, 1966), 57.

21. Genesis 3:12

22. Gien Karssen, *Her Name Is Woman*, book 2 (Colorado Springs, Colo.: NavPress, 1977), 159.

23. Janice Nunnally-Cox, *Foremothers* (New York: Seabury Press, 1981), 76.

24. Alice Ogden Bellis, *Helpmates, Harlots, Heroes* (Louisville, Ky.: Westminster /John Knox Press, 1994), 149.

25. Frederick Drimmer, *Daughters of Eve* (Norwalk, Conn.: C. R. Gibson, 1975), 78.

26. Richards and Richards, *Every Woman in the Bible*, 128.

27. Leviticus 15:28

28. George Arthur Buttrick, *Interpreter's Dictionary of the Bible*, vol. 1 (New York: Abingdon, 1962), 366.

29. Cook, *Exodus to Ruth*, 93.

30. 1 Samuel 21:5

31. Habakkuk 2:15

32. Deuteronomy 27:24

33. 2 Samuel 16:22

34. Isaiah 53:10

35. 2 Samuel 12:16,22

36. Preface to Psalm 51

37. 1 John 4:10

38. Proverbs 31:10

39. Lockyer, *All the Women of the Bible*, 36.

40. Matthew 1:6

Chapter 6: Herodias

1. Matthew 2:16

2. H. V. Morton, *Women of the Bible* (New York: Dodd, Mead & Company, 1941), 168.

3. Morton Bryan Wharton, *Famous Women of the New Testament* (Chicago: W. P. Blessing, 1890), 127.

4. Frances Vander Velde, *Women of the Bible* (Grand Rapids: Kregel, 1985), 186.

5. Joy Jacobs, *They Were Women Like Me* (Camp Hill, Pa.: Christian Publications, 1993), 19.

6. Ann Spangler and Jean E. Syswerda, *Women of the Bible* (Grand Rapids: Zondervan, 1999), 342.

7. Sue and Larry Richards, *Every Woman in the Bible* (Nashville: Nelson, 1999), 199.

8. Matthew Henry, *Matthew Henry's Commentary on the Whole Bible*, vol. 5 (1706; reprint, Peabody, Mass.: Hendrickson Publishers, 1991), 394.

9. Leviticus 18:16

10. Matthew 3:2

11. Matthew 3:4

12. F. C. Cook, ed., *Notes on the New Testament: The Gospels,* Barnes' Notes (1884; reprint, Grand Rapids: Baker, 1998), 351.

13. Mark 6:20, MSG

14. Alice Bach, *Women, Seduction, and Betrayal in Biblical Narrative* (Cambridge, England: Cambridge University Press, 1997), 227.

15. Esther 1:10–12

16. Ross Saunders, *Outrageous Women, Outrageous God* (Alexandria, New South Wales, Australia: E. J. Dwyer, 1996), 87.

17. Margaret E. Sangster, *The Women of the Bible* (New York: Christian Herald, 1911), 294.

18. Vander Velde, *Women of the Bible,* 187.

19. Colleen Reece, *Women of the Bible* (Uhrichsville, Ohio: Barbour, 1996), 97.

20. Herbert Lockyer, *All the Women of the Bible* (Grand Rapids, Mich.: Zondervan, 1967), 69.

21. Lockyer, *All the Women of the Bible.*

22. Jacobs, *They Were Women Like Me,* 15.

23. Morton, *Women of the Bible,* 171.

24. Wharton, *Famous Women of the New Testament,* 142.

25. Lockyer, *All the Women of the Bible,* 150.

26. Kenneth C. Davis, *Don't Know Much About the Bible* (New York: Morrow 1998), 368.

27. Bach, *Women, Seduction, and Betrayal,* 237.

28. Ecclesiastes 3:4

29. 2 Samuel 6:14

30. Psalm 150:4

31. Exodus 15:20

32. William F. Arndt and F. Wilbur Gingrich, *A Greek-English Lexicon of the New Testament and Other Early Christian Literature* (Chicago: University of Chicago Press, 1957), 587.

33. Bach, *Women, Seduction, and Betrayal,* 228.

34. Bach, *Women, Seduction, and Betrayal,* 230.

35. LaJoyce Martin, *Mother Eve's Garden Club* (Sisters, Ore.: Multnomah, 1993), 68.

36. Esther 5:3

37. Matthew 14:8

38. Mary Cartledge-Hayes, *To Love Delilah: Claiming the Women of the Bible* (San Diego: LuraMedia, 1990), 63.

39. Sylvia Charles, *Women in the Word* (South Plainfield, N. J.: Bridge Publishing, 1984), 163.

40. Bach, *Women, Seduction, and Betrayal,* 229.

41. Ethel Clark Lewis, *Portraits of Bible Women* (New York: Vantage Press, 1956), 112.

42. Spangler and Syswerda, *Women of the Bible,* 343.

43. Virginia Stem Owens, *Daughters of Eve* (Colorado Springs, Colo.: NavPress, 1995), 194.

44. Dwight L. Moody, T. De Witt Talmage, and Joseph Parker, *Bible Characters* (Chicago: Thomas W. Jackson Publishing Company, 1902), 256.

45. Morton, *Women of the Bible,* 171.

46. Luke 23:7–12

47. Owens, *Daughters of Eve,* 195.

48. Lockyer, *All the Women of the Bible,* 68.

Chapter 7: Tamar the Widow

1. Elizabeth Cady Stanton, *The Woman's Bible,* vol. 2 (1898; reprint, New York: Arno Press, 1972), 67.

2. Edith Deen, *All the Women of the Bible* (New York: Harper & Row, 1955), 41.

3. Alice Ogden Bellis, *Helpmates, Harlots, Heroes* (Louisville, Ky.: Westminster /John Knox Press, 1994), 92.

4. Clifton J. Allen, ed., *The Broadman Bible Commentary,* vol. 1 (Nashville: Broadman Press, 1969), 245.

5. James G. Murphy, ed., *A Commentary on the Book of Genesis,* Barnes' Notes (1873; reprint, Grand Rapids: Baker, 1998), 448.

6. Murphy, *A Commentary on the Book of Genesis,* 450.

7. Gerhard von Rad, *Genesis* (Philadelphia: Westminster Press, 1961), 357.

8. Murphy, *A Commentary on the Book of Genesis,* 448.

9. Barbara L. Thaw Ronson, *The Women of the Torah* (Northvale, N. J.: Jason Aronson, Inc., 1999), 170.

10. Jonathan Kirsch, *The Harlot by the Side of the Road* (New York: Ballantine Books, 1997), 137.

11. Rose Sallberg Kam, *Their Stories, Our Stories* (New York: Continuum Publishing, 1995), 72.

12. *Merriam-Webster's College Dictionary,* 10th ed., s.v. "onanism."

13. Ronson, *The Women of the Torah,* 172.

14. Proverbs 7:10

15. George Arthur Buttrick, *Interpreter's Dictionary of the Bible,* vol. 3 (New York: Abingdon, 1962), 932.

16. Ann Spangler and Jean E. Syswerda, *Women of the Bible* (Grand Rapids: Zondervan, 1999), 74.

17. Buttrick, *Interpreter's Dictionary of the Bible,* vol. 3, 932.

18. Matthew Henry, *Matthew Henry's Commentary on the Whole Bible,* vol. 1 (Peabody, Mass.: Hendrickson Publishers, 1991), 174.

19. Kirsch, *The Harlot,* 124.

20. Psalm 127:3

21. Leviticus 21:9

22. 2 Samuel 12:7

23. Kirsch, *The Harlot,* 143.

24. Gien Karssen, *Her Name Is Woman,* book 2 (Colorado Springs, Colo.: NavPress, 1977), 73.

25. Romans 3:10

26. Isaiah 64:6

27. Leviticus 18:15

28. Henry, *Matthew Henry's Commentary,* 175.

29. *Merriam-Webster's College Dictionary,* s.v. "breach."

30. Eugenia Price, *The Unique World of Women…in Bible Times and Now* (Grand Rapids: Zondervan, 1969), 51.

31. Matthew 1:2–16

Chapter 8: The Bleeding Woman

1. Colossians 4:14
2. Luke 5:31
3. Luke 8:42
4. Luke 8:42
5. William P. Barker, *Women and the Liberator* (Old Tappan, N. J.: Revell, 1972), 55.
6. George Arthur Buttrick, *Interpreter's Dictionary of the Bible,* vol. 1 (New York: Abingdon, 1962), 647.
7. Leviticus 15:26
8. Leviticus 15:27
9. Matthew 10:1, NASB
10. John 9:2
11. Joyce Hollyday, *Clothed with the Sun* (Louisville, Ky.: Westminster/ JohnKnox Press, 1994), 189.
12. Luke 8:43
13. Barker, *Women and the Liberator,* 57.
14. Psalm 130:5
15. Frederick Drimmer, *Daughters of Eve* (Norwalk, Conn.: C. R. Gibson, 1975), 33.
16. Hebrews 11:1
17. John 8:36
18. William Shakespeare, *Othello,* act 2, scene 3, line 379.
19. Herbert Lockyer, *All the Women of the Bible* (Grand Rapids, Mich.: Zondervan, 1967), 221.
20. Barker, *Women and the Liberator,* 59.
21. Ross Saunders, *Outrageous Women, Outrageous God* (Alexandria, New South Wales, Australia: E. J. Dwyer, 1996), 39.
22. Barker, *Women and the Liberator,* 60.
23. Frank E. Gaebelein, ed., *The Expositor's Bible Commentary,* vol. 8 (Grand Rapids, Mich.: Zondervan, 1984), 662.
24. Hollyday, *Clothed with the Sun,* 192.
25. Gaebelein, *The Expositor's Bible Commentary,* 662.
26. Lockyer, *All the Women of the Bible,* 221.

27. Lockyer, *All the Women of the Bible,* 222.

28. http://saints.catholic.org/saints/veronica2.html

29. Barker, *Women and the Liberator,* 61.

30. http://botanical.com/botanical/mgmh/s/speger76.html

31. http://www.keratin.com/ad/ad001.shtml

Conclusion: Rebel's Heart

1. Eugenia Price, *The Unique World of Women…in Bible Times and Now* (Grand Rapids: Zondervan, 1969), 52.

Discussion Questions

1. Sylvia Charles, *Women in the Word* (South Plainfield, N. J.: Bridge Publishing, 1984), 94.

Acknowledgments

Huge hugs to my editorial team at WaterBrook Press—Rebecca Price, Carol Bartley, Laura Barker, and Lisa Bergren. You are the very best encouragers an author could hope for.

Heartfelt thanks to my therapeutic friend Lois Luckett, MSW, LCSW, and Diane Noble, a precious writing sister, for reading every word and suggesting I change a few. Okay, more than a few!

Special thanks to Holly Oyler, who gave me a guided tour through the world of alopecia areata. You are a walking, talking miracle, dear woman. For more information about this form of hair loss, visit the Web site for the National Alopecia Areata Foundation at *www.naaf.org*.

Finally, endless thanks and boundless gratitude to my husband, who is my partner in all things. Your touch of wisdom graces every page, Bill. I love you with all my heart.

About the Author

Liz Curtis Higgs has one goal: to help women embrace the grace of God with joy and abandon! She's the author of more than thirty books, with 4.6 million copies in print. In her best-selling Bad Girls of the Bible series, Liz breathes new life into ancient tales about the most famous women in scriptural history, from Bathsheba to Mary Magdalene. Liz's award-winning historical novels, which transport the stories of Rebekah, Leah, Rachel, Dinah, Naomi, and Ruth to eighteenth-century Scotland, also invite readers to view biblical characters in a new light.

A seasoned professional speaker and Bible study teacher, Liz has toured with Women of Faith, Women of Joy, and Extraordinary Women. She has spoken for seventeen hundred other women's conferences, which has taken her to all fifty states in the United States and fourteen foreign countries, including Thailand, Portugal, South Africa, and New Zealand.

On the personal side, Liz is married to Bill Higgs, PhD, who serves as director of operations for her speaking and writing office. Louisville, Kentucky, is home for Liz and Bill, their grown children, and Liz's twin tabby cats, Boaz and Samson.

Follow Liz's online Bible study on www.LizCurtisHiggs.com,
and find her on www.Facebook.com/LizCurtisHiggs,
on www.Twitter.com/LizCurtisHiggs,
on www.Instagram.com/LizCurtisHiggs,
on www.Vimeo.com/LizCurtisHiggs,
and on www.Pinterest.com/LizCurtisHiggs.

MANY NAMES, MANY LEGENDS. ONE WOMAN, ONE GOD.

"A touching, beautiful look at one of the Bible's most captivating women."
—MARGARET FEINBERG

"An unparalleled feast of rich truth...and the most divine servings of grace."
—ANN VOSKAMP

The queen of Sheba's quest for wisdom will surprise you, challenge you, inspire you, change you. Shedding new light on this ancient biblical role model, Liz Curtis Higgs unveils timeless wisdom for all who aspire to please the King of kings.